WITHDRAWN
UTSA LIBRARIES

MANNERS
MAKYTH
MAN

THE PILGRIMAGE TO CANTERBURY
After the painting by Thomas Stothard, R.A.

MANNERS MAKYTH MAN

*An Anthology from the great writers illustrating
English manners and customs throughout
the centuries*

SELECTED AND EDITED BY
R. BRIMLEY JOHNSON

With Illustrations

KENNIKAT PRESS
Port Washington, N. Y./London

MANNERS MAKYTH MAN

First published circa 1925
Reissued in 1970 by Kennikat Press
Library of Congress Catalog Card No: 73-113338
ISBN 0-8046-0958-6

Manufactured by Taylor Publishing Company   Dallas, Texas

"On Wednesday (Sep., 1729) the Oration will be on the Skits of the Fashions, or a live gallery of family pictures in all ages; ruffs, muffs, puffs; shoes, wedding-shoes, two-shoes, slip-shoes, peels, clocks, pantofles, buskins, pantaloons, gaiters, shoulder-knots, perriwigs, head-dresses, modesties, tuckers, farthingales, corkins, minikin; slammerkins, ruffles, round robins, toilets, fans, patches; Dame, forsooth, Madam, My Lady, the wit and beauty of my Grannum; Winifred, Joan, Bridget, compared with our Winny, Jenny and Biddy; fine ladies and pretty gentlewomen; *being a general view of the beau monde from before Noah's flood to the year* 29. On Friday will be something better than last Tuesday. After each a bob at the times."

Announcement of John Henley, Orator Humbug—" President of the Butchers, Dean of Marrowbones and Cleavers, or Warden of Clare Market"—from his " gilt tub."

EDITOR'S NOTE

There can be no one best way of presenting a consecutive picture of English manners in the words of our great classics. Almost the whole of literature would contribute something to the full truth. Within a volume, it is only possible to select the most representative for the particular purpose in mind.

I have preferred to select from writers who speak for their own age, and have therefore, intentionally, avoided historical fiction. I should also remark that in my judgment, certain writers, particularly and justly associated in our minds with the accurate and lively description of manners, rather surprisingly do not contain any pictorial passage that would stand without its context. The fact accounts for the absence of some whose work in mass vividly portrays an age.

On the other hand, I have not made any selection from passages of no more than a few lines, which may describe a particular fashion or isolated scene, but would, I think, produce a disjointed and tiresome effect.

R.B.J.

CONTENTS

	Page
Introduction	19

CHAPTER I
CHAUCER TO SHAKESPEARE

Lords and Ladies

THE KNIGHT AND HIS SQUIRE	29
Chaucer's *Prologue*	
CHIVALRY AND A FAIR MAID	31
The Morte D'Arthur	
A "RIGHTFUL" COURTIER—AND OTHERS ..	37
Spenser's *Mother Hubbard*	
A PRIORESS	43
Chaucer's *Prologue*	

Law and Order

"IDLENESS, THE MOTHER OF THIEVES"	45
More's *Utopia*	
THE WATCH	50
Much Ado about Nothing	

The Commonalty

RECRUITING	58
"WHAT'S BECOME OF MY WIFE?"	62
A PAIR OF SHOES	64
Dekker's *A Shoemaker's Holiday*	

The Diversions

COURT PLAYERS	67
Shakespeare's *Hamlet*	
MASQUES AND COMMONERS	73
Ben Jonson's *Love Restor'd*	
A LESSON IN GALLANTRY	78
Ben Jonson's *Cynthia's Revels*	

CONTENTS

	Page
VILLAGE PLAYERS	82
A Midsummer Night's Dream	
RIDDLES AND PROPHECIES	93
Ben Jonson's *Cynthia's Revels*	

CHAPTER II

THE RESTORATION

At Court

A CORONATION	97
Evelyn's *Diary*	
CORONATION DAY	101
Pepys' *Diary*	
AN AUDIENCE	105
Evelyn's *Diary*	
"CREATIONS"	106
Pepys' *Diary*	
AN AMBASSADOR	108
Evelyn's *Diary*	
A RIVER PAGEANT	110
Evelyn's *Diary*	
A COURT BALL	110
Pepys' *Diary*	
FRENCH MODES	111
Evelyn's *Diary*	
A BANQUET AT WHITEHALL	113
Evelyn's *Diary*	
THE KING'S VEST	114
Pepys' *Diary*	
TO THE TREASURER'S	114
Pepys' *Diary*	

Public Spectacles

A PROCLAMATION	115
Evelyn's *Diary*	
A TRIAL	117
Evelyn's *Diary*	

CONTENTS

	Page
A Funeral	118
Evelyn's *Diary*	

The Diversions

	Page
The Frost	119
Evelyn's *Diary*	
"Monsieur Paquin's Digestors"	120
Evelyn's *Diary*	
A Dinner at the Guildhall	121
Pepys' *Diary*	
"Some Sort of Monkeys"	123
Evelyn's *Diary*	
A Wedding	124
Pepys' *Diary*	
The Bear Garden	126
Evelyn's *Diary*	
The Playhouse	127
Pepys' *Diary*	
Wax Candles and "All Things Civil"	127
Pepys' *Diary*	
Travelling	129
Pepys' *Diary*	
A Bet	135
Pepys' *Diary*	
Valentines	136
Pepys' *Diary*	

CHAPTER III

THE EIGHTEENTH CENTURY—I

Of Politeness

	Page
Town and Country Modes	139
The Spectator	
"At Least, be half-polite"	142
Lord Chesterfield's *Letters*	

CONTENTS

	Page
OF "MILDNESS" TO INFERIORS	143
Lord Chesterfield's *Letters*	
"AN AWKWARD FELLOW"	144
Lord Chesterfield's *Letters*	
AFFECTATION	145
Lord Chesterfield's *Letters*	
"FRENCH FOPPERIES"	146
The Spectator	
OF DANCING	150
Lord Chesterfield's *Letters*	
A DANCING MASTER	151
The Tatler	
LAUGHING	153
Lord Chesterfield's *Letters*	
ON WOMEN	154
Lord Chesterfield's *Letters*	

Of Dress

ON HOOPS	155
The Spectator	
ON HOODS	158
The Spectator	
THE HEAD-DRESS	160
The Spectator	

Domestic Economies

MY LITTLE REPUBLIC	164
Goldsmith's *The Vicar of Wakefield*	
RUSHES FOR CANDLES	165
White's *History of Selborne*	

The Diversions

THE OPERA	168
The Spectator	
A MIDNIGHT MASK	169
The Spectator	

CONTENTS

	Page
A PARTY	171
Goldsmith's *The Vicar of Wakefield*	
ON CLUBS	173
The Spectator	

CHAPTER IV

THE EIGHTEENTH CENTURY—II

Good Society

FANCY DRESS	179
Richardson's *Sir Charles Grandison*	
THE "EXQUISITES"	180
Smollett's *Roderick Random*	
"THERE'S NOTHING LIKE POLISH"	186
Sheridan's *The Rivals*	
"MISSES OF THE TON"	187
Fanny Burney's *Cecilia*	
THE "ENNUYÉ"	188
Fanny Burney's *Cecilia*	
"A VERY GREAT WRITER"	190
Fielding's *Amelia*	
MODERN EDUCATION	192
Richardson's *Sir Charles Grandison*	
THE PRESS	193
Sheridan's *School for Scandal*	
"A CLASS OF FEMALES"	195
Richardson's *Sir Charles Grandison*	
THE PROPOSAL	195
Richardson's *Sir Charles Grandison*	
"DAMNS HAVE HAD THEIR DAY"	200
Sheridan's *The Rivals*	

The Parish

THE VICAR	201
Crabbe's *The Borough*	

CONTENTS

		Page
THE PARSON		202
Crabbe's *The Village*		
A WISE LADY		203
Crabbe's *Parish Register*		
THE FARMER'S WIFE		205
Crabbe's *Parish Register*		
THE DOCTOR		205
Crabbe's *The Village*		
THE CARD PLAYER		206
Crabbe's *The Borough*		
THE POOR HOUSE		207
Crabbe's *The Borough*		

The Diversions

A MASQUERADE		208
Fanny Burney's *Cecilia*		
A PRIVATE BALL		214
Fanny Burney's *Evelina*		
"TWO WAYS OF EATING"		223
Smollett's *Roderick Random*		
SHOPS AND HAIR-DRESSING		225
Fanny Burney's *Evelina*		
AT VAUXHALL		226
Fielding's *Amelia*		
BATH		232
Sheridan's *The Rivals*		

CHAPTER V

THE NINETEENTH CENTURY—I

Gentility

MODERN GALLANTRY		233
Elia's *Essays*		
A MORNING CALL		238
Jane Austen's *Pride and Prejudice*		

CONTENTS

	Page
ON CALLING	240
Mrs. Gaskell's *Cranford*	
FRIENDSHIP	240
Jane Austen's *Northanger Abbey*	
A YEOMAN FARMER	242
Mrs. Gaskell's *Cranford*	
"A GENTLEMANLY OILMAN"	247
Elia's *Essays*	
PARTIES	249
Mrs. Gaskell's *Cranford*	
A GAME OF CARDS	252
Elia's *Essays*	
"A RATTLE"	258
Jane Austen's *Northanger Abbey*	
CHARADES	260
Jane Austen's *Emma*	
HOOPS	261
Maria Edgworth's *Belinda*	

Town and Country

A VILLAGE	265
Miss Mitford's *Our Village*	
THE DECAY OF BEGGARS	269
Elia's *Essays*	
A FARMER	272
Jane Austen's *Emma*	
A FARMERESS	275
Miss Mitford's *Our Village*	
ONCE A BEAUTY	279
Miss Mitford's *Our Village*	
A DAIRY WOMAN	281
Miss Mitford's *Our Village*	
"SIXPENCE A JOKE"	284
Elia's *Essays*	

CONTENTS

The Diversions

AN ASSEMBLY	289
Jane Austen's *Pride and Prejudice*	
A FÊTE	292
Maria Edgworth's *Belinda*	
WAGERS	294
Maria Edgworth's *Belinda*	
THE UPPER ROOMS, BATH	299
Jane Austen's *Northanger Abbey*	

CHAPTER VI

THE NINETEENTH CENTURY—II

Mayfair

AN OLD BEAU	303
Thackeray's *Pendennis*	
—AND HIS "TOILET"	306
Thackeray's *Pendennis*	
"A NEW GENERATION"	308
Thackeray's *Pendennis*	
A COMPANION	311
Thackeray's *Vanity Fair*	
"BELOW STAIRS"	314
Dicken's *Pickwick Papers*	

The Professions

DINNERS IN HALL	322
Thackeray's *Pendennis*	
"BEHIND THE SCENES"	326
Dicken's *Nicholas Nickleby*	

The Diversions

AT VAUXHALL	337
Thackeray's *Vanity Fair*	
A FANCY DRESS BREAKFAST	341
Dicken's *Pickwick Papers*	

CONTENTS

THE NINETEENTH CENTURY—III

Our Grandparents

		Page
TOWN AND COUNTRY		345
Trollope's *Doctor Thorne*		
HER FIRST BALL		346
Trollope's *Three Clerks*		
IN THE FASHION		354
Trollope's *Doctor Thorne*		
"SOMETHING FAST"		356
Trollope's *Three Clerks*		

The Professions

ON BOARD		360
Marryat's *Frank Mildmay*		
A PHYSICIAN		365
Trollope's *Doctor Thorne*		
A COURT-MARTIAL		367
Marryat's *Frank Mildmay*		
AN EXAMINATION		372
Trollope's *Frank Mildmay*		

LIST OF ILLUSTRATIONS

PILGRIMAGE TO CANTERBURY
After the painting by Thomas Stothard, R.A. .. *Frontispiece*

    Facing Page

SIR THOMAS MORE AND HIS FAMILY
From the drawing by Holbein at Basle 46

THE ENGLISH DANCING MASTER
Frontispiece of the book of that name, 1650 74

SAMUEL PEPYS
From the Medallion by David le Marchand 102

DRIVING A VAN OVER THE FROZEN SERPENTINE, 1826
From an old print 120

THE COCK-PIT
After Hogarth 126

THE EARL OF CHESTERFIELD
After the painting by Gainsborough 142

DR JOHNSON IN THE ANTE-ROOM OF LORD CHESTERFIELD
After a painting by E. M. Ward, R.A. 154

HUNTING THE SLIPPER ..
From an illustration by Thomas Rowlandson to *The Vicar of Wakefield* 172

THE COUNTESS'S DRESSING ROOM
From a painting by Hogarth, completed 1744 194

"GOOD-BYE"
From an engraving by J. M. Moreau 216

A NIGHT SCENE AT RANELAGH, MAY 6TH, 1752
From a print of the period 228

BALL AT RANELAGH ON THE BIRTHDAY OF GEORGE, PRINCE OF WALES, MAY 24TH, 1750 .. 244

THE SUPPER-PARTY
After J. M. Moreau 262

LIST OF ILLUSTRATIONS

	Facing Page
CARICATURE "RESTORATION DRESSES," 1789	290
CROPPED LOUNGERS IN BOND STREET, 1791	296
LADIES' DRESSES, 1816 From the *Lady's Magazine*	312
"MR. JOSEPH IN A STATE OF EXCITEMENT AT VAUXHALL" From a drawing by Thackeray in *Vanity Fair*	338
"MRS. LEO HUNTER RECEIVING THE COMPANY" From a drawing by Phiz in *The Pickwick Papers*	342
LADIES' DRESSES, EARLY VICTORIAN PERIOD From a fashion paper of the time	354
THE CHILDREN, EARLY VICTORIAN PERIOD From a fashion paper of the time	374

INTRODUCTION

With the progress of civilisation, manners deteriorate and decay, not precisely reverting to mere muscle, but continuously disclaiming more and more of form and phrase. Always parents, of each succeeding generation, deplore the lack of courtesy or poise in their young. Chivalry, we say, died long ago; the proprieties are forgotten; there are no ladies and gentlemen left in the world to-day—a world of noise and glare and self-assertion.

Wherefore the ritual of olden days, the changing codes of good-breeding, the almost forgotten antagonisms between true refinement and the "bejewelled apes," the well-born and the new rich, have acquired for us the glamour and the surprise of a genuine antique, glittering in ruffle and brocade.

All are themselves faded and gone; but their art lives. Through the word-portraits and painted scenes I have taken down from our old book-shelves, something yet speaks of how they lived and looked at life—obedient to or defying the Rules; some content with the passing hour, others searching the future with despair or hope. The way they lived reveals what manner of men they were.

I

Though, obviously, any divisions of time, or grouping in epochs, must be arbitrary, and only justified by convenience, certain general characteristics of progress, or change, clearly emerge from those adopted here: convenient stepping-stones for tracing the growth of man from Chaucer's Knight to the Victorian Beau.

In the first place, we note at once the clear-cut class-distinctions that remain unquestioned and unbridged up to Shakespeare; when the nobility simply used the commons for work and play as a part of their inheritance, whether privately owned or enslaved to the State. Only Art, as mediæval minstrel-jester afterwards vagabond player, and Learning, as scholar-priest later secluded in classic or legal courts, bear any resemblance to a middle, or professional, class. Sir Thomas More may protest already against the folly and injustice of a carelessly despotic Constitution; but the " Watch " survives to expose the Law most emphatically an ass.

" Ralph's as good a workman as any," but he must away to the wars; a wife left is a wife lost; for the low-born have but one rule of life, obedience; but one code of manners, respect.

There was romance and beauty in the ideal of chivalry to the Round Table or the Virgin Queen: an ideal of service, courage, tenderness, and restraint. Noble deeds, noble thoughts, noble dress, proclaimed nobility. Privilege recognised its responsibilities, and the greatest of all adventures was to protect the weak.

Yet the code was at once more simple and less sincere than in later centuries. Stately converse in formal assembly permitted the roughest of home talk; Launcelot's knightly perfections but thinly veiled the blackest treachery towards a generous and loyal friend. The most extravagant lip-homage of knight-errantry, whether in tournament or the Armada, was seldom inspired by respect for women, whom man neither loved nor trusted as he did his horse. They were tended and sheltered for his pride and pleasure;

trained to patience and obedience; held above work because not credited with a mind—save, it would seem, by Will of Avon, dreamer of dreams.

When at play, moreover, we see a like curious mingling of verbal subtlety and naively coarse fun, from the rough and tumble of the jousts to Bottom's buffoonery, alternating with the scholar's masque, and the conceits of euphemism.

Only in one respect, perhaps, were Arthur's Knights or the gallants of Elizabeth closer to modern times than some of their more civilised successors—in youth they were expected to play the Squire or court-page, disdaining no task, however menial, so it were training for manhood's honour.

II

Although diverted partially from normal development by reactions against Puritan severity, the Restoration presents an entirely different atmosphere of convention and standard of life: a big step towards modern conditions.

Whereas manners and dress were, in the beginning, the natural expression of real superiority—at least of type—if no guarantee of individual virtue, they have now little more meaning or significance than a livery of wealth and lineage. There are few duties and little honour attached to birth, which has rather acquired a license to idleness, ignorance, and reckless daring in crime. On the other hand, taste and wit are now discovered to be becoming in aristocrats; while nobility has lost its independence, its old position of father to the household, in sycophant waiting upon favour at Court. Fine clothes scarcely pretend to witness character; but a lapse in manners may prove the unpardonable sin.

Meanwhile, however, there has emerged a new power in the councils of State. The Peers, having abused their privileges, are now, in some measure, dependent upon men of commerce—a class created by the advance of civilisation and imperial adventure. The citizen has emerged from shop-keeping and the guilds of craftsmen; public opinion has learned to criticise and observe.

Never before or since has Fashion been so lavish in show, so precise in code, so exacting in rule; but it no longer offers a universally accepted model for conduct, or even the manly ideal of a patriot race.

That wonderful pair of diarists, who have preserved for us so vivid and intimate a portrait of the age, happen to have both betrayed the instincts of the snob, infinitely curious about the great, eager to imitate with discretion—where they may; but without even the affectation of approving what they record. They have moreover a code, conventions and a style of their own, the manners proper to their class—discriminating them from the mob, but not attaching them to the Court. Pepys has much to say of "the King's vest .... pinked with white silk under it," but writes with scarcely less enthusiasm of his own "new stuff suit, with a shoulder-belt."

There are now, moreover, gorgeous spectacles for the people—without the Palace or the Manor House; and we greatly question if the "very pretty fashion of drawing Valentines" was a prince's pastime.

Manners are now worn, and deliberately assumed, to conceal emotion and thought, not infrequently to falsify truth. Thus men may be kept apart by artificial barriers of convention, who have the same ideas, knowledge, and outlook. The surface of life is, indeed, brilliant and picturesque; its meaning lies deeply hid.

III

The eighteenth was a century of foundations: an age when men loved to construct and build. They had become conscious and argumentative about themselves. Hitherto we have compiled conventions by observation of records; from seeing what men were, deducting their aim or desire. At this period rules were drawn up, and manners became a formal art, scarcely a question so much of looks as of morals: a prosaic and material standard of somewhat cold reason, proud and confident of its judgment and information. The observers are now professional critics of men and life; once more linking propriety with conduct in itself scarcely beautiful or ideal.

True that Addison and Steele preached and taught with a kindly wit, as Goldsmith loved those he laughed at. But Lord Chesterfield, more typically, portrayed, with careful precision, the gentleman of his age, not necessarily of the Peerage, whose education and accomplishments were fundamentally artificial, directly calculated to deceive. Politeness was never natural; breeding enabled you to seem quite other than what wisdom counselled you to be. Fame and success depended upon the power to impose yourself upon others; polish was to be acquired by prudent vice.

This is, curiously enough, the first clear and official expression of a middle-class, later the destined defenders of strict morality, not yet despising an illustrious descent; who had discovered that man could *make* for himself a position he was not born to by the virtue which lay in clothes, cleanliness, conversation, and carriage. Now the unpardonable sin is to be awkward or coarse.

The theory of good behaviour and appearance is complex but stiff—not always, however, taught in one mode by different professors. To Addison the introduction of French modes was the indisputable sign of "foppery," though Chesterfield considered that no other nation really knew how to be polite.

Yet both acknowledge that excess, producing affectation, had already crept in, as we see it in the "exquisites" of Roderick Random, Bob Acres' "polish," and Fanny Burney's "Misses of the Ton": one and all imitation ladies and gentlemen—the social climbers of later centuries.

Now, moreover, the Court may lead, but can no longer create. We can sense the master-milliners behind the scene. Dress and decorum are unmistakably a question of public opinion, to some extent traditional and inherited, but ever taking new shapes in modification or defiance of the orthodox. There is no set, permanent, form of *noblesse oblige* in looks or deed.

Since fiction has meanwhile abandoned artificial romance for portraiture from life, we can see the men and women of the period more intimately than heretofore. The effect of dress and manners upon feeling, the details of social intercourse and class distinctions are dramatically presented, and there is no occasion for confusion or conjecture. Richardson, Fielding and their fellow-novelists have kept alive for us the youths whom Chesterfield sought to polish, the women for whom Addison pleaded intelligent consideration and some measure of comradeship with the dominant male.

It is indeed the precocious advent of feminity into public consciousness that marks, if it did not produce, many fundamental changes which now emerge— the greater variety and more rapid movement.

Fanny Burney proclaimed her sex. With exceptional advantages for the observation of manners, among sets not often simultaneously open to one writer, she made a fine use of her unique opportunities. For the first time men and women were drawn for us through the eyes of a clever girl, before she had lost the freshness and curiosity of youth, naturally more observant, and more interested in detail, than any masculine scribe. Many women attained some prominence at the birth of the middle-classes; but as novelists are the most popular, and the most intimate portrait-painters, they may ridicule absurdities out of fashion, reveal genuine refinement, and suggest reform. Evelina, no doubt, gave women the chance of improving themselves by reading—for did not Cecilia thus employ her time more profitably than Miss Larolles? She openly derided the popular association of tales with the Devil, and won the respect of statesmen and philosophers for fiction, by transforming the "evergreen follies" of circulating libraries into inventions for young people that were clean and merry and true. Certain great ladies of her day have asserted that, though gentlefolk may write to please their friends, to publish was to lose caste; and many years later, the first "heavy" reviewers of Charlotte Brontë and George Eliot declared that such novels were *not* written by pure women.

A more liberal verdict luckily prevailed; and prejudice, as usual, only served to establish the significance of the public gain. Fanny's own somewhat fastidious respectability was enough to prevent a scandal about her work; and we can scarcely exaggerate the advance to sense from sensibility given to women (the arbiters of fashion) by being allowed to read—supported, as it was, by the masterly writings of her successors.

One more new element arises here, or rather received recognition in literature—the life and character of the poor. From the beginning, they had been used—not entirely without sympathy and realistically enough, for comic relief; but Crabbe's little-known parish portraits anticipate material later developed, from Wordsworth to Dickens and George Gissing, with a depth of feeling and neatness of apt phrase, that gives a surprisingly modern touch to the correct poetic form. The lower classes have come into their own.

IV

In entering the nineteenth century, we are confronted with an immensely enlarged field and greatly increased variety of type. I have opened my chapter on this century with Lamb and Jane Austen; because their work looks forward, never behind its actual date.

In his relation to the public, Elia revives Addison and Steele as a kind of typical clubman, representing the sudden development of the Press—established chiefly by Leigh Hunt—which is itself a natural consequence of Dr. Johnson's revolt from the Patron, and the masterly conquest by Richardson and Fielding of the opportunities thus afforded for an appeal to the general reader. It was, as to a large extent it remains, the newspaper on which the people depend for culture; and if only the few were ready for Lamb in his own day, his audience has steadily grown with the years. Once more, the Press is most emphatically middle-class. Though it dare not omit Court gossip, this is not provided for the aristocracy, but for simple people in mean streets.

It was a little later, when trade had secured command of Empire, that Thackeray revived Society studies to please the professions in their contempt of shopkeepers, and Dickens indulged the kitchen-maid with naively coloured caricatures of my Lord and Lady as they appeared to reporters for the press.

Local colour is now evolved, to portray more accurately the variations of class and manners. Maria Edgworth invents the " national " novel—so quickly perfected by Scott; Miss Mitford continues Crabbe—with a difference; and Captain Marryat revives the sturdy realism of Smollet's naval portraits.

Jane Austen's generous loyalty to Fanny Burney has somehow failed, at present, to secure a general recognition for the pioneer of women novelists. But *Pride and Prejudice, Emma,* and above all *Persuasion* gave us a flawless mirror of the true nature of woman—not even yet fully interpreted by man—for whom the later generations are still awaiting a seer.

English youth under Victoria was immortalised in Pendennis and Clive Newcome, who did not desire Jane Austen wives, rather respecting the ladies of *Cranford*. Dickens supplied an almost complete picture of his vital and strenuous age, so confident of its own progress, so sure and optimistic of even better days to come—a jovial, exciting, and coloured surface of high lights and deep shadows, dramatically exaggerated into truth with sincere stage-emotion.

And we may leave the mid-Victorians in the capable hands of Anthony Trollope; a singularly well-balanced and typically English observer, who added a sound interpretation of provincial life to the London of Thackeray or Dickens, and Jane Austen's countryside.

There only remained for literature the emerging influence of the "Five Towns," which, like other phases of England characteristically late-Victorian, were more the parents of to-day than children of the past.

V

History reveals an almost unbroken advance towards simplicity in dress and manners, a continuously fuller emancipation from convention, and more natural manners. To-day we emphasise the veils and prohibitions of the Victorians; but they had travelled far from the pompous periods of Arthur, Sir Philip Sidney and Dr. Johnson; the flowing robes of Guinevere, Queen Elizabeth, and Lady Castlemaine; the stately courtesies of Sir Roger, the word-play of Wycherley, the Hoops and Head-dress laughed out of fashion by the Spectator.

Whether manners, as here revealed, are destined soon to become altogether extinct; how far the man beneath the clothes had in him the human nature we now so eagerly expose; I must leave the reader to determine. Whether to-day it is still true, as in earlier, more picturesque times, that "Manners makyth man," I will not say.

R. BRIMLEY JOHNSON.

MANNERS MAKYTH MAN

CHAPTER I

CHAUCER TO SHAKESPEARE

THE KNIGHT AND HIS SQUIRE
Chaucer's "PROLOGUE"

A KNIGHT ther was, and that a worthy man,   *Lords and*
That fro the tyme that he first bigan   *Ladies*
To ryden out, he loved chivalrye,
Trouthe and honour, fredom and curteisye.
Ful worthy was he in his lordes werre,
And thereto hadde he riden (no man ferre)
As wel in Christendom as hethenesse,
And ever honoured for his worthinesse.
    At Alisaundre he was, whan it was wonne ;
Ful ofte tyme he hadde the bord bigonne
Aboven alle naciouns in Pruce.
In Litton hadde he reysed and in Ruce,
No Christen man so ofte of his degree.
In Gernade at the sege eek hadde he be
Of Algezir, and riden in Belmarye.
At Lyeys was he, and at Satalye,
Whan they were wonne ; and in the Grete See.
At many a noble aryve hadde he be.

47 *werre*, war
48. *ferre*, further
52. *the bord bigonne*, crossed the sea
54. *reysed*, gone on a military expedition
60. *aryve*, disembarkation

At mortal batailles hadde he been fiftene,
And foughten for our feith at Tramissene
In listes thryes, and ay slayn his fo.
This ilke worthy knight had been also
Somtyme with the lord of Palatye,
Ageyn another hethen in Turkye:
And evermore he hadde a sovereyn prys.
And though that he were worthy, he was wys,
And of his port as meke as is a mayde.
He never yet no vileinye ne sayde
In al his lyf, un-to no maner wight.
He was a verray parfit gentil knight.
But for to tellen you of his array,
His hors were gode, but he was nat gay.
Of fustian he wered a gipoun
Al bismotered with his habergeoun;
For he was late y-come from his viage,
And wente for to doon his pilgrimage.

With him ther was his son, a yong Squyer,
A lovyere, and a lusy bachelor,
With lokkes crulle, as they were leyd in presse.
Of twenty yeer of age he was, I gesse.
Of his stature he was of evene lengthe,
And wonderly deliver, and greet of strengthe.
And he had been sometyme in chivachye,
In Flaunders, in Artoys, and Picardye,
And born him wel, as of so litel space,
In hope to stonden in his lady grace.
Embrouded was he, as it were a mede
A ful of fresshe floures, whyte and rede.

75. *gipoun*, doublet
76. *bismotered*, stained with rust
    babergeoun, coat of mail
81. *crulle*, curly
84. *deliver*, active
85. *chivachye*, cavalry

Singinge he was, or floytinge, all the day;
He was as fresh as is the month of May.
Short was his goune, with sleves longe and wyde.
Wel coude he sit on hors, and faire ryde.
He coude songes make and wel endyte,
Juste and eek daunce, and wel purtreye and wryte.
So hote he lovede, that by nightertale
He sleep namore than dooth a nightingale.
Curteys he was, lowly, and servisable,
And carf biforn his fader at the table . .

CHIVALRY AND A FAIR MAID

THE MORTE D'ARTHUR
Malory

This old baron had a daughter at that time, that was called the fair maid of Astolat, and ever she beheld Sir Launcelot wonderfully; and she cast such a love, wherefore she died; and her name was Elaine le Blaunch. So thus as she came to and fro, she was so hot in her love, that she thought Sir Launcelot should wear upon him at the jousts a token of hers. "Fair damsel," said Sir Launcelot, "and if I grant you that, ye may say I do more for your love than ever I did for lady or damsel." Then she remembered him that he would ride into the jousts disguised, and for because he had never before that time borne no manner of token of no damsel; then he bethought him that he would bear one of hers, that none of his blood thereby might know him. And then he said, "Fair damsel, I will grant you to wear a token of yours upon my helmet; and, therefore, what it is, show me." "Sir," said she, "it is a red sleeve of

91. *floytinge*, playing the flute   97. *nightertale*, night-time
96. *purtreye*, draw

mine, or scarlet, well embroidered with great pearls;" and so she brought it him. So Sir Launcelot received it, and said, " Never or this time did I so much for no damsel." And then Sir Launcelot betook the fair damsel his shield in keeping, and prayed her to keep it until he came again. And so that night he had merry rest and great cheer, for ever the fair damsel Elaine was about Sir Launcelot all the while that she might be suffered. . . . .

And so, on the morrow, when Sir Launcelot should depart, fair Elaine brought her father with her, and her two brethren, Sir Tirre and Sir Lavaine, and thus she said :

" My lord, Sir Launcelot, now I see that ye will depart, fair and courteous knight, have mercy upon me, and suffer me not to die for your love." " What would you that I did?" said Sir Launcelot. " I would have you unto my husband," said the maid Elaine. " Fair damsel, I thank you," said Sir Launcelot ; " but certainly," said he, " I cast me never to be married." " Then, fair knight," said she, " will ye be my love ?" " Jesu defend me !" said Sir Launcelot ; " for then should I reward your father and brother full evil for their great goodness." " Alas !" said she, " then must I needs die for your love." " Ye shall not," said Sir Launcelot ; " for wit ye will, fair damsel, that I might have been married and I had would ; but I never applied me to be married. But because, fair damsel, that ye will love me as ye say ye do, I will, for your good love and kindness, show you some goodness ; and that is this : That wheresoever ye will set your heart upon some good knight that will wed you, I shall give you together a thousand pounds yearly to you and to your heirs. Thus much will I give you, fair maid, for your kindness, and always while I live to be your own knight." " Of all this," said the damsel, " I will none ; for but if ye will wed me, or else be my love at the least, wit ye well, Sir Launcelot, my good days are done." "Fair damsel," said Sir Launcelot, " of these two things ye must pardon me." "Then she shrieked shrilly, and fell down to the ground in a swoon; and that gentlewoman bear her into her chamber, and there she made ever much sorrow. And then Sir Launcelot would depart; and there he asked Sir Lavaine what he would do? "What should I do," said Sir Lavaine, " but follow you, but if ye drive me from you." Then came Sir Bernard unto Sir Launcelot, and said unto him thus: "I cannot see but that my daughter, Elaine, will die for your sake." "I may not do thereto," said Sir Launcelot, " for that me sore repenteth. For I report me unto yourself, that my proffer is fair; and me repenteth," said Sir Launcelot, " that she loveth me as she doth. I was never the causer of it: for I report me unto your son, I early nor late proffered her bounty nor fair behests. And as for me,' said Sir Launcelot, " I dare do all that a good knight should do, that she is a clean maid for me, both for deed and for will; and I am right heavy of her distress; for she is a full fair maid, good and gentle, and right well taught." "Father," said Sir Lavaine, " I dare not make it good that she is a clean maid as for my lord, Sir Launcelot; but she doth as I do. For, sithence that I first saw my lord, Sir Launcelot, I could never depart from him; nor nought I will, and I may follow him." Then Sir Launcelot took his leave; and so they departed, and came to Winchester. And when King Arthur wist that Sir Launcelot was come whole and sound, the King made great joy of him; and so did Sir Gawaine and all the knights of the Round Table, except Sir Agravaine and Sir Mordred. And also Queen Guenever was waxed wrath with Sir Launcelot, and would by no means speak with him, but estranged herself from him; and Sir Launcelot made all the means that he might to speak with the Queen, but it would not be. . . .

Now speak we of the fair maid of Astolat, which made such sorrow day and night, that she never slept, eat, nor drank; and always she made her complaint unto Sir Launcelot. So when she had thus endured about ten days, that she felt that she must needs pass out of this world. Then she shrove her clean, and received her Creator; and ever she complained still upon Sir Launcelot. Then her ghostly father bade her leave such thoughts. Then said she, "Why should I leave such thoughts? am I not an earthly woman? and all the while the breath is in my body, I may complain. For my belief is, that I do none offence, though I love an earthly man; and I take God unto record, I never loved any but Sir Launcelot du Lake, nor never shall; and a maiden I am, for him and for all other. And sith it is the sufferance of God that I shall die for the love of so noble a knight, I beseech the high Father of heaven for to have mercy upon my soul; and that mine innumerable pains which I suffer may be allegiance of part of my sins. For our sweet Saviour, Jesu Christ," said the maiden, "I take thee to record, I was never greater offender against thy laws, but that I loved this noble knight, Sir Launcelot, out of all measure: and of myself, good Lord! I might not withstand the fervent love, wherefore I have my death." And then she called her father, Sir Bernard, and her brother, Sir Tirre; and heartily she prayed her father that her brother might write a letter like as she would indite it. And so her father granted it her. And, when the letter was written, word by word, as she had devised, then she prayed her father that she might be watched until she were dead. "And while my body is whole let this letter be put into my right hand, and my hand bound fast with the letter until that I be cold; and let me be put in a fair bed, with all the richest clothes that I have about me. And so let my bed, with all my rich clothes, be laid with me in a chariot to the next place whereas the Thames is; and there let me be put in a barge, and but one man with me, such as ye trust, to steer me thither, and that my barge be covered with black samite over and over. Thus, Father, I beseech you let it be done." So her father granted her faithfully that all this thing should be done like as she had devised. Then her father and her brother made great dole; for, when this was done, anon she died. And so, when she was dead, the corpse, and the bed, and all, were led the next way unto the Thames; and there was a man, and the corpse and all, were put in a barge on the Thames; and so the man steered the barge to Westminster, and there he rode a great while to and fro or any man discovered it.

So, by fortune, King Arthur and Queen Guenever were speaking together at a window : and so as they looked into the Thames, they espied the black barge, and had marvel what it might mean. Then the King called Sir Kaye, and showed him it. "Sir," said Sir Kaye, "wit ye well that there is some new tidings." "Go ye thither," said the King unto Sir Kaye, "and take with you Sir Brandiles and Sir Agravaine, and bring me ready word what is there." Then these three knights departed and came to the barge, and went in; and there they found the fairest corpse, lying on a rich bed, that ever they saw, and a poor man sitting in the end of the barge, and no word would he speak. So these three knights returned unto the King again, and told him what they had found. "That fair corpse will I see," said King Arthur. And then the King took the Queen by the hand, and went thither. Then the King made the barge to be holden fast; and then the King and the Queen went in with certain knights with them; and there they saw a fair gentlewoman, lying in a rich bed, covered unto her middle with many rich clothes, and all was cloth of gold: and she lay as though she had smiled. Then the Queen espied the letter in the right hand, and told the King thereof. Then the King took it in his hand, and said, " Now I am sure this letter will tell what she was, and why she is come hither." Then the King and the Queen went out of the barge; and the King commanded certain men to wait upon the barge. And so when the King was come within his chamber, he called many knights about him, and said " that he would wit openly what was written within that letter." Then the King broke it open, and made a clerk to read it. And this was the intent of the letter :

" Most noble knight, my lord, Sir Launcelot du Lake, now hath death made us two at debate for your love. I was your love, that men call the Fair Maiden of Astolat; therefore unto all ladies I make my moan. Yet for my soul that ye pray, and bury me at the least and offer me my mass penny. This is my last request: and a clean maid I died, I take God to my witness. Pray for my soul, Sir Launcelot, as thou art a knight peerless." This was all the substance of the letter. And when it was read, the Queen and all the knights wept for pity of the doleful complaints. Then was Sir Launcelot sent for; and when he was come, King Arthur made the letter to be read to him. And when Sir Launcelot had heard it, word by word, he said, " My lord, King Arthur, wit you well that I am right heavy of the death of this fair damsel. God knoweth I was never causer of her death by my will; and that I will report me unto her own brother here, he is Sir Lavaine. I will not say nay," said Sir Launcelot, " but that she was both fair and good;

and much was I beholden unto her: but she loved me out of measure." "Ye might have showed her, said the Queen, "some bounty and gentleness, that ye might have preserved her life." "Madam," said Sir Launcelot, "she would none other way be answered, but that she would be my wife, or else my love; and of these two I would not grant her; but I proffered her for her good love, which she showed me, a thousand pounds yearly to her and her heirs, and to wed any manner of knight that she could find best to love in her heart. For, madam," said Sir Launcelot, "I love not to be constrained to love; for love must arise of the heart, and not by constraint." "That is truth," said King Arthur and many knights; "love is free in himself, and never will be bound; for where he is bound, he loseth himself. Then," said the King unto Sir Launcelot, "it will be your worship that ye oversee that she be buried worshipfully." "Sir," said Sir Launcelot, "that shall be done as I can best devise." And so many knights went thither to behold the fair dead maid. And on the morrow she was richly buried, and Sir Launcelot offered her mass penny; and all the knights of the Round Table that were there, at that time, offered with Sir Launcelot. And then, when all was done, the poor man went again with the barge.

A "RIGHTFUL" COURTIER AND OTHERS

MOTHER HUBBERD
Spenser

But the right gentle minde would bite his lip,
To heare the Javell so good men to nip;
For, though the vulgar yeeld an open eare,
And common Courtiers love to gybe and fleare
At everie thing which they hear spoken ill,

And the best speaches with ill meaning spill,
Yet the brave Courtier, in whose beauteous thought
Regard of honour harbours more than ought,
Doth loath such base condition, to backbite
Anies good name for envie or despite,
He stands on tearmes of honourable minde,
Ne will be carried with the common winde
Of Courts inconstant mutabilitie,
Ne after everie tattling fable flie ;
But heares and sees the follies of the rest,
And thereof gathers for himselfe the best.
He will not creepe, nor crouche with fained face,
But walkes upright with comely stedfast pace,
And unto all doth yeeld due curtesie ;
But not with kissed hand belowe the knee,
As that same Apish crue is wont to doo ;
For he disdaines himselfe t'embase theretoo.
He hates fowle leasings, and vile flatterie,
Two filthie blots in noble gentrie ;
And lothefull idleness he doth detest,
The canker worme of everie gentle brest ;
The which to banish with faire exercise
Of knightly feates, he daylie doth devise :
Now menaging the mouthes of stubborn steedes,
Now practising the proofe of warlike deedes,
Now his bright arms assaying, now his speare,
Now the nigh aymed ring away to beare.
At other times he casts to sew the chace
Of swift wilde beasts, or runne on foote a race,
T'enlarge his breath (large breath in armies most
    needfull)
Or els by wrestling to wex strong and heedfull,
Or his stiffe armes to stretch with Eughen bowe,
And manly legs, still passing too and fro,
Without a gowned beast him fast beside,
A vaine ensample of the Persian pride ;
Who, after he had woune th'Assyrian foe,

Did ever after scorne on foote to goe.
Thus when this Courtly Gentleman with toyle
Himselfe hath wearied, he doth recoyle
Unto his rest, and there with sweete delight
Of musicks skill revives his toyled spright;
Or els with Loves, and Ladies gentle sports,
The joy of youth, himself he recomforts;
Or lastly, when the bodie list to pause,
His minde unto the Muses he withdrawes:
Sweete Ladie Muses, Ladies of delight,
Delights of Life, and ornaments of light!
With whom he close confers with wise discourse,
Of Natures workes, of heavens continuall course,
Of forreine lands, of people different,
Of kingdomes change, of divers government,
Of dreadfull battailes of renowned knights;
With which he kindleth his ambitious sprights.
To like desire and praise of noble fame,
The only upshot whereto he doth ayme;
For all his minde on honour fixed is,
To which he levels all his purposes,
And in his Princes service spends his dayes,
Not so much for to game, or for to raise
Himselfe to high degree, as for his grace,
And in his liking to winne worthie place,
Through due deserts and comely carriage,
In whatso please employ his personage,
That may be matter meete to gaine him praise:
For he is fit to use in all assayes
Whether for Armes and warlike amenaunce,
Or else for wise and civill governaunce.
For he is practiz'd well in policie,
And thereto doth his Courting most applie:
To learn the enterdeale of Princes strange,
To marke th' intent of Counsells, and the change
Of states, and eke of private men somewhile,
Supplanted by fine falsehood and faire guile;

Of all the which he gathereth what is fit
T'enrich the storehouse of his powerfull wit,
Which through wise speaches and grave conference
He daylie eekes, and brings to excellence.
   Such is the rightfull Courtier in his kinde,
But unto such the Ape lent not his minde:
Such were for him no fit companions,
Such would descrie his lewd conditions;
But the young lustie gallants he did chose
To follow, meete to whom he might disclose
His witlesse pleasance, and ill pleasing vein.
A thousand wayes he them could entertaine,
With all the thriftless games that may be found;
With mumming and with masking all around,
With dice, with cards, with balliards farre unfit,
With shuttlecocks, misseeming manlie wit,
With courtizans, and costly riotize,
Whereof still somewhat to his share did rize:
Ne, them to pleasure, would he sometimes scorne
A Pandares coat (so basely was he borne).
Thereto he could fine loving verses frame,
And play the Poet oft. But ah! for shame
Let not sweete Poets praise, whose onely pride
Is virtue to advaunce, and vice deride
Be with the worke of losels wit defamed.
Ne let such verses Poetrie be named!
Yet he the name on him would rashly take,
Maugre the sacred Muses, and it make
A servant to the vile affection
Of such, as he depended most upon;
And with the sugrie sweete thereof allure
Chast Ladies eares to fantasies impure.
   To such delights the noble wits he led
Which him reliev'd, and their vaine humours fed
With fruitless follies and unsound delights.
But if perhaps into their noble sprights
Desire of honor or brave thoughts of armes

Did ever creepe, then with his wicked charmes
And strong conceipts he would it drive away,
Ne suffer it to house there halfe a day.
And whenso love of letters did inspire
Their gentle wits, and kindle wise desire,
That chieflie doth each noble minde adorne
Then he would scoffe at learning and else scorne
The Sectaries thereof, as people base
And simple men, which never came in place
Of world affaires, but, in dark corners mewd,
Muttred of matters as their bookes them shewd,
Ne other knowledge ever did attaine,
But with their gownes their gravitie maintaine.
From them he would his impudent lewde speach
Against Gods holie Ministers oft reach,
And mock Divines and their profession.
What else then did he by progression,
But mocke high God Himselfe, whom they professe?
But what car'd he for God, or godlinesse?
All his care was himselfe how to advaunce,
And to uphold his courtly countenance.
By all the cunning meanes he could devise:
Were it by honest wayes, or otherwise,
He made small choyce; yet sure his honestie
Got him small gaines, but shameles flatterie,
And filthie brocage, and unseemly shifts,
And borowe base, and some good Ladies gifts:
But the best helpe, which chiefly him sustain'd,
Was his man Raynolds purchase which he gain'd.
For he was school'd by kinde in all the skill
Of close conveyance, and each practise ill
Of coosinage and cleanly knaverie,
Which oft maintain'd his masters braverie.
Besides, he usde another slipprie slight,
In taking on himselfe, in common sight,
False personages fit for everie sted,
With which be thousands cleanly coosined:

Now like a Merchant, Merchants to deceive,
With whom his credit he did often leave.
In gage for his gay Masters hopelesse dett :
Now like a Lawyer, when he land would lett,
Or sell fee-simples in his Master's name,
Which he had never, nor ought like the same.
Then would he be a Broker, and draw in
Both wares and money, by exchange to win :
Then would he seeme a Farmer that would sell
Bargaines of woods, which he did lately fell,
Or corne, or cattle, or such other ware,
Thereby to coosin men not well aware :
Of all the which there came a secret fee,
To th'Ape, that he his countenance might bee.
 Besides all this, he us'd oft to beguile
Poore suters, that in Court did haunt some while ;
For he would learne their business secretly,
And then informe his Master hastely,
That he by means might cast them to prevent,
And beg the sute the other ment.
Or otherwise false Reynold would abuse
The simple suter, and wish him to chuse
His Master, being one of great regard
In Court, to compas anie sute not hard,
In case his paines were recompenst with reason.
So would he worke the silly man by treason
To buy his Master's frivolous good will,
That had not power to doo him good or ill.
So pitifull a thing is Suters state !
Most miserable man, whom wicked fate
Hath brought to Court, to sue for had ywist,
That few have found, and manie one hath mist !
Full little knowest thou, that hast not tride,
What hell it is in suing long to bide :
To loose good dayes, that might be better spent ;
To wast long nights in pensive discontent ;
To speed to-day, to be put back to-morrow ;

To feed on hope, to pine with feare and sorrow;
To have thy Princes grace, yet want her Peeres;
To have thy asking, yet waite manie yeeres;
To fret thy soule with crosses and with cares;
To lat thy heart through comfortlesse dispaires;
To fawne, to crowche, to waite, to ride, to ronne,
To spend, to give, to want, to be undonne.
Unhappie wight, borne to disastrous end,
That doth his life in so long tendance spend!
    Who ever leaves sweet home, where meane estate
In safe assurance, without strife or hate,
Finds all things needfull for contentment meeke,
And will to Court for shadowes vaine to seeke,
Or hope to gaine, himselfe will a daw trie:
That curse God send unto mine enemie!
For none but such as this bold Ape, unblest,
Can ever thrive in that unluckie quest;
Or such as hath a Reynold to his man,
That by his shifts his Master furnish can.
But yet this Foxe could not so closely hide
His craftie feates, but that they were descride
At length by such as sate in justics seate,
Who for the same him fowlie did entreate;
And having worthily him punished,
Out of the Court for ever banished.

A PRIORESS

Chaucer's "PROLOGUE"

THER was also a Nonne, a Prioresse,
That of hir smyling was ful simple and coy;
Hir gretteste ooth was but by sëynt Loy;   120
And she was cleped madame Eglentyne.
Ful wel she song the service divyne,

    121. *cleped*, called.

Entuned in hir nose ful semely;
And Frensh she spak ful faire and fetishly,
After the scole of Stratford atte Bowe,
For Frensh of Paris was to hir unknowe.
At mete wel y-taught was she with-alle;
She leet no morsel from hir lippes falle,
Ne wette hir fingers in hir sauce depe.
Wel coude she carie a morsel, and wel kepe,   130
That no drope ne fille up-on hir brest.
In curteisye was set ful much hir lest.
Hir over lippe wyped she so clene,
That in hir coppe was no ferthing sene
Of grece, whan she dronken hadde hir draughte. 135
Ful semely after hir mete she raughte,
And sikerly she was of great disport,
And ful plesaunt, and amiable of port,
And peyned hir to countrefete chere
Of court, and been estatlich of manere,   140
And to ben holden digne of reverence,
But, for to spoken of hir conscience,
She was so charitable and so pitous,
She wolde wepe, if that she sawe a mous
Caught in a trappe, if it were deed or bledde. 145
Of smale houndes had she, that she fedde
With rosted flesh, or milk and wastel-breed.
But sore weep she if oon of hem were deed,
Or if men smoot it with a yerde smerte : ,
And al was conscience and tendre herte.   150
Ful semely hir wimpel pinched was;
Hir nose tretys; hir eyen greye as glas;
Hir mouth ful smal, and ther-to softe and reed;
But sikerly she hadde a fair forhead;

  124. *fetishly*, elegantly. 140. *estatlich*, stately
  132. *lest*, happiness 147. *washtel-breed*, fine cake
  136. *raughti*, left the table 149. *yerde*, stick
  137. *sikerly*, certainly 151. *wimpel*, hood
      152. *tretys*, well-shaped

It was almost a spanne brood, I trowe;   155
For, hardily, she was nat undergrowe.
Ful fetis was hir cloke, as I was war.
Of smal coral aboute hir arm she bar
A peire of bedes, gauded al with grene;
And ther-on heng a broche of gold ful shene,   160
On which ther was first write a crowned A,
And after, *Amor vincit omnia.*

"IDLENESS, THE MOTHER OF THIEVES"

UTOPIA
More

 This punishment of theves passeth the limites   *Law and*
of justice, and is also very hurtefull to the weale   *Order*
publique. For it is to extreame and cruel a punishment for thefte, and yet not sufficient to refrayne
and withhold men from thefte. For simple thefte
is not so great an offense, that it owght to be
punished with death. Neither ther is any punishment so horrible, that it can kepe them from stealynge,
which have no other craft, whereby to get their
living. Therfore in this poynte, not you onlye,
but also the most part of the world, be like euyll
scholemaisters, which be readyer to beate, then to
teache, their scholers. For great and horrible punish-
mentes be appointed for theves, whereas much rather
provision should have ben made, that there were some
meanes, whereby they myght get their livyng, so that
no man shoulde be dryven to this extreme neces-
sitie, firste to steale, and then to dye. Yes (quod he)
this matter is wel ynough provided for already.
There be handy craftes, there is husbandrye to gette
their livynge by, if they would not willingly be nought.
Nay, quod I, you shall not skape so; for first

---

157. *fetis*, handsome

of all, I wyll speake nothynge of them, that come home oute of the warres, maymed and lame, as not longe a go, oute of Blacke heath fielde, and a litell before that, out of the warres in France: suche, I saye, as put their lives in ieoperdye for the weale publiques or the kynges sake, and by reason of weakeness and lamenesse be not hable to occupye their olde craftes, and be to aged to lerne new; of them I wyll speake nothing, forasmuch as warres have their ordinarie recourse. But let us considre those thinges that chaunce daily before our eyes. First there is a great numbre of gentlemen, which can not be content to live idle themselves, lyke dorres, of yat whiche other have laboured for: their tenauntes I meane, whom they polle and shave to the quicke, by reisyng their rentes (for this onlye poynte of frugalitie do they vse, men els through their lauasse and prodigall spendynge, hable to brynge theymselfes to verye beggerye) these gentlemen, I say, do not only live in idlenesse themselfes, but also carrye about with them at their tailes a great flock or traine of idle and loyterynge servingmen, which never learned any craft wherby to get their livynges. These men, as sone as their mayster is dead, or be sicke themselfes, be incontinent thrust out of dores. For gentlemen hadde rather keepe idle persones, then sicke men, and many times the dead mans heyre is not hable to mainteine so great a house, and kepe so many serving men as his father dyd. Then in the meane season they that be thus destitute of service, either starve for honger, or manfullye playe the theves. For what would you have them to do? When they have wandred abrode so longe, untyl they have worne threde bare their apparell, and also appairid their helth. Then gentlemen because of their pale and sickely faces, and patched cotes, wil not take them into service. And husbandmen dare not set them a worke:

SIR THOMAS MORE AND HIS FAMILY
From the drawing by Holbein at Basle.

knowynge wel ynoughe that he is nothing mete to doe trewe and faythful service to a poore man wyth a spade and a mattoke for small wages and hard fare, whyche beynge deyntely and tenderly pampered up in ydilnes and pleasure, was wont with a sworde and a buckler by hys syde to iette through the strete with a bragginge loke, and to thynke hym selfe to good to be anye mans mate. Naye by saynt Mary sir (quod the lawier) not so. For this kinde of men muste we make moste of. For in them as men of stowter stomaches, bolder spirites, and manlyer courages then handycraftes men and plowemen be, doth consiste the whole powre, strength and puissaunce of oure army, when we muste fight in battayle. Forsothe sir as well you myghte saye (quod I) yat for warres sake you muste cheryshe theves. For suerly you shall never lacke theves, whyles you have them. No nor theves be not the most false and faynt harted soldiers, nor souldioius be not cowardlete theves: so wil thees ii craftes agree together . . . No nor those same handy crafte men of yours in Cities, nor yet the rude and vplandish plowmen of the countreye, are not supposed to be greatly affraryde of your gentlemens idle servingmen, vnlesse it be suche as be not of body or stature correspondent to their strength and courage, orels whose bolde stomakes be discouraged throughe povertie. Thus you may see, that it is not to be feared lest they shoulde be effeminated, if thei were brought up in good craftes and laboursome workes, whereby to gette their livynges, whose stoute and sturdy bodyes (for gentlemen vouchsafe to corrupte and spill none but picked and chosen men) now either by reason of rest and idlenesse be brought to weakenesse: orels by easy and womanly exercises be made feble and vnhable to endure hardnesse. Truly howe so ever the case standeth, thys me thinkith is nothing auayeable to the weale publeque, for warre sake, which you never have, but when you wyl your selfes to keepe and mainteyn an unnumerable flocke of that sort of men, that be so troublesome and noyous in peace. Whereof you ought to have a thowsand times more regarde, then of warre. But yet this is not only the necessary cause of stealing. There is another, whych, as I suppose, is p [ro]per and peculiar to you Englishmen alone. What is that, quod the Cardinal? forsoth my lorde (quod I) your shepe that were wont to be so meke and tame, and so smal eaters, now, as I heare saye, be become so great devourers and so wylde, that they eate up, and swallow downe the very men them selfes. They consume, destroye, and devoure whole fieldes, howses, and cities. For looke in what partes of the realme doth growe the fynest, and therefore dearest woll, there noble men, and gentlemen: yea and certeyn Abbottes, holy men no doubt, not contenting them selfes with the yearely revenues and profytes, that were wont to grow to theyr forefathers and predecessours of their landes, nor beynge content that they live in rest and pleasure nothing profiting, yea much noyinge the weale publique: leave no grounde for tillage, thei inclose al into pastures: thei throw doune houses, they plucke downe townes, and leave nothing standynge, but only the churche to be made a shepehowse. And as thoughe you lost no small quantity of grounde by forests, chases, laundes and parkes, those good holy men turne all dwellinge places and all glebeland into desolation and wildernes. Therefore that on covetous and unsatiable cormaraunte and very plage of his natyve countrey maye compasse about and inclose many thousand akers of grounde to gether within one pale or hedge, the husbandmen be thrust owte of their owne, or els either by coveyne and fraude, or by violent oppression they be put besydes it, or by wronges and iniuries thei be so weried, that they be compelled to sell all : by one meanes therfore or by other, either by hooke or crooke they muste needes departe awaye, poore, selye, wretched, soules, men, women, husbands, wives, fatherless children, widowes, wofull mothers, with their yonge babes, and their houshold smal in substance, and muche in numbre, as husbandrye requireth manye handes. Awaye thei trudge, I say, out of their knowen and accustomed houses, fyndynge no place to reste in. All their housholdestuffe, which is verye little woorthe, thoughe it might well abide the sale: yet beeynge sodainely thruste oute, they be constrayned to sell it for a thing of nought. And when they have wandered abrode tyll that be spent, what can they then els doo but steale, and then instly pardy be hanged, or els go about a beggyng. And yet then also they be caste in prison as vagaboundes, because they go aboute and worke not : whom no man wyl set a worke, though thei never so willingly profre themselves therto. For one Shephearde or Heardman is ynough to eate up that grounde with cattel, to the occupying whereof about husbandrye manye handes were requisite. . . . Thus the unreasonable covetousnes of a few hath turned yat thing to the vtter vndoing of your ylande, in the whiche thynge the chiefe felicitie of your realme did consist. For this great dearth of victualles causeth men to kepe as little houses, and as smale hospitalitie as they possible maye, and to put away their servauntes : whether, I pray you, but a beggynge : or elles (whyche these gentell bloudes, and stoute stomackes, wyll sooner get their myndes unto) a stealing ? Nowe to amende the matter, to this wretched beggerye, and miserable povertie is ioyned greate wantonnes, importunate superfluitie, and excessive riote. For not only gentle mennes servauntes, but also handicrafte men : yea and almooste the ploughmen of the countrey, with al other sortes of people, vse muche strange and proude newe-fanglenes in their apparell, and to muche prodigall riotte, and sumptuous fare at their table. Nowe bawdes, quienes, whoores, harlottes, strumpettes, brothel houses, stewes, and yet an other stewes, wynetauernes, ale houses, and tiplinge houses, with so manye noughtie, lewde, and vnlawfull games, as dyce, cardes, tables, tennis, boules, coytes, do not all these sende the haunters of them streyghte a stealynge when theyr money is gone? Caste oute these pernicyous abhominations, make a lawe, that they, whiche plucked downe fermes, and townes of husbandrye, shal reedifie them, or els yelde, and uprender the possession thereof to suche, as wil go to the cost of buylding them anewe. Suffer not these riche men to bie up al, to ingrosse, and forstalle, and with their monopolie to kepe the market alone as please them. Let not so many be brought vp in idelnes, let husbandry and tillage be restored, let clothe-workinge be renewed, that ther may be honest labours for this idill sort to passe their tyme in profitablye, whiche hitherto either povertie hath caused to be theves, or elles nowe be either vagabondes, or idil serving men, and shortelye wilbe theves.

THE WATCH

MUCH ADO ABOUT NOTHING
Shakespeare

A Street

Enter Dogberry *and* Verges *with the* Watch.
Dog. Are you good men and true?
Verg. Yea, or else it were pity but they should suffer salvation, body and soul.
Dog. Nay, that were a punishment too good for them, if they should have any allegiance in them, being chosen for the prince's watch.

Verg. Well, give them their charge, neighbour Dogberry.
Dog. First, who think you the most desartless man to be constable?
First Watch. Hugh Otecake, sir, or George Seacole; for they can write and read.
Dog. Come hither, neighbour Seacole. God hath blessed you with a good name: to be a well-favoured man is the gift of fortune; but to write and read comes by nature.
Sec. Watch. Both which, master constable,—
Dog. You have: I knew it would be your answer. Well, for your favour, sir, why, give God thanks, and make no boast of it; and for your writing and reading, let that appear when there is no need of such vanity. You are thought here to be the most senseless and fit man for the constable of the watch; therefore bear you the lantern. Ths is your charge: you shall comprehend all vagrom man; you are to bid any man stand, in the prince's name.
Sec. Watch. How if a' will not stand?
Dog. Why, then, take no note of him, but let him go; and presently call the rest of the watch together, and thank God you are rid of a knave.
Verg. If he will not stand when he is bidden, he is none of the prince's subjects.
Dog. True, and they are to meddle with none but the prince's subjects. You shall also make no noise in the streets; for the watch to babble and to talk is most tolerable and not to be endured.
Watch. We will rather sleep than talk; we know what belongs to a watch.
Dog. Why, you speak like an ancient and most quiet watchman; for I cannot see how sleeping should offend: only, have a care that your bills be not stolen. Well, you are to call at all the alehouses, and bid those that are drunk get them to bed.

Watch. How if they will not?

Dog. Why, then let them alone till they are sober: if they make you not then the better answer, you may say they are not the men you took them for.

Watch. Well, sir.

Dog. If you meet a thief, you may suspect him, by virtue of your office, to be no true man; and, for such kind of men, the less you meddle or make with them, the more is for your honesty.

Watch. If we know him to be a thief, shall we not lay hands on him?

Dog. Truly, by your office, you may; but I think they that touch pitch will be defiled: the most peaceable way for you, if you do take a thief, is to let him show himself what he is, and steal out of your company.

Verg. You have been always called a merciful man, partner.

Dog. Truly, I would not hang a dog by my will, much more a man who hath any honesty in him.

Verg. If you hear a child crying in the night, you must call to the nurse and bid her still it.

Watch. How if the nurse be asleep and will not hear us?

Dog. Why, then, depart in peace, and let the child wake her with crying; for the ewe that will not hear her lamb when it baes will never answer a calf when he bleats.

Verg. 'Tis very true.

Dog. This is the end of the charge:—you, constable, are to present the prince's own person; if you meet the prince in the night, you may stay him.

Verg. Nay, by 'r lady, that I think I cannot.

Dog. Five shillings to one on't, with any man that knows the statues, he may stay him: marry not without the prince be willing; for, indeed, the watch ought to offend no man; and it is an offence to stay a man against his will.

Verg. By'r lady, I think it be so.

Dog. Ha, ah, ha! Well, masters, good-night: an there be any matter of weight chances, call up me: Keep your fellows' counsels and your own; and good night. Come, neighbour.

Watch. Well, masters, we hear our charge: let us go sit here upon the church-bench till two, and then all to bed.

Dog. One word more, honest neighbours. I pray you, watch about Signior Leonato's door; for the wedding being there to-morrow, there is a great coil to-night. Adieu: be vigitant, I beseech you.

[*Exeunt* DOGBERRY AND VERGES.]

Enter BORACHIO *and* CONRADE

Bora. What, Conrade!
Watch. [*Aside*]. Peace! Stir not.
Bora. Conrade, I say!
Con. Here, man; I am at thy elbow.
Bora. Mass, and my elbow itched; I thought there would a scab follow.
Con. I will owe thee an answer for that: and now forward with thy tale.
Bora. Stand thee close, then, under this penthouse, for it drizzles rain; and I will, like a true drunkard, utter all to thee.
Watch. [*Aside*]. Some treason, masters; yet stand close.
Bora. Therefore know I have earned of Don John a thousand ducats.
Con. Is it possible that any villany should be so dear?
Bora. Thou shouldst rather ask, if it were possible any villany should be so rich; for when rich villains have need of poor ones, poor ones may make what price they will.
Con. I wonder at it.

Bora. That shows thou art unconfirmed. Thou knowest that the fashion of a doublet, or a hat, or a cloak, is nothing to a man.

Con. Yes, it is apparel.

Bora. I mean, the fashion.

Con. Yes, the fashion is the fashion.

Bora. Tush! I may as well say the fool's the fool. But seest thou not what a deformed thief this fashion is?

Watch. [*Aside*]. I know that Deformed; a' has been a vile thief this seven year; a' goes up and down like a gentleman: I remember his name.

Bora. Didst thou not hear somebody?

Con. No: 'twas the vane on the house.

Bora. Seest thou not, I say, what a deformed thief this fashion is? how giddily a' turns about all the hot bloods between fourteen and five-and-thirty? Sometimes fashioning them like Pharaoh's soldiers in the reechy painting, sometime like god Bel's priests in the old church-window, sometime like the shaven Hercules in the smirched worm-eaten tapestry, where his codpiece seems as massy as his club!

Con. All this I see; and I see that the fashion wears out more apparel than the man. But art not thou thyself giddy with the fashion too, that thou has shifted out of thy tale into telling me of the fashion?

Bora. Not so, neither: but know that I have to-night wooed Margaret, the Lady Hero's gentlewoman, by the name of Hero: she leans me out at her mistress's chamber-window, bids me a thousand times good-night,—I tell this tale vilely:—I should first tell thee how the Prince, Claudio and my master, planted and placed and possessed by my master Don John, saw afar off in the orchard this amiable encounter.

Con. And thought they Margaret was Hero?

Bora. Two of them did, the prince and Claudio; but the devil my master knew she was Margaret; and partly by his oaths, which first possessed them, partly by the dark night, which did deceive them, but chiefly by my villany, which did confirm any slander that Don John had made, away went Claudio enraged; swore he would meet her, as he was appointed, next morning at the temple, and there, before the whole congregation, shame her with what he saw o'er night, and send her home again without a husband.

First Watch. We charge you, in the prince's name, stand!

Sec. Watch. Call up the night master constable. We have here recovered the most dangerous piece of lechery that ever was known in the common-wealth.

First Watch. And one Deformed is one of them: I know him; a' wears a lock.

Con. Masters, masters.—

Sec. Watch. You'll be made bring Deformed forth. I warrant you.

Con. Masters,——

First Watch. Never speak: we charge you let us obey you to go with us.

Bora. We are like to prove a goodly commodity, being taken up of these men's bills.

Con. A commodity in question, I warrant you. Come, we'll obey you.

[*Exeunt.*]

A Prison.

Enter DOGBERRY, VERGES, *and* SEXTON, *in gowns*; *and the* WATCH, *with* CONRADE *and* BORACHIO.

Dog. Is our abode dissembly appeared?

Verg. O, a stool and a cushion for the sexton.

Sex. Which be the malefactors?

Dog. Marry, that am I and my partner

Verg. Nay, that's certain; we have the exhibition to examine.

Sex. But which are the offenders that are to be examined? let them come before master constable.

Dog. Yea, marry, let them come before me. What is your name, friend?

Bora. Borachio.

Dog. Pray, write down, Borachio. Yours, sirrah?

Con. I am a gentleman, sir, and my name is Conrade.

Dog. Write down, master gentleman Conrade. Masters, do you serve God?

Con.} Yea, sir, we hope.
Bora.

Dog. Write down, that they hope they serve God: and write God first; for God defend but God should go before such villains! Masters, it is proved already that you are little better than false knaves; and it will go near to be thought so shortly. How answer you for yourselves?

Con. Marry, sir, we say we are none.

Dog. A marvellous witty fellow, I assure you; but I will go about with him. Come you hither, sirrah; a word in your ear: sir, I say to you, it is thought you are false knaves.

Bora. Sir, I say to you we are none.

Dog. Well, stand aside. 'Fore God, they are both in a tale. Have you writ down, that they are none?

Sex. Master Constable, you go not the way to examine: you must call forth the watch that are their accusers.

Dog. Yea, marry, that's the eftest way. Let the watch come forth. Masters, I charge you, in the prince's name, accuse these men.

First Watch. This man said, sir, that Don John, the prince's brother, was a villain.

Dog. Write down, Prince John a villain. Why, this is flat perjury, to call a prince's brother villain.

Bora. Master Constable—,

Dog. Pray thee, fellow, peace : I do not like thy look, I promise thee.

Sex. What heard you him say else?

Sec. Watch. Marry, that he had received a thousand ducats of Don John for accusing the Lady Hero wrongfully.

Dog. Flat burglary as ever was committed.

Verg. Yea, by mass, that it is.

Sex. What else, fellow?

First Watch. And that Count Claudio did mean, upon his words, to disgrace Hero before the whole assembly, and not marry her.

Dog. O villain! thou wilt be condemned into everlasting redemption for this.

Sex. What else?

Watch. This is all.

Sex. And this is more, masters, than you can deny. Prince John is this morning secretly stolen away; Hero was in this manner accused, in this very manner refused, and upon the grief of this suddenly died. Master Constable, let these men be bound, and brought to Leonato's : I will go before and show him their examination.

[*Exit.*]

Dog. Come, let them be opinioned.

Verg. Let them be in the hands——

Con. Off, coxcomb!

Dog. God's my life, where's the sexton? let him write down, the prince's officer, coxcomb. Come, bind them. Thou naughty varlet!

Con. Away! you are an ass, you are an ass.

Dog. Dost thou not suspect my place? dost thou not suspect my years? O that he were here to write me down an ass! But, masters, remember that

I am an ass; though it be not written down, yet forget not that I am an ass. No, thou villain, thou art full of piety, as shall be proved upon thee by good witness. I am a wise fellow; and, which is more, an officer; and, which is more, a householder; and, which is more, as pretty a piece of flesh as any is in Messina; and one that knows the law, go to; and a rich fellow enough, go to; and a fellow that hath had losses; and one that hath two gowns, and every thing handsome about him. Bring him away. O that I had been writ down an ass !

[*Exeunt.*]

RECRUITING

A SHOEMAKER'S HOLIDAY
Dekker

A Street in London

The Commonalty

To Lacy, Askew, enter SIMON EYRE, MARGERY *his wife,* HODGE, FIRK, JANE, *and* RALPH *with a pair of shoes.*

Eyre. Leave whining, leave whining ! Away with this whimpering, this puling, these blubbering tears, and these wet eyes ! I'll get thy husband discharged, I warrant thee, sweet Jane; go to !

Hodge. Master, here be the captains.

Eyre. Peace, Hodge; hush, ye knave, hush !

Firk. Here be the cavaliers and the colonels, master.

Eyre. Peace, Firk; peace, my fine Firk ! Stand by with your pishery-pashery, away ! I am a man of the best presence; I'll speak to them, and they were Popes—Gentlemen, captains, colonels, commanders ! Brave men, brave leaders, may it please you to give me audience. I am Simon Eyre, the mad shoemaker of Tower Street; this wench with the mealy mouth that will never tire, is my wife, I can tell you; here's Hodge, my man and my foreman; here's Firk, my fine firking journeyman, and this is blubbered Jane. All we come to be suitors for this honest Ralph. Keep him at home, and as I am a true shoemaker and a gentleman of the gentle craft, buy spurs yourselves, and I'll find ye boots these seven years.

Marg. Seven years, husband?

Eyre. Peace, midriff, peace! I know what I do. Peace!

Firk. Truly, master cormorant, you shall do God good service to let Ralph and his wife stay together. She's a young new-married woman; if you take her husband away from her a night, you undo her; she may beg in the daytime; for he's as good a workman at a prick and an awl, as any is in our trade.

Jane. O let him stay, else I shall be undone.

Firk. Ay, truly, she shall be laid at one side like a pair of old shoes else, and be occupied for no use.

Lacy. Truly, my friends, it lies not in my powers: The Londoners are pressed, paid, and set forth by the lord mayor; I cannot change a man.

Hodge. Why, then you were as good be a corporal as a colonel, if you cannot discharge one good fellow; and I tell you true, I think you do more than you can answer, to press a man within a year and a day of his marriage.

Eyre. Well said, melancholy Hodge; gramercy, my fine foreman.

Marg. Truly, gentleman, it were ill done for such as you, to stand so stiffly against a poor young wife, considering her case, she is new-married, but let that pass: I pray, deal not roughly with her; her husband is a young man, and but newly entered, but let that pass.

Eyre. Away with your pishery-pashery, your pols and your edipols! Peace, midriff; silence, Cicely Bumtrinket! Let your head speak.

Firk. Yea, and the horns, too, master.

Eyre. Too soon, my fine Firk, too soon! Peace, scoundrels! See you this man? Captains, you will not release him? Well, let him go; he's a proper shot; let him vanish! Peace, Jane, dry up thy tears, they'll make his powder dankish. Take him, brave men; Hector of Troy was an hackney to him. Hercules and those termagant scoundrels, Prince Arthur's Round-table—by the Lord of Ludgate—ne'er fed such a tall, such a dapper swordsman; by the life of Pharaoh, a brave resolute swordsman! Peace, Jane; I say no more, mad knaves.

Firk. See, see, Hodge, how my master raves in commendation of Ralph!

Hodge. Ralph, th'art a gull, by this hand, and thou goest not.

Askew. I am glad, good Master Eyre, it is my hap
To meet so resolute a soldier.
Trust me, for your report and love to him,
A common slight regard shall not respect him.

Lacy. Is thy name Ralph?

Ralph. Yes, sir.

Lacy. Give me thy hand;
Thou shalt not want, as I am a gentleman.
Woman, be patient; God, no doubt, will send
Thy husband safe again; but he must go,
His country's quarrel says it shall be so.

Hodge. Th'art a gull, by my stirrup, if thou dost not go. I will not have thee strike thy gimlet into these weak vessels; prick thine enemies, Ralph.

Enter DODGER.

Dodger. My lord, your uncle on the Tower-hill
Stays with the lord mayor and the aldermen,
And doth request you with all speed you may,
To hasten thither.

Askew. Cousin, let's go.

Lacy. Dodger, run you before, tell them we come
This Dodger is mine uncle's parasite.
       [*Exit Dodger.*]

The arrant'st varlet that e'er breathed on earth;
He sets more discord in a noble house
By one day's broaching of his pickthank tales,
Than can be salved again in twenty years,
And he, I fear, shall go with us to France,
To pry into our actions.
 Askew.   Therefore, coz,
It shall behove you to be circumspect.
 Lacy. Fear not, good cousin.—Ralph, hie to your colours.
 Ralph. I must, because there's no remedy;
But, gentle master and my loving dame,
As you have always been a friend to me,
So in mine absence think upon my wife.
 Jane. Alas, my Ralph.
 Marg. She cannot speak for weeping.
 Eyre. Peace, you cracked groats, you mustard tokens, disquiet not the brave soldier. Go thy ways, Ralph!
 Jane. Ay, ay, you bid him go; what shall I do when he is gone?
 Firk. Why be doing with me or my fellow Hodge; be not idle.
 Eyre. Let me see thy hand, Jane. This fine hand, this white hand, these pretty fingers must spin, must card, must work; work, you bombast-cotton-candle-quean; work for your living, with a pox to you.— Hold thee, Ralph, here's five sixpences for thee; fight for the honour of the gentle craft, for the gentlemen shoemakers, the courageous cordwainers, the flower of St. Martin's, the mad knaves of Bedlam, Fleet Street, Tower Street and Whitechapel; crack me the crowns of the French knaves; a pox on them,

crack them; fight by the Lord of Ludgate; fight, my fine boy!

Firk. Here, Ralph, here's three twopences; two carry into France, the third shall wash our souls at parting, for sorrow is dry. For my sake, firk the *Basa mon cues*.

Hodge. Ralph, I am heavy at parting; but here's a shilling for thee. God send thee to cram thy slops with French crowns, and thy enemies' bellies with bullets.

Ralph. I thank you, master, and I thank you all.
Now, gentle wife, my loving lovely Jane,
Rich men, at parting, give their wives rich gifts,
Jewels and rings, to grace their lily hands.
Thou know'st our trade makes rings for women's
    heels:
Here take this pair of shoes, cut out by Hodge,
Stitched by my fellow Firk, seamed by myself,
Made up and pinked with letters for thy name.
Wear them, my dear Jane, for thy husband's sake;
And every morning, when thou pull'st them on,
Remember me, and pray for my return.
Make much of them; for I have made them so,
That I can know them from a thousand mo.

WHAT'S BECOME OF MY WIFE?

A SHOEMAKER'S HOLIDAY
Dekker

Room in Eyre's house

To Firk, Margery, Hans, Hodge, enter Ralph, lame.

Hodge. What, fellow Ralph? Mistress, look here, Jane's husband! Why, how now, lame? Hans, make much of him, he's a brother of our trade, a good workman, and a tall soldier.

Hans. You be welcome, broder.

Marg. Perdy, I knew him not. How doſt thou, good Ralph? I am glad to see thee well.

Ralph. I would to God you saw me, dame, as well as when I went from London into France.

Marg. Truſt me, I am sorry, Ralph, to see thee impotent. Lord, how the wars have made him sunburnt! The left leg is not well; 'twas a fair gift of God the infirmity took not hold a little higher, considering thou cameſt from France; but let that pass.

Ralph. I am glad to see you well, and I rejoice
To hear that God hath bleſt my maſter so
Since my departure.

Marg. Yea, truly, Ralph, I thank my Maker.: but let that pass.

Hodge. And, sirrah Ralph, what news, what news in France?

Ralph. Tell me, good Roger, firſt, what news in England? How does my Jane? When didſt thou see my wife?
Where lives my poor heart? She'll be poor indeed,
Now I want limbs to get whereon to feed.

Hodge. Limbs? Haſt thou not hands, man? Thou shalt never see a shoemaker want bread, though he have but three fingers on a hand.

Ralph. Yet all this while I hear not of my Jane.

Marg. O Ralph, your wife,—perdy, we know not what's become of her. She was here a while, and because she was married, grew more ſtately than became her; I checked her, and so forth; away she flung, never returned, nor said bye nor bah; and, Ralph, you know, "ka me, ka thee." And so, as I tell ye—Roger, is not Firk come yet?

Hodge. No, forsooth.

Marg. And so, indeed, we heard not of her, but I hear she lives in London; but let that pass. If she had wanted, she might have opened her case to me or my husband, or to any of my men ; I am sure, there's not any of them, perdy, but would have done her good to his power. Hans, look if Firk be come.

Hans. Yaw. ik sal. vro.
[*Exit* Hans.]

Marg. And so, as I said—but, Ralph, why dost thou weep ? Thou knowest that naked we came out of our mother's womb, and naked we must return ; and, therefore, thank God for all things.

Hodge. No, faith, Jane is a stranger here ; but, Ralph, pull up a good heart, I know thou hast one. Thy wife, man, is in London ; one told me, he saw her a while ago very brave and neat ; we'll ferret her out, an' London hold her.

Marg. Alas, poor soul, he's overcome with sorrow; he does but as I do, weep for the loss of any good thing. But, Ralph, get thee in, call for some meat and drink, thou shalt find me worshipful towards thee.

Ralph. I thank you, dame ; since I want limbs and lands, I'll trust to God, my good friends, and my hands.
[*Exit*]

A PAIR OF SHOES

A SHOEMAKER'S HOLIDAY
Dekker

A Street before Hodge's Shop

Enter a SERVING-MAN

Serv. Let' me see now, the sign of the Last in Tower Street. Mass, yonder's the house. What-haw ! Who's within ?

Enter RALPH

Ralph. Who calls there ? What want you, sir ?

Serv. Marry, I would have a pair of shoes made for a gentlewoman against to-morrow morning. What, can you do them ?

Ralph. Yes, sir, you shall have them. But what length's her foot?

Serv. Why you must make them in all parts like this shoe; but, at any hand, fail not to do them, for the gentlewoman is to be married very early in the morning.

Ralph. How? by this shoe must it be made? by this? Are you sure, sir, by this?

Serv. How, by this? Am I sure, by this? Art thou in thy wits? I tell thee, I must have a pair of shoes dost thou mark me? a pair of shoes, two shoes, made by this very shoe, this same shoe, against to-morrow morning by four a clock. Dost understand me? Canst thou do't?

Ralph. Yes, sir, yes—I—I—I can do't. By this shoe, you say? I should know this shoe. Yes, sir, yes, by this shoe, I can do't. Four a clock, well. Whither shall I bring them?

Serv. To the sign of the Golden Ball in Watling Street; enquire for one Master Hammon, a gentleman, my master.

Ralph. Yea, sir; by this shoe, you say?

Serv. I say, Master Hammon at the Golden Ball; he's the bridegroom, and those shoes are for his bride.

Ralph. They shall be done by this shoe; well, well, Master Hammon at the Golden Shoe—I would say, the Golden Ball; very well, very well. But I pray you sir,, where must Master Hammon be married?

Serv. At Saint Faith's Church, under Paul's. But what's that to thee? Prithee, dispatch those shoes, and so farewell.

[*Exit*]

Ralph. By this shoe, said he. How am I amazed. At this strange accident! Upon my life, This was the very shoe I gave my wife, When I was pressed for France; since when, alas!

I never could hear of her; it is the same,
And Hammon's bride no other but my Jane.

Enter FIRK.

Firk. 'Snails, Ralph, thou hast lost thy part of three pots, a countryman of mine gave me to breakfast.

Ralph. I care not; I have found a better thing.

Firk. A thing? away! Is it a man's thing, or a woman's thing?

Ralph. Firk, dost thou know this shoe?

Firk. No, by my troth; neither doth that know me! I have no acquaintance with it, 'tis a mere stranger to me.

Ralph. Why, then I do; this shoe, I durst be sworn,
Once covered the instep of my Jane.
This is her size, her breadth, thus trod my love;
These true-love knots I pricked; I hold my life,
By this old shoe I shall find out my wife.

Firk. Ha, ha! Old shoe, that wert new! How a murrain came this ague-fit of foolishness upon thee?

Ralph. Thus, Firk; even now here came a serving-man;
By this shoe would he have a new pair made
Against to-morrow morning for his mistress,
That's to be married to a gentleman.
And why may not this be my sweet Jane?

Firk. And why may'st not thou be my sweet ass? Ha, ha!

Ralph. Well, laugh and spare not! But the truth is this:
Against to-morrow morning I'll provide
A lusty crew of honest shoemakers,
To watch the going of the bride to church.
If she prove Jane, I'll take her in despite
From Hammon and the devil, were he by.
If it be not my Jane, what remedy?

Hereof I am sure, I shall live till I die,
Although I never with a woman lie.
[Exit]

Firk. Thou lie with a woman to build nothing but Cripple-gates ! Well, God sends fools fortune, and it may be, he may light upon his matrimony by such a device; for wedding and hanging goes by destiny. *[Exit]*

COURT PLAYERS

HAMLET
Shakespeare

Flourish of trumpets within

Guildenstern. There are the players.

Hamlet. Gentlemen, you are welcome to Elsinore. Your hands, come then: the appurtenance of welcome is fashion and ceremony: let me comply with you in this garb, lest my extent to the players, which, I tell you must show fairly outward, should more appear like entertainment than yours. You are welcome: but my uncle-father and aunt-mother are deceived.

Guil. In what, my dear lord?

Ham. I am but mad north-north-west: when the wind is southerly I know a hawk from a handsaw.

Re-enter Polonius.

Pol. Well be with you, gentlemen!

Ham. Hark you, Guildenstern; and you too: at each ear a hearer: that great baby you see there is not yet out of his swaddling-clouts.

Rosencrantz. Happily he's the second time come to them; for they say an old man is twice a child.

Ham. I will prophesy he comes to tell me of the players: mark it. You say right, sir: o'Monday morning; 'twas so, indeed.

The Diversions

Pol. My lord, I have news to tell you.

Ham. My lord, I have news to tell you. When Roscius was an actor in Rome,—

Pol. The actors are come hither, my lord.

Ham. Buz, buz!

Pol. Upon my honour,—

Ham. Then came each actor on his ass,—

Pol, The best actors in the world, either for tragedy, comedy, history, pastoral, pastoral-comical, historical-pastoral, tragical-historical, tragical-comical-historical-pastoral, scene individable, or poem unlimited : Seneca cannot be too heavy, nor Plautus too light. For the law of writ and the liberty, these are the only men.

Ham. O Jephthah, judge of Israel, what a treasure had'st thou!

Pol. What a treasure had he, my lord?

Ham. Why,

' One fair daughter, and no more,
  The which he loved passing well.'

Pol. .[*Aside*]. Still on my daughter.

Ham. Am I not i' the right, old Jephthah?

Pol. If you call me Jephthah, my lord, I have a daughter that I love passing well.

Ham. Nay, that follows not.

Pol. What follows, then, my lord?

Ham. Why,

' As by lot, God wot,'

And then you know,

' It came to pass, as most like it was,'—

The first row of the pious chanson will show you more ; for look, where my abridgement comes.

Enter four or five Players.

You are welcome, masters ; welcome all. I am glad to see thee well. Welcome, good friends. O, my old friend! Why thy face is valanced since I saw thee last ; comest thou to beard me in Denmark?

What, my young lady and mistress! By 'r Lady, your ladyship is nearer to heaven than when I saw you last, by the altitude of a chopine. Pray God, your voice, like a piece of uncurrent gold, be not cracked within the ring. Masters, you are all welcome. We'll e'en to 't like French falconers, fly at any thing we see: we'll have a speech straight: come, give us a taste of your quality; come, a passionate speech.

First Play. What speech, my good lord?

Ham. I heard thee speak me a speech once, but it was never acted; or, if it was, not above once; for the play, I remember, pleased not the million; 'twas caviare to the general: but it was—as I received it, and others, whose judgements in such matters cried in the top of mine—an excellent play, well digested in the scenes, set down with as much modesty as cunning. I remember, one said there were no sallets in the lines to make the matter savoury, nor no matter in the phrase that might indict the author of affectation; but called it an honest method, as wholesome as sweet, and by very much more handsome than fine. One speech in it I chiefly loved: 'twas Æneas' tale to Dido; and thereabout of it especially, where he speaks of Priam's slaughter: if it live in your memory, begin at this line; let me see, let me, see;

' The rugged Pyrrhus, like th' Hyrcanian beast,'—
It is not so: it begins with ' Pyrrhus.'

' The rugged Pyrrhus, he whose sable arms,
  Black as his purpose, did the night resemble
  When he lay couched in the ominous horse,
  Hath now this dread and black complexion
    smear'd
  With heraldry more dismal: head to foot
  Now is he total gules; horridly trick'd
  With blood of fathers, mothers, daughters, sons,
  Baked and impasted with the parching streets,
  That lend a tyrannous and a damned light

   To their lord's murder : roasted in wrath and fire,
  And thus o'er-sized with coagulate gore,
  With eyes like carbuncles, the hellish Pyrrhus
  Old grandsire Priam seeks.'
  So, proceed you.
 Pol. 'Fore God, my lord, well spoken, with good accent and good discretion.
 First Play.   ' Anon he finds him
  Striking too short at Greeks ; his antique sword
  Rebellious to his arm, lies where it falls,
  Repugnant to command : unequal match'd,
  Pyrrhus at Priam drives ; in rage strikes wide ;
  But with the whiff and wind of his fell sword
  The unnerved father falls. Then senseless Ilium,
  Seeming to feel this blow, with flaming top
  Stoops to his base, and with a hideous crash
  Takes prisoner Pyrrhus' ear : for, lo ! his sword,
  Which was declining on the milky head
  Of reverend Priam, seem'd i' the air to stick :
  So, as a painted tyrant, Pyrrhus stood,
  And like a neutral to his will and matter,
  Did nothing.
  But as we often see, against some storm,
  A silence in the heavens, the rack stand still,
  The bold winds speechless and the orb below
  As hush as death, anon the dreadful thunder
  Doth rend the region, so after Pyrrhus' pause
  Aroused vengeance sets him new a-work ;
  And never did the Cyclops' hammers fall
  On Mars's armour, forged for proof eterne,
  With less remorse than Pyrrhus' bleeding sword
  Now falls on Priam.
  Out, out, thou strumpet, Fortune ! All you gods,
  In general synod take away her power,
  Break all the spokes and fellies from her wheel,
  And bowl the round nave down the hill of heaven
  As low as to the fiends !'

Pol. This is too long.
Ham. It shall to the barber's, with your beard. Prithee, say on: he's for a jig or a tale of bawdry, or he sleeps: say on: come to Hecuba.
First Play. 'But who, O, who had seen the
    mobled queen—'
Ham. 'The mobled queen?'
Pol. That's good; 'mobled queen' is good.
First Play. 'Run barefoot up and down, threaten-
    ing the flames
With bisson rheum; a clout upon that head
Where late the diadem stood; and for a robe,
About her lank and all o'er-teemed loins,
A blanket, in the alarm of fear caught up:
Who this had seen, with tongue in venom steep'd
'Gainst Fortune's state would treason have pro-
    nounced:
But if the gods themselves did see her then,
When she saw Pyrrhus make malicious sport
In mincing with his sword her husband's limbs,
The instant burst of clamour that she made,
Unless things mortal move them not at all,
Would have made mitch the burning eyes of
    heaven
And passion in the gods.'
Pol. Look, whether he has not turned his colour and has tears in's eyes. Prithee, no more.
Ham. 'Tis well; I'll have thee speak out the rest of this soon. Good my lord, will you see the players well bestowed? Do you hear, let them be well used, for they are the abstract and brief chronicles of the time: after your death you were better have a bad epitaph than their ill report while you live.
Pol. My lord, I will use them according to their desert.
Ham. God's bodykins, man, much better: use every man after his desert, and who shall 'scape

whipping? Use them after your own honour and dignity: the less they deserve, the more merit is in your bounty.

A hall in the castle.

Enter HAMLET *and* PLAYERS.

Ham. Speak the speech, I pray you, as I pronounced it to you, trippingly on the tongue: but if you mouth it, as many of your players do, I had as lief the town-crier spoke my lines. Nor do not saw the air too much with your hand, thus; but use all gently: for in the very torrent, tempest, and, as I may say, whirlwind of your passion, you must acquire and beget a temperance that may give it smoothness. O, it offends me to the soul to hear a robustious perwig-pated fellow tear a passion to tatters, to very rags, to split the ears of the groundlings, who, for the most part are capable of nothing but inexplicable dumb-shows and noise: I would have such a fellow whipped for o'erdoing termagant; it out-herods Herod: pray you, avoid it.

First Play. I warrant your honour.

Ham. Be not too tame neither, but let your own discretion be your tutor: suit the action to the word, the word to the action; with this special observance, that you o'erstep not the modesty of nature: for anything so overdone is from the purpose of playing, whose end, both at the first and now, was and is, to hold, as 'twere, the mirror up to nature; to show virtue her own feature, scorn her own image, and the very age and body of the time his form and pressure. Now this overdone or come tardy off, though it make the unskilful laugh, cannot but make the judicious grieve; the censure of the which one must in your allowance o'erweigh a whole theatre of others. O, there be players that I have seen play, and heard others praise, and that highly, not to speak it profanely, that neither having the accent of Christians nor the gait of Christian, pagan, nor man, have so strutted and bellowed, that I have thought some of nature's journeymen had made men, and not made them well, they imitated humanity so abominably.

First Play. I hope we have reformed that indifferently with us, sir.

Ham. O, reform it altogether. And let those that play your clowns speak no more than is set down for them: for there be of them that will themselves laugh, to set on some quantity of barren spectators to laugh too, though in the mean time some necessary question of the play be then to be considered: that's villanous, and shows a most pitiful ambition in the fool that uses it. Go, make you ready.

[*Exeunt* PLAYERS]

MASQUES AND COMMONERS

LOVE RESTOR'D
Ben Jonson

The KING *and* COURT *being seated and in expectation.*
Enter MASQUERADO.

I would I could make them a show myself! In troth, ladies, I pity you all. You are in expectation of a device to-night, and I am afraid you can do little else but expect it. Though I dare not show my face, I can speak truth under a vizard. Good faith, an't please your majesty, your Masquers are all at a stand; I cannot think your majesty will see any show to-night, at least worth your patience. Some two hours since, we were in that forwardness, our dances learned, our masquing attire on and attired. A pretty fine speech was taken up of the poet too, which if he never be paid for now, it's no matter; his wit costs him nothing. Unless we should come in like a morrice-dance, and whistle our ballad ourselves, I know not what we should do: we have neither musician to play our tunes, but the wild music here; and the rogue playboy, that acts Cupid, is got so hoarse, your majesty cannot hear him half the breadth of your chair.

Enter PLUTUS, *as Cupid.*

See, they have thrust him out, at adventure. We humbly beseech your majesty to bear with us. We had both hope and purpose it should have been better, howsoever we are lost in it.

Plu. What makes this light, feather'd vanity here? away, impertinent folly! Infect not this assembly.

Masq. How, boy!

Plu. Thou common corruption of all manners and places that admit thee.

Masq. Have you recovered your voice to rail at me?

Plu. No, vizarded impudence. I am neither player nor masquer; but the god himself, whose deity is here profaned by thee. Thou, and thy like, think yourselves authorized in this place to all license of surquedry. But you shall find custom hath not so grafted you here, but you may be rent up, and thrown out as unprofitable evils. I tell thee, I will have no more masquing; I will not buy a false and fleeting delight so dear: the merry madness of one hour shall not cost me the repentance of an age.

Enter ROBIN GOODFELLOW

Rob. How! no masque, no masque? I pray you say, are you sure on't? no masque, indeed! What do I here then? can you tell?

Masq. No, faith.

Rob. Slight, I'll be gone again, an there be no

The title page of the book of that name, 1650.

masque; there's a jest. Pray you resolve me. Is there any? or no? a masque?

Plu. Who are you?

Rob. Nay, I'll tell you that when I can. Does any body know themselves here, think you? I would fain know if there be a masque or no.

Plu. There is none, nor shall be, sir; does that satisfy you?

Rob. Slight, a fine trick! a piece of England's joy, this! Are these your court sports? would I had kept me to my gambols o' the country still, selling of fish, short service, shoeing the wild mare, or roasting of robin-redbreast. These were better, than, after all this time, no masque: you look at me. I have recovered myself now for you, I am the honest plain country spirit, and harmless; Robin Goodfellow, he that sweeps the hearth and the house clean, riddles† for the country maids, and does all their other drudgery, while they are at hot-cockles: one that has discoursed with your court spirits ere now; but was fain to-night to run a thousand hazards to arrive at this place; never poor goblin was so put to his shifts to get in to see nothing. So many thorny difficulties as I have past, deserved the best masque; the whole shop of the revels. I would you would admit some of my feats, but I have little hope of that, i' faith, you let me in so hardly.

Plu. Sir, here's no place for them nor you. Your rude food-fellowship must seek some other sphere for your admitty.

Rob. Nay, so your stiff-necked porter told me at the gate, but not in so good words. His staff spoke somewhat to that boisterous sense: I am sure he concluded all in a non-entry, which made me e'en climb over the wall, and in by the wood yard, so to the terrace, where when I came, I found the oaks of the guard

†riddles = passes the embers through a sieve.

more unmoved, and one of them, upon whose arm I hung, shoved me off o'the ladder, and dropt me down like an acorn. 'Twas well there was not a sow in the verge, I had been eaten up else. Then I heard some talk of the carpenters' way, and I attempted that; but there the wooden rogues let a huge trapdoor fall on my head. If I had not been a spirit, I had been mazarded. Though I confess I am none of those subtle ones, that can creep through at a key-hole, or the cracked pane of a window. I must come in at a door, which made me once think of a trunk; but that I would not imitate so Catholic a coxcomb as Coryat. Therefore I took another course. I watched what kind of persons the door most opened to, and one of their shapes I would belie to get in with. First I came with authority, and said, I was an engineer, and belonged to the motions. They asked me if I was the fighting bear of last year, and laughed me out of that, and said the motions were ceased. Then I took another figure, of an old tire-woman; but tired under that too, for none of the masquers would take note of me, the mark was out of my mouth. Then I pretended to be a musician, marry I could not shew mine instrument, and that bred a discord. Now there was nothing left for me that I could presently think on, but a feather-maker of Blackfriars, and in that shape I told them, Surely I must come in, let it be opened unto me; but they all made as light of me, as of my feathers; and wondered how I could be a Puritan, being of so vain a vocation. I answered, We are all masquers sometimes: with which they knock'd Hypocrisy o'the pate, and made room for a bombard man, that brought bouge* for a country lady or two, that fainted, he said, with fasting for the fine sight since seven o'clock in the morning. O how it grieved me, that I was prevented of that shape, and

*Bouge=provisions.

had not touched on it in time, it liked me so well;
but I thought I would offer at it yet. Marry,
before I could procure my properties, alarum came
that some of the whimlens had too much; and one
shewed how fruitfully they had watered his head, as
he stood under the grices; and another came out,
complaining of a cataract shot into his eyes by a
planet, as he was star-gazing. There was that device
defeated! By this time I saw a fine citizen's wife or
two let in; and that figure provoked me exceedingly
to take it; which I had no sooner done, but one of
the black-guards had his hand in my vestry, and was
groping of me as nimbly as the Christmas cut-purse.
He thought he might be bold with me, because I
had not a husband in sight to squeak to. I was glad
to forego my form, to be rid of his hot steeming
affection, it so smelt of the boiling house. Forty
other devices I had of wiremen and the chandrie, and
I know not what else: but all succeeded alike. I
offered money too, but that could not be done so
privately, as it durst be taken, for the danger of an
example. At last, a troop of strangers came to the
door, with whom I made myself sure to enter: but
before I could mix, they were all let in, and I left
alone without, for want of an interpreter. Which,
when I was fain to be to myself, a Colossus [of] the
company told me, I had English enough to carry me
to bed; with which all the other statues of flesh
laughed. Never till then did I know the want of an
hook and a piece of beef, to have baited three or four
of those goodly wide mouths with. In this despair,
when all invention and translation too failed me, I
e'en went back, and stuck to this shape you see me in
of mine own, with my broom and my candles, and
came on confidently, giving out, I was a part of
the Device: at which, though they had little to do
with wit, yet, because some on't might be used here

to-night, contrary to their knowledge, they thought it fit, way should be made for me; and, as it fall out, to small purpose.

A LESSON IN GALLANTRY

CYNTHIA'S REVELS
Ben Jonson

Enter AMORPHUS, *followed by* ASOTUS *and his* TAILOR.

Amo. A little more forward: so, sir. Now go in, discloak yourself and come forth. [*Exit* ASOTUS]. Tailor, bestow thy absence upon us; and be not prodigal of this secret, but to a dear customer.

[*Exit* TAILOR]

Re-enter ASOTUS

'Tis well enter'd, sir. Stay, you come on too fast; your pace is too impetuous. Imagine this to be the palace of your pleasure, or place where your lady is pleased to be seen. First, you present yourself, thus: and spying her, you fall off, and walk some two turns; in which time, it is to be supposed, your passion hath sufficiently whited your face, then, stifling a sigh or two, and closing your lips, with a trembling boldness, and bold terror, you advance yourself forforward. Prove this much, I pray you.

Aso. Yes, sir;—pray Jove I can light on it! Here, I come in, you say, and present myself?

Amo. Good.

Aso. And then I spy her, and walk off?

Amo' Very good.

Aso. Now, sir, I stifle, and advance forward?

Amo. Trembling.

Aso. Yes, sir, trembling; I shall do it better when I come to it. And what must I speak now?

Amo. Marry, you shall say; *Dear Beauty,* or *sweet Honour* (or by what other title you please to remember her), *methinks you are melancholy.* This is, if she be alone now, and discompanied.

Aso. Well, sir, I'll enter again; her title shall be *My dear Lindabrides.*

Amo. Lindabrides!

Aso. Ay, sir, the emperor Alicandroe's daughter, and the prince Meridian's sister, in *the Knight of the Sun*; she should have been married to him, but that the princess Claridiana——

Amo. O, you betray your reading.

Aso. Nay, sir, I have read history, I am a little humanitian. Interrupt me not, good sir. *My dear Lindabrides,—my dear Lindabrides,—my dear Lindabrides, methinks you are melancholy.*

Amo. Ay, and take her by the rosy-fingered hand.

Aso. Must I so: O!—*My dear Lindabrides, methinks you are melancholy.*

Amo. Or thus, sir. *All variety of divine pleasures, choice sports, sweet music, rich fare, brave attire, soft beds, and silken thoughts, attend this dear beauty.*

Aso. Believe me, that's pretty. *All variety of divine pleasures, choice sports, sweet music, rich fare, brave attire, soft beds, and silken thoughts, attend this dear beauty.*

Amo. And then, offering to kiss her hand, if she shall coily recoil, and signify your repulse, you are to re-enforce yourself with:

> *More than most fair lady.*
> *Let not the rigour of your just disdain*
> *Thus coarsely censure of your servant's zeal.*

And withal, protest her to be the only and absolute unparallel'd creature you do adore, and admire, and respect, and reverence, in this Court, corner of the world, or kingdom.

Aso. This is hard, by my faith. I'll begin it all again.

Amo. Do so, and I will act it for your lady.

Aso. Will you vouchsafe, sir? *All variety of divine pleasures, choice sports, sweet music, rich fare, brave attire, soft beds, and silken thoughts, attend this dear beauty.*

Amo. So, sir, pray you, away.

Aso. More than most fair lady
Let not the rigour of your just disdain
Thus coarsely censure of your servant's zeal;
I protest you are the only, and absolute, unapparell'd

Amo. Unparallel'd.

Aso. Unparallel'd creature, I do adore, and admire, and respect, and reverence, *in this corner of the world or kingdom.*

Amo. This is, if she abide you. But now, put the case she should be passant when you enter, as thus: you are to frame your gait thereafter, and call upon her, *lady, nymph, sweet refuge, star of our court.* Then, if she be guardant, here; you are to come on, and, laterally disposing yourself, swear by her blushing and well-coloured cheek, the bright dye of her hair, her ivory teeth, (though they be ebony), or some such white and innocent oath, to induce you. If regardant, then maintain your station, brisk and ripe, show the supple motion of your pliant body, but in chief of your knee, and hand, which cannot but arride her proud humour exceedingly.

Aso. I conceive you, sir. I shall perform all these things in good time, I doubt not, they do so hit me.

Amo. Well, sir, I am your lady; make use of any of these beginnings, or some other out of your invention; and prove how you can hold up, and follow it. Say, say.

Asso. Yes, sir. *My dear Lindabrides.*

Amo. No, you affect that Lindabrides too much;

and let me tell you it is not so courtly. Your pedant should provide you some parcels of French, or some pretty commodity of Italian, to commence with, if you would be exotic and exquisite.

Aso. Yes, sir, he was at my lodging t'other morning, I gave him a doublet.

Amo. Double your benevolence, and give him the hose too; clothe you his body, he will help to apparel your mind. But now, see what your proper genius can perform alone, without adjection of any other Minerva.

Aso. I comprehend you, sir.

Amo. I do stand you, sir; fall back to your first place. Good, passing well: very properly pursued.

Aso. Beautiful, ambiguous, and sufficient lady, what! are you all alone?

Amo. We would be, sir, if you should leave us.

Aso. I am at your beauty's appointment, bright angel; but—

Amo. What but?

Aso. No harm, more than most fair feature.

Amo. That touch relish'd well.

Aso. But I protest—

Amo. And why should you protest?

Aso. For good will, dear esteem'd madam, and I hope your ladyship will so conceive of it:
And will, in time, return from your disdain,
And rue the suff'rance of our friendly pain.

Amo. O, that piece was excellent! If you could pick out more of these play-articles, and, as occasion shall salute you, embroider or damask your discourse with them, persuade your soul, it would most judiciously commend you. Come, this was a well discharged and auspicious bout. Prove the second.

Aso. Lady, I cannot ruffle it in red and yellow.

Amo. Why, if you can revel it in white, sir, 'tis sufficient.

Aso. Say you so, sweet lady! Lan, tede, de, de, de, dant, dant, dant, dante. [Sings and dances]. No, in good faith, madam, whosoever told you ladyship so, abused you; but I would be glad to meet your ladyship in a measure.

Amo. Me, sir! Belike you measure me by yourself, then?

Aso. Would I might, fair feature.

Amo. And what were you the better, if you might?

Aso. The better it please you to ask, fair lady.

Amo. Why, this was ravishing, and most acutely continued. Well, spend not your humour too much, you have now competently exercised your conceit: this, once or twice a day, will render you an accomplished, elaborate, and well-levell'd gallant. Convey in your courting-stock, we will in the heat of this go visit the nymph's chamber.

[*Exeunt*]

VILLAGE PLAYERS

A MIDSUMMER NIGHT'S DREAM
Shakespeare

The Wood. TITANIA *lying asleep*
Enter QUINCE, SNUG, BOTTOM, FLUTE, SNOUT *and* STARVELING

Bot. Are we all met?

Quin. Pat, pat; and here's a marvellous convenient place for our rehearsal. This green plot shall be our stage, this hawthorn-brake our tiring-house; and we will do it in action as we will do it before the duke.

Bot. Peter Quince,—

Quin. What sayest thou, Bully Bottom?

Bot. There are things in this comedy of Pyramus and Thisby that will never please. First, Pyramus must draw a sword to kill himself; which the ladies cannot abide. How answer you that?

Snout. By'r lakin', a parlous fear.

Star. I believe we must leave the killing out, when all is done.

Bot. Not a whit: I have a device to make all well. Write me a prologue; and let the prologue seem to say, we will do no harm with our swords, and that Pyramus is not killed indeed; and, for the more better assurance, tell them that I Pyramus am not Pyramus, but Bottom the weaver: this will put them out of fear.

Quin. Well, we will have such a prologue; and it shall be written in eight and six.

Bot. No, make it two more; let it be written in eight and eight.

Snout. Will not the ladies be afeard of the lion?

Star. I fear it, I promise you.

Bot. Masters, you ought to consider with your selves: to bring in,—God shield us!—a lion among ladies, is a most dreadful thing; for there is not a more fearful wild-fowl than your lion living: and we ought to look to't.

Snout. Therefore another prologue must tell he is not a lion.

Bot. Nay, you must name his name, and half his face must be seen through the lion's neck; and he himself must speak through, saying thus, or to the same defect,—'Ladies,' or, 'Fair ladies,—I would wish you,'—or, 'I would request you,'—or, 'I would entreat you,—not to fear, not to tremble: my life for yours. If you think I am come hither as a lion, it were pity of my life: no, I am no such thing; I am a man as other men are:' and there indeed let him name his name, and tell them plainly, he is Snug the joiner.

Quin. Well, it shall be so. But there is two hard

things; that is, to bring the moonlight into a chamber; for, you know, Pyramus and Thisby meet by moonlight.

Snout. Doth the moon shine that night we play our play?

Bot. A calendar, a calendar! look in the almanac; find out moonshine, find out moonshine.

Quin. Yes, it doth shine that night.

Bot. Why, then may you leave a casement of the great chamber window, where we play, open, and the moon may shine in at the casement.

Quin. Ay; or else one must come in with a bush of thorns and a lantern, and say he comes to disfigure, or to present, the person of moonshine. Then, there is another thing: we must have a wall in the great chamber; for Pyramus and Thisby, says the story, did talk through the chink of a wall.

Snout. You can never bring in a wall. What say you, Bottom?

Bot. Some man or other must present wall: and let him have some plaster, or some loam, or some rough-cast about him, to signify wall; and let him hold his fingers thus, and through that cranny shall Pyramus and Thisby whisper.

Quin. If that may be, then all is well. Come, sit down, every mother's son, and rehearse your parts. Pyramus, you begin: when you have spoken your speech, enter into that brake: and so everyone according to his cue.

Enter PUCK *behind.*

Puck. What hempen home-spun have we swaggering here,
So near the cradle of the fairy queen?
What, a play toward! I'll be an auditor;
An actor too perhaps, if I see cause.

Quin. Speak, Pyramus. Thisby, stand forth.

Bot. Thisby, the flowers of odious savours sweet,—

Quin. Odours, odours.
Bot. —odours savours sweet:
So hath thy breath, my dearest Thisby dear.
But hark, a voice! Stay thou but here awhile,
 And by and by I will to thee appear.   [*Exit*]
 Puck. A stranger Pyramus than e'er played here.
   [*Exit*]
 Flu. Must I speak now?
 Quin. Ay, marry, must you; for you must understand he goes but to see a noise that he heard, and is to come again.
 Flu. Most radiant Pyramus, most lily-white of
   hue,
Of colour like the red rose on triumphant brier,
Most briskly juvenal, and eke most lovely Jew,
 As true as truest horse, that yet would never tire,
I'll meet thee, Pyramus, at Ninny's tomb.
 Quiu. 'Ninus' tomb,' than: why you must not speak that yet; that you answer to Pyramus: you speak all your part at once, cues and all. Pyramus enter: your cue is past; it is, ' never tire.'

The Palace of Theseus.

To THESEUS, HIPPOLYTA, PHILOSTRATE, LYSANDER, DEMETRIUS, HERMIA, HELENA, *enter* QUINCE *for the Prologue.*
 Pro. If we offend, it is with our good will.
 That you should think, we come out to offend,
But with good will. To show our simple skill,
 That is the true beginning of der end.
Consider, then, we come but in despite.
 We do not come, as minding to content you,
Our true intent is. All for your delight,
 We are not here. That you should here repent you,
The actors are at hand; and, by their show,
You shall know all, that you are like to know.
 The. This fellow doth not stand upon points.

Lys. He hath rid his prologue like a rough colt; he knows not the stop. A good moral, my lord: it is not enough to speak, but to speak true.

Hip. Indeed he hath played on his prologue like a child on a recorder; a sound, but not in government.

The. His speech was like a tangled chain; nothing impaired, but all disordered. Who is next?

Enter Pyramus *and* Thisbe, Wall, Moonshine, *and* Lion.

Pro. Gentles, perchance you wonder at this show;
   But wonder on, till truth make all things plain.
This man is Pyramus, if you would know;
   This beauteous lady Thisby is certain.
This man, with lime and rough-cast, doth present
   Wall, that vile Wall which did these lovers sunder;
And through Wall's chink, poor souls, they are content
   To whisper. At the which let no man wonder.
This man, with lanthorn, dog, and bush of thorn,
   Presenteth Moonshine; for, if you will know,
By moonshine did these lovers think no scorn
   To meet at Ninus' tomb, there, there to woo.
This grisly beast, which Lion hight by name,
The trusty Thisby, coming first by night,
Did scare away, or rather did affright;
And, as she fled, her mantle she did fall,
   Which Lion vile with bloody mouth did stain.
Anon comes Pyramus, sweet youth and tall,
   And finds his trusty Thisby's mantle slain:
Whereat, with blade, with bloody blameful blade,
   He bravely broach'd his boiling bloody breast,
And Thisby, tarrying in mulberry shade,
   His dagger drew, and died. For all the rest,
Let Lion, Moonshine, Wall, and lovers twain
   At large discourse, while here they do remain.

Exeunt Prologue, Pyramus, Thisbe, Lion *and* Moonshine.

The. I wonder if the lion be to speak.

Dem. No wonder, my lord: one lion may, when many asses do.

Wall. In this same interlude it doth befall
That I, one Snout by name, present a wall;
And such a wall, as I would have you think,
That had in it a crannied hole or chink,
Through which the lovers, Pyramus and Thisby,
Did whisper often very secretly.
This loam, this rough-cast, and this stone, doth show
That I am that same wall; the truth is so:
And this the cranny is, right and sinister,
Through which the fearful lovers are to whisper.

The. Would you desire lime and hair to speak better?

Dem. It is the wittiest partition that ever I heard discourse, my lord.

The. Pyramus draws near the wall: silence!

Re-enter PYRAMUS.

Pyr. O grim-look'd night! O night with hue so black!
O night, which ever art when day is not!
O night, O night! alack, alack, alack,
   I fear my Thisby's promise is forgot!
And thou, O wall, O sweet, O lovely wall,
   That stand'st between her father's ground and mine!
Thou wall, O wall, O sweet and lovely wall,
   Show me thy chink, to blink through with mine eyne!

[WALL *holds up his fingers*]

Thanks, courteous wall: Jove shield thee well for this!
But what see I? No Thisby do I see,
O wicked wall, through whom I see no bliss!
Cursed be thy stones for thus deceiving me!

The. The wall, methinks, being sensible, should curse again.

Pyr. No, in truth, sir, he should not. 'Deceiving me' is Thisbe's cue: she is to enter now, and I am to spy her through the wall. You shall see, it will fall pat as I told you. Yonder she comes.

Re-enter THISBE.

This. O wall, full often hast thou heard my moans,
For parting my fair Pyramus and me!
My cherry lips have often kiss'd thy stones,
 Thy stones with lime and hair knit up in thee.
Pyr. I see a voice: now will I to the chink,
To spy an I can hear my Thisby's face.
Thisby!
This. My love thou art, my love I think.
Pyr. Think what thou wilt, I am thy lover's grace,
And, like Limander, am I trusty still.
This. And I like Helen, till the Fates me kill.
Pyr. Not Shafalus to Procrus was so true.
This. As Shafalus to Procrus, I to you.
Pyr. O, kiss me through the hole of this vile wall!
This. I kiss the wall's hole, not your lips at all.
Pyr. Wilt thou at Ninny's tomb meet me straightway?
This. 'Tide life,' tide death, I come without delay.

[*Exeunt* PYRAMUS *and* THISBE]

Wall. Thus have I, wall, my part discharged so;
And, being done, thus wall away do go.

[*Exit*]

The. Now is the mural down between the two neighbours.
Dem. No remedy, my lord, when walls are so wilful to hear without warning.
Hip. This is the silliest stuff that ever I heard.
The. The best in this kind are but shadows; and the worse are no worse, if imagination amend them.

Hip. It must be your imagination, then, and not theirs.

The. If we imagine no worse of them than they of themselves, they may pass for excellent men. Here come two noble beasts in, a man and a lion.

Re-enter LION *and* MOONSHINE.

Lion. You, ladies, you, whose gentle hearts do fear
The smallest monstrous mouse that creeps on floor,
May now perchance both quake and tremble here,
When lion rough in wildest rage doth roar.
Then know that I, one Snug the joiner, am
A lion-fell, nor else no lion's dam;
For, if I should as lion come in strife
Into this place, 'twere pity on my life.

The. A very gentle beast, and of a good conscience.

Dem. The very best at a beast, my lord, that e'er I saw.

Lys. This lion is a very fox for his valour.

The. True; and a goose for his discretion.

Dem. Not so, my lord; for his valour cannot carry his discretion; and the fox carries the goose.

The. His discretion, I am sure, cannot carry his valour; for the goose carries not the fox. It is well: leave it to his discretion, and let us listen to the moon.

Moon. This lanthorn doth the horned moon present;—

Dem. He should have worn the horns on his head.

The. He is no crescent, and his horns are invisible within the circumference.

Moon. This lanthorn doth the horned moon present;
Myself the man i' the moon do seem to be.

The. This is the greatest error of all the rest: the man should be put into the lantern. How is it else the man i' the moon?

Dem. He dares not come there for the candle; for, you see, it is already in snuff.

Hip. I am aweary of this moon: would he would change!

The. It appears, by his small light of discretion, that he is in the wane; but yet, in courtesy, in all reason, we must stay the time.

Lys. Proceed, Moon.

Moon. All that I have to say, is, to tell you that the lanthorn is the moon; I, the man i' the moon; this thorn-bush, my thorn-bush; and this dog, my dog.

Dem. Why, all these should be in the lantern; for all these are in the moon. But, silence! here comes Thisbe.

Re-enter THISBE.

This. This is old Ninny's tomb. Where is my love?

Lion. [*Roaring*]. Oh——   [THISBE *runs off*]

Dem. Well roared, Lion.

The. Well run, Thisbe.

Hip. Well shone, Moon. Truly, the moon shines with a good grace.

[*The* LION *shakes* THISBE'S *mantle, and exit*]

The. Well moused, Lion.

Dem. And then came Pyramus.

Lys. And so the lion vanished.

Re-enter PYRAMUS

Pyr. Sweet Moon, I thank thee for thy sunny beams;
I thank thee, Moon, for shining now so bright;
For, by thy gracious, golden, glittering gleams,
I trust to take of truest Thisby sight.
     But stay, O spite!
     But mark, poor knight,
What dreadful dole is here!
     Eyes, so you see?
     How can it be?

O dainty duck ! O dear !
    Thy mantle good,
    What, stain'd with blood !
Approach, ye Furies fell !
    O Fates, come, come,
    Cut thread and thrum ;
Quail, crush, conclude, and quell !

The. This passion, and the death of a dear friend, would go near to make a man look sad.

Hip. Beshrew my heart, but I pity the man.

Pyr. O wherefore, Nature, did'st thou lions frame?
Since lion vile hath here deflowered my dear :
Which is—no, no—which was the fairest dame
That lived, that loved, that liked, that look'd with
    cheer.
    Come, tears, confound ;
    Out, sword, and wound
The pap of Pyramus ;
    Ay, that left pap,
    Where heart doth hop :   [*Stabs himself*]
Thus die I, thus, thus, thus.
    Now am I dead,
    Now am I fled ;
My soul is in the sky :
    Tongue, lose thy light ;
    Moon, take thy flight :   [*Exit Moonshine*]
Now die, die, die, die, die.   [*Dies*]

Dem. No die, but an ace, for him ; for he is but one.

Lys. Less than an ace, man ; for he is dead ; he is nothing.

The. With the help of a surgeon he might yet recover, and prove an ass.

Hip. How chance Moonshine is gone before Thisbe comes back and finds her lover ?

The. She will find him by starlight. Here she comes ; and her passion ends the play.

Re-enter THISBE.

Hip. Methinks she should not use a long one for such a Pyramus : I hope she will be brief.

Dem. A mote will turn the balance, which Pyramus, which Thisbe, is the better ; he for a man, God warrant us ; she for a woman, God bless us.

Lys. She hath spied him already with those sweet eyes.

Dem. And thus she means, videlicet :—

This. Alseep, my love ?
What, dead, my dove ?
O Pyramus, arise !
Speak, speak. Quite dumb ?
Dead, dead ? A tomb
Must cover thy sweet eyes.
These lily lips,
This cherry nose,
These yellow cowslip cheeks,
Are gone, are gone :
Lovers, make moan:
His eyes were green as leeks.
O Sisters Three,
Come, come to me,
With hands as pale as milk :
Lay them in gore,
Since you have shore
With shears his thread of silk.
Tongue, not a word :
Come, trusty sword ;
Come, blade, my breast imbrue :   [*Stabs herself*]
And, farewell, friends ;
Thus Thisbe ends :
Adieu, adieu, adieu.   [*Dies*]

The. Moonshine and Lion are left to bury the dead.

Dem. Ay, and Wall too.

Bot. [*Starting up*]. No, I assure you ; the wall is down that parted their fathers. Will it please you to see the epilogue, or to hear a Bergomask dance between two of our company?

The. No epilogue, I pray you; for your play needs no excuse. Never excuse; for when the players are all dead, there need none be blamed. Marry, if he that writ it had played Pyramus and hanged himself in Thisbe's garter, it would have been a fine tragedy: and so it is, truly; and very notably discharged. But come, your Bergomask: let your epilogue alone.

RIDDLES AND PROPHECIES
CYNTHIA'S REVELS
Ben Jonson

PHANTASTE, PHILANTIA, ARGURION, MORIA, HEDON, ANAIDES, AMORPHUS, ASOTUS.

Phi. For spots sake let's have some Riddles or Purposes, ho!

Pha. No, faith, your Prophecies are best, the t'other are stale.

Phi. Prophecies! we cannot all sit in at them; we shall make a confusion. No; what call'd you that we had in the forenoon?

Pha. Substantives and adjectives, is it not, Hedon?
Pha. Ay that. Who begins?
Pha. I have thought; speak your adjectives, sirs.
Phi. But do not you change them.
Pha. Not I. Who says?
Mor. Odoriferous.
Phi. Popular.
Arg. Humble.
Ana. White-liver'd.
Hed. Barbarous.
Amo. Pythagorical.
Hed. Yours, signior.
Aso. What must I do, sir?

Amo. Give forth your adjective with the rest; as prosperous, good, fair, sweet, well—

Hed. Any thing that hath not been spoken.

Aso. Yes sir, well spoken shall be mine.

Pha. What have you all done?

All. Ay.

Pha. Then the substantive is Breeches. Why *odoriferous* breeches, guardian?

Mor. Odoriferous,—because odoriferous: that which contains most variety of savour and smell we say is most odoriferous; now breeches, I presume, are incident to that variety, and therefore odoriferous breeches.

Pha. Well, we must take it howsoever. Who's next? Philautia?

Phi. Popular.

Pha. Why *popular* breeches?

Phi. Marry, that is, when they are not content to be generally noted in court, but will press forth on common stages and broker's stalls, to the public view of the world.

Pha. Good. Why *humble* breeches, Argurion?

Arg. Humble! because they use to be sat upon; besides, if you tie them not up, their property is to fall down about your heels.

Mer. She has worn the breeches, it seems, which have done so.

Pha. But why *white-liver'd*?

Ana. Why! are not their linings white? Besides when they come in swaggering company, and will pocket up any thing, may they not properly be said to be white-liver'd?

Pha. O yes, we must not deny it. And why *barbarous*, Hedon?

Hed. Barbarous! because commonly, when you have worn your breeches sufficiently, you give them to your barber.

Amo. That's good; but how *Pythagorical*?
Phi. Ay, Amorphus, why Pythagorical breeches?
Amo. O most kindly of all; 'tis a conceit of that fortune, I am bold to hug my brain for.
Pha. How is it, exquisite Amorphus?
Amo. O, I am rapt with it, 'tis so fit, so proper, so happy—
Phi. Nay, do not rack us thus.
Amo. I never truly relish'd myself before. Give me your ears. Breeches, Pythagorical, by reason of their transmigration into several shapes.
Mor. Most rare, in sweet troth. Marry this young gentleman, for his well-spoken—
Pha. Ay, why *well-spoken* breeches?
Aso. Well-spoken! Marry, well-spoken because —whatsoever they speak is well-taken; and whatsoever is well-taken is well-spoken.
Mor. Excellent! believe me.
Aso. Not so, ladies, neither.
Hed. But why breeches, now?
Pha. Breeches, *quasi* bear-riches; when a gallant bears all his riches in his breeches.
Amo. Most fortunately etymologised.
Pha. Nay, we have another sport afore this, of A thing done, and who did it, etc.
Phi. Ay, good Phantaste, let's have that: distribute the places.
Pha. Why, I imagine, A thing done; Hedon thinks, who did it; Moria, with what it was done; Anaides, where it was done; Argurion, when it was done; Amorphus, for what cause was it done; you, Philautia, what followed upon the doing of it; and this gentleman, who would have done it better. What? is it conceived about?
All. Yes, yes.
Pha. Then speak you, sir, *Who would have done it better*?

Aso. How! does it begin at me?

Pha. Yes, sir: this play is called the Crab, it goes backward.

Aso. May I not name myself?

Phi. If you please, sir, and dare abide the venture of it.

Aso. Then I would have done it better, whatever it is.

Pha. No doubt on't, sir; a good confidence. *What followed upon the act*, Philautia?

Phi. A few heat drops, and a month's mirth.

Pha. *For what cause*, Amorphus?

Amo. For the delight of ladies.

Pha. *When*, Argurion?

Arg. Last progress.

Pha. *Where*, Anaides?

Ana. Why, in a pair of pain'd slops.

Pha. *With what*, Moria?

Mor. With a glyster.

Pha. *Who*, Hedon?

Hed. A traveller.

Pha. Then the thing done was, *An oration was made*. Rehearse. An oration was made—

Hed. By a traveller—

Mor. With a glyster—

Ana. In a pair of pain'd slops—

Arg. Last progress—

Amo. For the delight of ladies—

Phi. A few heat drops, and a month's mirth followed.

Pha. And, this silent gentleman would have done it better.

CHAPTER II

THE RESTORATION

A CORONATION
Evelyn's DIARY

April 23, 1661. Was the coronation of his Majesty *At Court* Charles II, in the Abby Church of Westminster; at all which ceremonie I was present. The King and all his Nobility went to the Tower, I accompanying my Lord Viscount Mordaunt part of the way; this was on Sunday the 22nd, but indeede his Majestie went not til early this morning, and proceeded from thence to Westminster in this order:

First went the Duke of York's Horse Guards. Messengers of the Chamber. 136 Esquires to the Knights of the Bath, each of whom had two, most richly habited. The Knight Harbinger, Serjeant Porter. Sewers of the Chamber. Quarter Waiters. Six Clearks of Chancery. Clearke of the Signet. Clearke of the Priory Seale. Clearks of the Council, of the Parliament, and of the Crowne. Chaplaines in ordinary having dignities 10. Kings Advocats and Remembrancer. Council at Law. Members of the Chancery. Puisne Serjeants. Kings Attorney and Solicitor. Kings eldest Serjeant. Secretaries of the French and Latine tongue. Gent. Ushers, Daily Waiters, Sewers, Carvers, and Cupbearers in ordinary. Esquires of the Body 4. Masters of Standing offices being no Councillors, *viz.* of the

Tents, Revels, Ceremonies, Armorie, Wardrobe, Ordnance, Requests, Chamberlaine of the Exchequer. Barons of the Exchequer. Judges. Lord Chiefe Baron. Lord C. Justice of the Common Pleas. Master of the Rolls. Lord C. Justice of England. Trumpets. Gentlemen of the Privy Chamber. Knights of the Bath, 68, in crimson robes exceeding rich and the noblest shew of the whole cavalcade, his Majestie excepted. Knt. Marshall. Treasurer of the Chamber. Master of the Jewells. Lords of the Privy Council. Comptroller of the Household. Treasurer of the Household. Trumpets. Serjeant Trumpet. Two Pursuivants at Armes. Barons. Two Pursuivants at Armes. Viscounts. Two Heraulds. Earles. Lord Chamberlaine of the Household. Two Heraulds. Marquisses. Dukes. Heralds Clarencieux and Norroy. Lord Chancellor. Lord High Steward of England. Two persons representing the Dukes of Normandy and Aquitain, *viz*. Sir Richard Fanshawe and Sir Herbert Price, in fantastiq habits of the time. Gentlemen Ushers. Garter. Lord Maior of London. The Duke of York alone (the rest by two's). Lord High Constable of England. Lord Great Chamberlaine of England. The Sword borne by the Earle Marshal of England. The KING in royal robes and equipage. Afterwards follow'd Equerries, Footemen, Gent. Pensioners. Master of the Horse leading a horse richly caparison'd. Vice Chamberlaine. Captain of the Pensioners. Captain of the Guard. The Guard. The Horse Guard. The Troope of Volunteers with many other Officers and Gentlemen.

This magnificent traine on horseback, as rich as embroidery, velvet, cloth of gold and silver, and jewells, could make them and their prancing horses, proceeded thro' the streetes strew'd with flowers, houses hung with rich tapessry, windoes and balconies full of ladies; the London Militia lining the ways, and the several Companies with their banners and loud musiq rank'd in their orders; the fountains running wine, bells ringing, with speeches made at the severall triumphal arches; at that of the Temple Barr (neere which I stood) the Lord Maior was receiv'd by the Bayliff of Westminster, who in a scarlet robe made a speech. Thence with joyful acclamations his Majestie passed to Whitehall. Bonfires at night.

The next day, being St. George's, he went by water to Westminster Abby. Wher his Majestie was enter'd, the Deane and Prebendaries brought all the regalia, and deliver'd them to severall Noblemen to beare before the King, who met them at the west doore of the Church singing an anthem, to the Quire. Then came the Peers in their robes and coronets in their hands, til his Majestic was plac'd on a throne elevated before the altar. Then the Bishop of London (the Archbishop of Canterbury being sick) went to every side of the throne to present the King to the People, asking if they would have him for their King and do him homage; at this they shouted four times *God save King Charles the Second*! Then an anthem was sung. Then his Majestie attended by 3 Bishops went up to the altar, and he offer'd a pall and a pound of gold. Afterwards he sate downe in another chaire during the sermon, which was preach'd by Dr. Morley then Bishop of Worcester. After sermon the King tooke his oath before the altar to maintain the Religion, Magna Charta, and Laws of the Land. The hymn *Veni S. Sp.* follow'd, and then the Litany by 2 Bishops. Then the Archbishop of Canterbury, present but much indispos'd and weake, said *Lift up your hearts*; at which the King rose up and put off his robes and upper garments, and was in a waistcoate so opened in divers places that the Archb'p might commodiously anoint him, first in the palmes of his hands, when an anthem was sung and a prayer read; then his breast and twixt the shoulders, bending of both armes, and lastly on the crowne of the head, with apposite hymns and prayers at each anoynting; this done, the Deane clos'd and button'd up the waistcoate. Then was a coyfe put on, and the cobbium, syndon, or dalmatic, and over this a supertunic of cloth of gold, with buskins and sandals of the same, spurs, and the sword, a prayer being first said over it by the Archbishop on the altar before t'was girt on by the Lord Chamberlaine. Then the armill, mantle, etc. Then the Archbishop plac'd the crowne imperial on the altar pray'd over it, and set it on his Majestie's head, at which all the Peers put on their coronets. Anthems and rare musiq, with lutes, viols, trumpets, organs, and voices, were then heard, and the Archbishop put a ring on his Majestie's finger. The King next offer'd his sword on the altar, which being redeemed was drawn and borne before him. Then the Archbishop deliver'd him the sceptre with the dove in one hand, and in the other the sceptre with the globe. Then the King kneeling, the Archbishop pronounce'd the blessing. The King then ascending againe his Royal Throne, whilst *Te Deum* was singing, all the Peeres did their homage, by everyone touching his crowne. The Archbishop and the rest of the Bishops first kissing the King; who receiv'd the holy sacrament, and so disrob'd, yet with the crowne imperial on his head, and accompanied with all the Nobility in the former order, he went on foote upon blew cloth, which was spread and reach'd from the West dore of the Abby to Westminster stayres, when he tooke water in a triumphal barge to Whitehall, where was extraordinary feasting.

THE RESTORATION

CORONATION DAY
Pepys' Diary

April 23rd, 1661. About four I rose and got to the Abbey, where I followed Sir J. Denham, the surveyor, with some company he was leading in. And with much ado, by the favour of Mr. Cooper, his man, did get up into a great scaffold across the north end of the Abbey, where with a great deal of patience I sat from past four till eleven before the King came in. And a great pleasure it was to see the Abbey raised in the middle, all covered with red, and a throne (that is, a chair) and footstool on the top of it; and all the officers of all kinds, so much as the very fiddlers, in red vests. At last comes in the Dean and Prebendaries of Westminster, with the Bishops (many of them in cloth of gold copes), and after them the Nobility, all in their Parliament robes, which was a most magnificent sight. Then the Duke and the King with a sceptre (carried by my Lord Sandwich) and sword and wand before him, and the crown too. The King in his robes, bareheaded, which was very fine. And after all had placed themselves, there was a sermon and the service; and then in the choir at the high altar the King passed through all the ceremonies of the Coronation, which to my great grief I and most in the Abbey could not see. The crown being put upon his head, a great shout began, and he came forth to the throne, and there passed through more ceremonies: as taking the oath, and having things read to him by the Bishop: and his lords (who put on their caps as soon as the King put on his crown) and bishops came, and kneeled before him. And three times the King-at-Arms went to the three open places on the scaffold, and proclaimed, that if any one could show any reason why Charles Stewart should not be King of England, that now he should come and

speak. And a General Pardon also was read by the
Lord Chancellor, and medals flung up and down by my
Lord Cornwallis, of silver, but I could not come by
any. But so great a noise that I could make but little
of the music; and indeed, it was lost to everybody.
I went out a little while before the King had done all
his ceremonies, and went round the Abbey to Westminster Hall, all the way within rails, and 10,000
people with the ground covered with blue cloth; and
scaffolds all the way. Into the Hall I got, where it
was very fine with hangings and scaffolds one upon
another, full of brave ladies; and my wife in one
little one, on the right hand. Here I stayed walking
up and down, and at last upon one of the side stalls
I stood and saw the King come in with all the persons
(but the soldiers) that were yesterday in the cavalcade;
and a most pleasant sight it was to see them in their
several robes. And the King came in with his crown
on, and his sceptre in his hand, under a canopy borne
up by six silver staves, carried by Barons of the Cinque
Ports, and little bells at every end. And after a long
time he got up to the farther end, and all set themselves down at their several tables; and that was also
a brave sight: and the King's first course carried up
by the Knights of the Bath. And many fine ceremonies there was of the Herald's leading up people
before him, and bowing; and my Lord of Albemarle's going to the kitchen and eating a bit of the
first dish that was to go to the King's table. But,
above all, was these three Lords, Northumberland,
and Suffolk, and the Duke of Ormond, coming before
the courses on horseback, and staying so all dinner-
time, and at last bringing up (Dymcock) the King's
Champion, all in armour on horseback, with his spear
and target carried before him. And a Herald pro-
proclaims 'That if any dare deny Charles Stewart to
be lawful King of England, here was a Champion

From the Medallion by David le Marchand in the British Museum.

THE RESTORATION

that would fight with him'; and with these words, the Champion flings down his gauntlet, and all this he do three times in his going up towards the King's table. At last, when he is come, the King drinks to him, and then sends him the cup, which is of gold, and he drinks it off, and then rides back again with the cup in his hand. I went from table to table to see the Bishops and all others at their dinner, and was infinitely pleased with it. And at the Lord's table I met with William Howe, and he spoke to my Lord for me, and he did give him four rabbits and a pullet, and so Mr. Creed and I got Mr. Minshell to give us some bread, and so we at a stall ate it, as everybody else did what they could get. I took a great deal of pleasure to go up and down, and look upon the ladies, and to hear the music of all sorts, but above all the 24 violins. About six at night they had dined, and I went up to my wife. And strange it is to think that these two days have held up fair till now that all is done, and the King gone out of the Hall; and then it fell a-raining and thundering and lightening as I have not seen it do for some years; which people did take great notice of. God's blessing of the work of these two days, which is a foolery to take too much notice of such things. I observed little disorder in all this, only the King's footmen had got hold of the canopy, and would keep it from the Barons of the Cinque Ports, which they endeavoured to force from them again, but could not do it till my Lord Duke of Albemarle caused it to be put into Sir R. Pye's hand till to-morrow to be decided. At Mr. Bowyer's; a great deal of company, some I knew, others I did not. Here we stayed upon the leads and below till it was late, expecting to see the fireworks, but they were not performed to-night; only the City had a light like a glory round about it, with bonfires. At last I went to King Street, and there sent Crockford to my father's and my house, to tell them I could not come home to-night, because of the dirt, and a coach could not be had. And so I took my wife and Mrs. Frankleyn (who I proffered the civility of lying with my wife at Mrs. Hunt's to-night) to Axe Yard, in which, at the further end, there were three great bonfires, and a great many gallants, men and women; and they laid hold of us, and would have us drink the King's health upon our knees, kneeling upon a faggot, which we all did, they drinking to us one after another, which we thought a strange frolic; but these gallants continued there a great while, and I wondered to see how the ladies did tipple. At last I sent my wife and her bedfellow to bed, and Mr. Hunt and I went in with Mr. Thornbury (who did give the company all their wine, he being yeoman of the wine-cellar to the King); and there, with his wife and two of his sisters, and some gallant sparks that were there, we drank the King's health, and nothing else, till one of the gentlemen fell down stark drunk, and there lay; and I went to my Lord's pretty well. But no sooner a-bed with Mr. Shepley but my head began to turn, and I to vomit and if ever I was foxed, it was now, which I cannot say yet, because I fell asleep, and slept till morning. Thus did the day end with joy everywhere; and blessed be God, I have not heard of any mischance to anybody through it all, but only to Serjeant Glynne, whose horse fell upon him yesterday, and is like to kill him, which people do please themselves to see how just God is to punish the rogue at such a time as this: he being now one of the King's Serjeants, and rode in the cavalcade with Maynard, to whom people wish the same fortune. There was also this night, in Kihg Street, a woman had her eye put out by a boy's flinging a firebrand into the coach. Now, after all this, I can say, that, besides the pleasure of the sight of these glorious things, I may now shut my eyes against any other objects, nor for the future trouble myself to see things of state and show, as being sure never to see the like again in this world.

AN AUDIENCE

Evelyn's DIARY

Dec. 29, 1662. Saw the audience of the Muscovy Ambassador which was with extraordinary state, his retinue being numerous, all clad in vests of severall colours, with buskins after the Eastern manner; their caps of fur; tunicks richly embrodred with gold and pearls made a glorious shew. The King being seated under a canopie in the Banquetting house, the Secretary of the Embassy went before the Ambassador in a grave march, holding up his master's letters of credence in a crimson taffeta scarfe before his forehead. The Ambassador then deliver'd it with a profound reverence to the King, who gave it to our Secretary of State; it was written in a long and lofty style. Then came in the presents, borne by 165 of his retinue, consisting of mantles and other large pieces lined with sable, black fox and ermine; Persian carpets, the ground cloth of gold and velvet; hawks, such as they sayd never came the like; horses said to be Persian; bowes and arrows, &c. These borne by so long a traine rendered it very extraordinary. Wind musiq play'd all the while in the galleries above. This finish'd, the Ambassador was convey'd by the Master of the Ceremonies to York House, where he was treated with a banquet which cost £200 as I was assur'd.

"CREATIONS"

Pepys' DIARY

April 20th, 1661. Comes my boy to tell me that the Duke of York had sent for all the principal officers, etc., to come to him to-day. So I went by water to Mr. Coventry's, and there stayed and talked a good while with him till all the rest came. We went up and saw the Duke dress himself, and in his night habit he is a very plain man. Then he sent us to his closet, where we saw among other things two very fine chests, covered with gold and Indian varnish, given him by the East Indy Company of Holland. The Duke comes; and after he had told us that the fleet was designed for Algiers (which was kept from us till now), we did advise about many things as to the fitting of the fleet, and so went away. After that to my Lord's, where Sir W. Pen came to me, and dined with my Lord. After dinner he and others that dined there went away; and then my Lord looked upon his pages' and footmen's liveries which are come home to-day, and will be handsome, though not gaudy. Then with my Lady and my Lady Wright to Whitehall; and in the Banqueting House saw the King create my Lord Chancellor and several others Earls, and Mr. Crewe and several others Barons; the first being led up by Heralds and five old Earls to the King, and there the patent is read, and the King puts on his vest, and sword, and coronet, and gives him the patent. And then he kisseth the King's hand, and rises and stands covered before the King. And the same for each Baron, only he is led up by three of the old Barons. And they are girt with swords before they go to the King. That being done (which was very pleasant to see their habits), I carried my Lady back, and there I found my Lord angry, for that his page had let my Lord's new beaver hat be changed for an old hat; then I went away, and with Mr. Creed to the Exchange, and bought some things, as gloves and bandstrings, etc. So back to the Cockpit; and there, by the favour of one Mr. Bowman, he and I got in, and there saw the King and Duke of York and his Duchess (which is a plain woman, and like her mother, my Lady Chancellor). And so saw *The Humorsome Lieutenant* acted before the King, but not very well done. But my pleasure was great to see the manner of it, and so many great beauties, but, above all, Mrs. Palmer, with whom the King do discover a great deal of familiarity. So Mr. Creed and I (the play being done) went to Mrs. Harper's, and there sat and drank, it being about twelve at night. The ways being so dirty, and stopped up with the rails which are this day set up in the streets, I could not go home, but went with him to his lodgings at Mr. Ware's, and there lay all night.

21st. (Lord's day.) In the morning we were troubled to hear it rain as it did, because of the great show to-morrow. Dined with Dr. Thomas Pepys and Dr. Fairbrother; and all our talk about to-morrow's show, and our trouble that it is like to be a wet day. All the way is so thronged with people to see the triumphal arches, that I could hardly pass for them. Home, people being at church, and I got home unseen, and so up to my chamber, and set down these last five or six days' diaries.

22nd. The King's going from the Tower to Whitehall. Up early, and made myself as fine as I could, and put on my velvet coat, the first day that I put it on, though made half a year ago. And being ready, Sir W. Batten, my Lady, and his two daughters, and his son and wife, and Sir W. Pen and his son and I went to Mr. Young's, the flagmaker in Cornhill; and there we had a good room to ourselves, with wine and good cake, and saw the show very well. In which it is impossible to relate the glory of this day, expressed in the clothes of them that rode, and their horses and horse-clothes. Among others, my Lord Sandwich's embroidery and diamonds were not ordinary among them. The Knights of the Bath was a brave sight of itself; and their Esquires, among which Mr. Armiger was an Esquire to one of the Knights. Remarkable were the two men that represent the Dukes of Normandy and Aquitaine. The Bishops came next after Barons, which is the higher place; which makes me think that the next Parliament they will be called to the House of Lords. My Lord Monk rode bare after the King, and led in his hand a spare horse, as being Master of the Horse. The King, in a most rich embroidered suit and cloak, looked most noble. Wadlow, the vintner, at the Devil in Fleet Street, did lead a fine company of soldiers, all young, comely men, in white doublets. There followed the Vice-Chamberlain, Sir G. Carteret, a company of men all like Turks; but I know not yet what they are for. The streets all gravelled, and the houses hung with carpets before them, made brave show, and the ladies out of the windows. So glorious was the show with gold and silver, that we were not able to look at it, our eyes at last being so much overcome. Both the King and the Duke of York took notice of us, as they saw us at the window. In the evening, by water to Whitehall to my Lord's, and there I spoke with my Lord. He talked with me about his suit, which was made in France, and cost him £200, and very rich it is with embroidery.

AN AMBASSADOR

Evelyn's Diary

24 Feb. 1682. This evening I was at the entertainment of the Morocco Ambassador at the Dutchesse

of Portsmouth's glorious apartments at Whitehall, where was a greate banquet of sweetmeates and musiq, but at which both the Ambassador and his retinue behaved themselves with extraordinary moderation and modesty, tho' plac'd about a long table a lady betweene two Moores, and amongst these were the King's natural children, *viz.* Lady Lichfield and Sussex, the Dutchess of Portsmouth, Nelly, &c. concubines and cattill of that sort, as splendid as jewells and excesse of bravery could make them. The Moores neither admiring nor seeming to regard any thing, furniture or the like, with any earnestnesse, and but decently tasting of the banquet. They dranke a little milk and water, but not a drop of wine; they also dranke of a sorbet and jacolatt; did not looke aboute, or stare on the ladies, or expresse the least suprize, but with a courtly negligence in pace, countenance and whole behaviour, answering only to such questions as were ask'd with a greate deale of wit and gallantrie, and so gravely tooke leave with this compliment, ' That God would blesse the Dutchess of Portsmouth and the Prince her soun, meaning the little Duke of Richmond.' The King came in at the latter end, just as the Ambassador was going away. In this manner was this slave (for he was no more at home) entertain'd by most of the nobility in towne, and went often to Hide Park on horseback, where he and his retinue shew'd their extraordinary activity in horsemanship, and flinging and catching their launces at full speede; they rid very short, and could stand upright at full speede, managing their spears with incredible agility. He went sometimes to the theatres, where upon any foolish or fantastical action, he could not forbear laughing, but he endeavour'd to hide it with extraordinary modesty and gravity. In a word, the Russian Ambassador, still at Court, behav'd himselfe like a clowne compar'd to this civil heathen.

A RIVER PAGEANT

Evelyn's DIARY

23/viii/1662. I was spectator of the most magnificent triumph that ever floated on the Thames; considering the innumerable boates and vessells, dress'd and adorn'd with all imaginable pomp, but above all the thrones, arches, pageants, and other representations, stately barges of the Lord Maior and Companies, with various inventions, musiq and peales of ordnance both from the vessels and the shore, going to meete and conduct the new Queene from Hampton Court to Whitehall, at the first time of her coming to towne. In my opinion it far exceeded all the Venetian Bucentoras, etc., on the Ascension, when they go to espouse the Adriatic. His Majestie and the Queene came in an antiq-shap'd open vessell, cover'd with a state or canopy of cloth of gold, made in form of a cupola, supported with high Corinthian pillars, wreath'd with flowers, festoons, and garlands. I was in our new-built vessell, sailing amongst them.

A COURT BALL

Pepys' DIARY

15*th November*, 1666.

15th. To Mrs. Pierce's, where I find her as fine as possible, and Mr. Pierce going to the ball at night at Court, it being the Queen's birthday. I also to the ball, and with much ado got up to the loft, where with much trouble I could see very well. Anon the house grew full, and the candles light, and the King and Queen and all the ladies sat; and it was, indeed, a glorious sight to see Mrs. Stewart in black and white lace, and her head and shoulders dressed with diamonds, and the like many great ladies more, only the Queen none; and the King in his rich vest of some rich silk and silver trimming, as the Duke of York and all the dancers were, some of cloth of silver, and others of other sorts, exceeding rich. Presently after the King was come in, he took the Queen, and about fourteen more couple there was, and began the bransles. As many of the men as I can remember presently were the King, Duke of York, Prince Rupert, Duke of Monmouth, Duke of Buckingham Lord Douglas, Mr (George) Hamilton, Colonel Russell, Mr. Griffith, Lord Ossory, Lord Rochester; and of the ladies, the Queen, Duchess of York, Mrs. Stewart, Duchess of Monmouth, Lady Essex Howard, Mrs. Temple, Swede's Ambassadress, Lady Arlington, Lord George Barkeley's daughter, and many others I remember not; but all most excellently dressed in rich petticoats and gowns, and diamonds, and pearls. After the bransles, then to a corant, and now and then a French dance; but that so rare that the corants grew tiresome, that I wished it done. Only Mrs. Stewart danced mighty finely, and many French dances, specially one the King called the New Dance, which was very pretty; but, upon the whole matter, the business of the dancing of itself was not extraordinary pleasing. But the clothes and the sight of the persons were indeed very pleasing, and worth my coming, being never likely to see more gallantry while I live, if I should come twenty times. About twelve at night it broke up. So away home with my wife, who was displeased with the dull dancing, and satisfied with the clothes and persons. My Lady Castlemaine, without whom all is nothing, being there, very rich, though not dancing.

FRENCH MODES
Evelyn's DIARY

18 Oct. 1666. To Court. It being the first time his Majesty put himself solemnly into the Eastern

fashion of vest, changeing doublet, stiff collar, band and cloake, into a comely dress, after the Persian mode with girdle or straps, and shoe strings and garters into bouckles, of which some were set with precious stones, resolving never to alter it, and to leave the French mode, which had hitherto obtain'd to our greate expence and reproch. Upon which divers courtiers and gentlemen gave his Majesty gold by way of wager that he would not persist in this resolution. I had sometime before presented an invective against that unconstancy, and our so much affecting the French fashion, to his Majesty, in which I tooke occasion to describe the comlinesse and usefulnesse of the Persian clothing, in the very same manner his Majesty now clad himself. This pamphlet I intitl'd ' Tyrannus, or the Mode,' and gave it to his Majesty to reade. I do not impute to this discourse the change which soon happen'd, but it was an identity that I could not but take notice of.

This night was acted my Lord Broghill's tragedy call'd ' Mustapha ' before their Majesties at Court, at which I was present, very seldom going to the publiq theaters for many reasons, now as they were abused to an atheistical liberty, fowle and undecent women now (and never till now) permitted to appear and act, who inflaming severall young noblemen and gallants, became their misses, and to some their wives; witness the Earle of Oxford, Sir R. Howard, P. Rupert, the Earle of Dorset, and another greater person than any of them, who fell into their snares to the reproch of their noble families, and ruine of both body and soule. I was invited by my Lord Chamberlaine to see this tragedy, exceedingly well written, thogh in my mind I did not approve of any such pastime in a season of such judgments and calamities.

A BANQUET AT WHITEHALL
Evelyn's DIARY

22 April 1667. Saw the sumptuous supper in the Banquetting-house at White-hall on the eve of St. George's day, where were all the Companions of the Order of the Garter. 23. In the morning his Majesty went to Chapell with the Knights of the Garter all in their habits and robes, usher'd by the Heraulds; after the first service they went in procession, the youngest first, the Sovereigne last, with the Prelate of the Order and Dean, who had about his neck the booke of the Statutes of the Order, and then the Chancellor of the Order (old Sir Hen. de Vic) who wore the purse about his neck; then the Heraulds and Garter King at Arms, Clarencieux, Black Rod. But before the Prelate and Deane of Windsor went the Gentlemen of the Chapell, and Choristers singing as they marched; behind them two Doctors of Musick in damask robes; this procession was about the Courts of White-hall. Then returning to their stalls and seates in the Chapell, plac'd under each Knights coate armour and titles, the second service began: then the King offer'd at the altar, an anthem was sung, then the rest of the Knights offer'd, and lastly proceeded to the Banquetting-house to a greate feast. The King sat on an elevated throne at the upper end at a table alone, the Knights at a table on the right hand, reaching all the length of the roome; over against them a cupboard of rich gilded plate; at the lower end the musick; on the balusters above, wind musick, trumpets and kettle-drums. The King was serv'd by the Lords and Pensioners, who brought up the dishes. About the middle of the dinner the Knights drank the King's health, then the King theirs, when the trumpets and musick plaied and sounded, the guns going off at the Tower. At the banquet came in the Queene and stood

by the King's left hand, but did not sit. Then was the banquetting stuff flung about the roome profusely. In truth the croud was so greate, that tho' I staied all the supper the day before, I now staied no longer than this sport began, for feare of disorder. The cheere was extraordinary, each Knight having forty dishes to his messe, piled up five or six high. The roome hung with the richest tapessry.

THE KING'S VEST

Pepys' Diary

15th Oct. 1667. This day the King begins to put on his vest, and I did see several persons of the House of Lords and Commons too, great courtiers, who are in it; being a long cassock close to the body, of black cloth, and pinked with white silk under it, and a coat over it, and the legs ruffled with black ribbon like a pigeon's leg; and, upon the whole, I wish the King may keep it, for it is a very fine and handsome garment.
May 17, 1668.
17th. (Lord's day). Up, and put on my new stuff-suit, with a shoulder-belt, according to the new fashion, and the bands of my vest and tunic laced with silk lace, of the colour of my suit; and so, very handsome, to church.

TO THE TREASURER'S

Pepys' Diary

March 4. 1669.
4th. To the Treasurer's house, where the Duke of York is, and his Duchess; and there we find them at dinner in the great room, unhung; and there was with them my Lady Duchess of Monmouth, the Countess of Falmouth, Castlemaine, Henrietta Hyde (my Lady

Hinchingbroke's sister), and my Lady Peterborough. And after dinner Sir Jer. Smith and I were invited down to dinner with some of the Maids of Honour, namely, Mrs. Ogle, Blake, and Howard; which did me good to have the honour to dine with, and look on them; and the Mother of the Maids, and Mrs. Howard, the Mother of the Maid of Honour of that name, and the Duke's housekeeper here. Here was also Monsieur Blancfort, Sir Richard Powell, Colonel Villiers, Sir Jonathan Trelawny, and others. And here drank most excellent, and great variety, and plenty of wines, more than I have drank, at once, these seven years, but yet did me no great hurt. Having dined very merrily, and understanding by Blancfort how angry the Duke of York was about their offering to send Saville to the Gate-house, among the rogues, and then observing how this company, both the ladies and all, are of a gang, and did drink a health to the union of the two brothers, and talking of others as their enemies, they parted, and so we up; and there I did find the Duke of York and Duchess, with all the great ladies, sitting upon a carpet, on the ground, there being no chairs, playing at ' I love my love with an A, because he is so and so; and I hate him with an A, because of this and that ' : and some of them, but particularly the Duchess herself and my Lady Castlemaine, were very witty. This done, they took barge, and I with Sir J. Smith to Captain Cox's; and there to talk, and left them.

A PROCLAMATION
Evelyn's DIARY

4 *Feb.* 1685.

Then were the Council sworn, and Proclamation order'd to be publish'd, that all Officers should continue in their stations, that there might be no failure of

Public Spectacles

public justice, till his further pleasure should be known Then the King rose, the Lords accompanying him to his bed-chamber, where, whilst he repos'd himselfe tired indeede as he was with griefe and watching, they return'd againe into the Council-chamber to take order for the *proclaiming* his Majesty, which (after some debate) they consented should be in the very forme his grandfather K. James I was, after the death of Queene Elizabeth; as likewise that the Lords, &c. should proceed in their coaches thro' the Citty for the more solemnity of it. Upon this was I, and severall other Gentlemen waiting in the Privy-gallerie, admitted into the Council-chamber to be witnesse of what was resolv'd on. Thence with the Lords, the Lord Marshall and Heraulds, and other Crowne Officers being ready, we first went to White-hall-gate, where the Lords stood on foote bare-headed, whilst the Herauld proclaim'd his Majesty's title to the Imperial Crowne and Succession according to the forme, the trumpets and kettle-drums having first sounded 3 times, which ended with the people's acclamations. Then a Herauld call'd the Lords' coaches according to rank, myselfe accompanying the solemnity in my Lord Cornwallis's coach, first to Temple Barr, where the Lord Maior and his brethren met us on horseback, in all their formalities, and proclaim'd the King; hence to the Exchange in Cornhill, and so we return'd in the order we set forth. Being come to White-hall, we all went and kiss'd the King and Queene's hands. He had been on the bed, but was now risen and in his undresse. The Queene was in bed in her appartment, but put forth her hand, seeming to be much afflicted, as I believe she was, having deported herselfe so decently upon all occasions since she came into England, which made her universally belov'd.

A TRIAL
Evelyn's DIARY

30 Nov. 1680. This signal day begun the trial (at which I was present) of my Lord Viscount Stafford, for conspiring the death of the King; second sonn to my Lord Thomas Howard Earle of Arundel and Surry, Earle Marishall of England and grandfather to the present Duke of Norfolk, whom I so well knew, and from which excellent person I received so many favours. It was likewise his birth-day. The trial was in Westminster Hall, before the King, Lords, and Commons, just in the same manner as 40 yeares past, the greate and wise Earle of Strafford (there being but one letter differing their names) receiv'd his trial for pretended ill government in Ireland, in the very same place, this Lord Stafford's father being then High Steward. The place of sitting was now exalted some considerable height from the paved floore of the Hall, with a stage of boards. The throne, woolpacks for the Judges, long formes for the Peeres, chaire for the Lord Steward, exactly ranged, as in the House of Lords. The sides on both hands scaffolded to the very roofe for the Members of the House of Commons. At the upper end and on the right side of the King's state, was a box for his Majesty, and on the left others for the greate ladyes, and over heade a gallerie for Ambassadors and public Ministers. At the lower end or entrance was a barr, and place for the prisoner, the Lieutenant of the Tower of London, the axe-bearer and guards, my Lord Stafford's two daughters, the Marchionesse of Winchester being one; there was likewise a box for my Lord to retire into. At the right hand, in another box, somewhat higher, stood the Witnesses; at the left the Managers, in the name of the Commons of England, viz. Serjeant Maynard (the greate lawyer) the same who prosecuted

the cause against the Earle of Strafford 40 yeares before, being now neere 80 yeares of age, Sir William Jones, late Attorney General, Sir Francis Winnington, a famous pleader, and Mr. Treby now recorder of London, not appearing in their gownes as lawyers, but in their cloakes and swords as representing the Commons of England: to these were joined Mr. Hampden, Dr. Sacheverell, Mr. Poule, Col. Titus, Sir Tho. Lee, all gentlemen of quality, and noted parliamentary men. The two first dayes, in which were read the commission and impeachment, were but a tedious entrance into matter of fact, at which I was but little present. But on Thursday I was commodiously seated amongst the Commons, when the witnesses were sworn and examined. The principal witnesses were Mr. Oates (who call'd himself Dr.) Mr. Dugdale, and Tuberville. Oates swore that he deliver'd a commission to Viscount Stafford from the Pope, to be Paymaster Generall to an army intended to be rais'd. Dugdale, that being at Lord Aston's, the prisoner dealt with him plainly to murder his Majestie: and Tuberville, that at Paris he had also proposed the same to him.

A FUNERAL

Evelyn's DIARY

6/3/1652. Saw the magnificent funeral of that Arch-rebel Ireton, carried in pomp from Somerset House to Westminster, accompanied with divers regiments of souldiers horse and foote; then marched the mourners, General Cromwell (his father-in-law), his mock-parliament-men, officers, and 40 poore men in gownes, 3 led horses in housings of black cloth, 2 led in black velvet, and his charging-horse all cover'd over with embrodery and gold on crimson velvet; then the gyydons, ensignes, 4 heraulds carrying the armes of the State (as they cal'd it), namely, the red crosse and Ireland, with the casq, wreath, sword, spurrs, &c.; next, a chariot canopied of black velvet and 6 horses, in which was the corps; the pall held up by the mourners on foote; the mace and sword with other marks of his charge in Ireland (where he died of the plague), carried before in black scarfs. Thus in a grave pace, drums cover'd with cloth, souldiers reversing their armes, they proceeded through the streetes in a very solemn manner. This Ireton was a stout rebell, and had been very bloudy to the King's party, witnesse his severity at Colchester, when in cold blood he put to death those gallant gentlemen, Sir Cha. Lucas and Sir George Lisle. My co. R. Fanshawe came to visit me and informe me of many considerable affaires. Sir Henry Hubert presented me with his brother my Lord Cherbourie's book ' De Veritate.'

THE FROST

Evelyn's Diary

24 Jan. 1684. The frost continuing more and more severe, the Thames before London was still planted with boothes in formal streetes, all sorts of trades and shops furnish'd and full of commodities, even to a printing presse, where the people and ladyes tooke a fancy to have their names printed, and the day and yeare set down when printed on the Thames; this humour tooke so universally, that 'twas estimated the printer gain'd £5 a day, for printing a line onely, at sixpence a name, besides what he got by ballads, &c. Coaches plied from Westminster to the Temple, and from several other staires to and fro, as in the streetes, sleds, sliding with skeetes, a bull-baiting, horse and

Diversions

coach races, puppet plays and interludes, cookes, tipling, and other lewd places, so that it seem'd to be a baccanalian triumph, or carnival on the water, whilst it was a severe judgment on the land, the trees not onely splitting as if by lightning-struck, but men and cattle perishing in divers places, and the very seas so lock'd up with ice, that no vessels could stir out or come in. The fowles, fish, and birds, and all our exotiq plants and greenes universally perishing. Many parkes of deer were destroied, and all sorts of fuell so deare, that there were greate contributions to preserve the poore alive. Nor was this severe weather much lesse intense in most parts of Europe, even as far as Spaine and the most Southern tracts. London, by reason of the excessive coldnesse of the aire hindering the ascent of the smoke, was so fill'd with the fuliginous steame of the sea-coale, that hardly could one see crosse the streetes, and this filling the lungs with its grosse particles, exceedingly obstructed the breast so as one could scarcely breath. There was no water to be had from the pipes and engines, nor could the brewers and divers other tradesmen worke, and every moment was full of disastrous accidents.

"MONSIEUR PAQUIN'S DIGESTORS"

Evelyn's Diary

12 April 1682. I went this afternoon with severall of the Royal Society to a supper which was all dress'd, both fish and flesh, in Monsieur Papin's Digestors, by which the hardest bones of beefe itselfe, and mutton, were made as soft as cheese, without water or other liquor, and with lesse than 8 ounces of coales, producing an incredible quantity of gravy; and for close of all a jelly made of the bones of beef, the best for clearness and good relish, and the most delicious that I

"On Tuesday, the 17th of January, 1826, Mr. Henry Hunt, Junr., for a bet of 100 Guineas made with a Noble Lord of sporting celebrity, drove his Father's Matchless Blacking Van with four blood horses upon the Ice over the Serpentine at its broadest point." *Morning Chronicle, Jan.* 18, 1826.

From a lithograph in the British Museum.

had ever seene or tasted. We eat pike and other fish bones, and all without impediment; but nothing exceeded the pigeons, which tasted just as if bake'd in a pie, all these being stew'd in their own juice, without any addition of water save what swam about the Digester, as *in balneo*; the natural juice of all these provisions acting on the grosser substances, reduc'd the hardest bones to tendernesse; but it is best descanted with more particulars for extracting tinctures, preserving and stewing fruite, and saving fuel, in Dr. Papin's booke, publish'd and dedicated to our Society, of which he is a member. He is since gone to Venice with the late Resident here (and also a Member of our Society), who carried this excellent mechanic, philosopher, and physician, to set up a philosophical meeting in that city. This philosophical supper caus'd much mirth amongst us, and exceedingly pleas'd all the company. I sent a glass of jelley to my wife, to the reproach of all that the ladies ever made of the best hartshorn.

A DINNER AT THE GUILDHALL

Pepys' Diary

Oct. 29th, 1663.

29th. To Guildhall; and, meeting with Mr. Proby, Sir R. Ford's son, and Lieutenant-Colonel Baron, a City commander, we went up and down to see the tables; where under every salt there was a bill of fare, and at the end of the table the persons proper for the table. Many were the tables, but none in the Hall but the Mayor's and the Lords of the Privy Council that had napkins or knives, which was very strange. We went into the Buttery, and there stayed and talked, and then into the Hall again, and there wine was offered, and they drank, I only drinking some hypocras, which do not break my vow, it being, to the best of my present judgement, only a mixed compound drink, and not any wine. If I am mistaken, God forgive me! but I do hope and think I am not. By and by met with Creed: and we, with the others, went within the several Courts, and there saw the tables prepared for the Ladies, and Judges, and Bishops: all great signs of a great dinner to come. By and by, about one o'clock, before the Lord Mayor came, came into the Hall, from the room where they were first led into, the Chancellor (Archbishop before him), with the Lords of the Council, and other Bishops, and they to dinner. Anon comes the Lord Mayor, who went up to the lords, and then to the other tables to bid welcome; and so all to dinner. I sat near Proby, Baron, and Creed at the Marchant Strangers' table; where ten good dishes to a mess, with plenty of wine of all sorts, of which I drank none; but it was very unpleasing that we had no napkins nor change of trenchers, and drank out of earthen pitchers and wooden dishes. It happened that after the lords had half dined came the French Ambassador up to the lords table, where he was to have sat: he would not sit down nor dine with the Lord Mayor, who was not yet come, nor have a table to himself, which was offered; but in a discontent went away again. After I had dined, I and Creed rose and went up and down the house, and up to the ladies' room, and there stayed gazing upon them. But though there were many and fine, both young and old, yet I could not discern one handsome face there; which was very strange. I expected music, but there was none but only trumpets and drums, which displeased me. The dinner, it seems, is made by the Mayor and two Sheriffs for the time being, the Mayor paying one half, and they the other. And the whole, Proby says, is reckoned to come to about £700 or £800 at most

THE RESTORATION

Being wearied with looking upon a company of ugly women, Creed and I went away, and took coach, and through Cheapside, and there saw the pageants, which were very silly. The Queen mends apace, they say: but yet talks idle still.

"SOME SORT OF MONKEYS"
Evelyn's DIARY

19 June, 1682. The Bantame, or East India Ambassadors (at this time we had in London the Russian, Moroccan, and Indian Ambassadors), being invited to dine at Lord Geo. Berkeleys (now Earl), I went to the entertainment to contemplate the exotic guests. They were both very hard-favour'd and much resembling in countenance some sort of monkeys. We eate at two tables, the Ambassadors and interpreter by themselves. Their garments were rich Indian silks, flowered with gold, *viz.* a close waistcoate to their knees, drawers, naked legs, and on their heads capps made like fruit-baskets. They wore poison'd daggers at their bosoms, the hafts carv'd with some ugly serpents or devils heads, exceeding keene, and of Damasco metal. They wore no sword. The second Ambassador (sent it seemes to succeed in case the first should die by the way in so tedious a journey), having ben at Mecca, wore a Turkish or Arab sash, a little part of the linnen hanging downe behinde his neck, with some other difference of habite, and was halfe a Negro, bare legg'd and naked feete, and deem'd a very holy man. They sate cross-legg'd like Turks, and sometimes in the posture of apes and monkeys; their nailes and teeth black as jet, and shining, which being the effect, as to their teeth, of perpetually chewing betel to preserve them from the tooth-ache, much raging in their country, is esteem'd beautifull.

The first Ambassador was of an olive hue, a flat face, narrow eyes, squat nose, and Moorish lips, no haire appeared; they wore several rings of silver, gold, and copper on their fingers, which was a token of knighthood or nobility. They were of Java Major, whose Princes have been turn'd Mahometans not above 50 yeares since, the inhabitants are still pagans and idolators. They seem'd of a dull and heavy constitution, not wondering at any thing they saw, but exceedingly astonished how our Law gave us property in our estates, and so thinking we were all Kings, for they could not be made to comprehend how subjects could possess anything but at the pleasure of their Prince, they being all slaves; they were pleas'd with the notion, and admir'd our happinesse. They were very sober, and I believe subtle in their way. Their meate was cook'd, carried up, and they attended by several fat slaves, who had no covering save drawers, which appear'd very uncouth and loathsome. They eate their pilaw and other spoone meate without spoones, taking up their pottage in the hollow of their fingers, and very dexterously flung it into their mouths without spilling a drop.

A WEDDING

Pepys' Diary

31st July, 1665.

31st. Up, and very betimes by six o'clock at Deptford, and there find Sir G. Carteret, and my Lady ready to go; I being in my new-coloured silk suit, and coat trimmed with gold buttons and gold broad lace round my hands, very rich and fine. By water to the Ferry, where, when we came, no coach there; and tide of ebb so far spent as the horse-boat could not get off on the other side the river to bring away the coach. So we were fain to stay there in the unlucky Isle of Dogs, in a chill place, the morning cool, and wind fresh, about two if not three hours, to our great discontent. Yet, being upon a pleasant errand, and seeing that it could not be helped, we did bear it very patiently; and it was worth my observing to see how, upon these two scores, Sir G. Carteret, the most passionate man in the world, and that was in greatest haste to be gone, did bear with it, and very pleasant all the while, at least not troubled so much as to fret and storm at it. Anon the coach comes; in the meantime there coming a News thither with his horse to go over, that told us he did come from Islington this morning; and that Proctor, the vintner of the Mitre in Wood Street, and his son are dead this morning there, of the plague; he having laid out abundance of money there, and was the greatest vintner for some time in London for great entertainments. We, fearing the canonical hour would be past before we got thither, did, with a great deal of unwillingness, send away the licence and wedding-ring. So that when we came, though we drove hard with six horses, yet we found them gone from home; and, going towards the church, met them coming from church, which troubled us. But, however, that trouble was soon over; hearing it was well done: they being both in their old clothes: my Lord Crewe giving her, there being three coachfuls of them. The young lady mighty sad, which troubled me; but yet I think it was only her gravity in a little greater degree than usual. All saluted her, but I did not, till my Lady Sandwich did ask me whether I saluted her or no. So to dinner, and very merry we were; but in such a sober way as never almost any wedding was in so great families; but it was much better. After dinner company divided, some to cards, others to talk. My

Lady Sandwich and I up to settle accounts, and pay her some money. And mighty kind she is to me, and would fain have had me gone down for company with her to Hinchingbroke; but for my life I cannot. At night to supper, and so to talk; and which, methought, was the most extraordinary thing, all of us to prayers as usual, and the young bride and bridegroom too; and so, after prayers, soberly to bed; only I got into the bridegroom's chamber while he undressed himself, and there was very merry, till he was called to the bride's chamber, and into bed they went. I kissed the bride in bed, and so the curtains drawn with the greatest gravity that could be, and so good-night. But the modesty and gravity of this business was so decent, that it was to me indeed ten times more delightful than if it had been twenty times more merry and jovial.

THE BEAR GARDEN
Evelyn's DIARY

16 June, 1670. I went with some friends to the Bear Garden, where was cock-fighting, dog-fighting, beare and bull baiting, it being a famous day for all these butcherly sports, or rather barbarous cruelties. The bulls did exceeding well, but the Irish wolfe-dog exceeded, which was a tall grey hound, a stately creature indeede, who beate a cruell mastiff. One of the bulls toss'd a dog full into a *lady's lap*, as she sate in one of the boxes at a considerable height from the arena. Two poore dogs were kill'd, and so all ended with the ape on horseback, and I most heartily weary of the rude and dirty pastime, which I had not seene, I think, in twenty yeares before.

THE ROYAL COCK PIT
After Hogarth.

THE PLAYHOUSE

Pepys' DIARY

5th March 1666.

5th. I find my Lord Brouncker and Mrs. Williams, and they would of their own accord, though I had never obliged them, nor my wife neither, with one visit for many of theirs, go see my house and my wife; which I showed them, and made them welcome with wine and China oranges (now a great rarity since the war; none to be had). My house happened to be mighty clean, and did me great honour, and they mightily pleased with it.

19th. After dinner we walked to the King's playhouse, all in dirt, they being altering of the stage to make it wider. But God knows when they will begin to act again; but my business here was to see the inside of the stage and all the tiring-rooms and machines; and, indeed, it was a sight worthy seeing. But to see their clothes, and the various sorts, and what a mixture of things there was; here a wooden leg, there a ruff, here a hobby-horse, there a crown, would make a man split himself to see with laughing: and particularly Lacy's wardrobe, and Shotrell's. But then again to think how fine they show on the stage by candle-light, and how poor things they are to look at too near hand, is not pleasant at all. The machines are fine, and the paintings very pretty.

WAX CANDLES AND "ALL THINGS CIVIL"

Pepys' DIARY

12*th February*, 1667.

12th. This done, T. Killigrew and I to talk; and he tells me how the audience at his house is not above half so much as it used to be before the late fire. That Knipp is like to make the best actor that ever came upon the stage, she understanding so well: that they are going to give her £30 a year more. That the stage is now by his pains a thousand times better and more glorious than ever heretofore. Now, wax-candles, and many of them; then, not above 3 lbs. of tallow; now, all things civil, no rudeness anywhere; then, as in a bear-garden: then, two or three fiddlers; now, nine or ten of the best; then, nothing but rushes upon the ground, and everything else mean; now, all otherwise: then, the Queen seldom and the King never would come; now, not the King only for state, but all civil people do think they may come as well as any. He tells me that he hath gone several times, eight or ten times he tells me, hence to Rome, to hear good music; so much he loves it, though he never did sing or play a note. That he hath ever endeavoured in the late King's time and in this to introduce good music, but he never could do it, there never having been any music here better than ballads. Nay, says 'Hermit poor' and 'Chevy Chase' was all the music we had; and yet no fiddlers get so much money as ours do here, which speaks our rudeness still. That he hath gathered our Italians from several Courts in Christendom, to come to make a concert for the King, which he do give £220 a year apiece to: but badly paid, and do come in the room of keeping four ridiculous gondolas, he having got the King to put them away, and lay out money this way; and indeed I do commend him for it, for I think it is a very noble undertaking. He do intend to have some times of the year these operas to be performed at the two present theatres, since he is defeated in what he intended in Moorfields on purpose for it; and he tells me plainly that the City audience was as good as the Court, but now they are most gone. Baptista tells me that Giacomo Charissimi is still alive at Rome, who was master to Vinnecotio, who is one of the Italians that the King hath here, and the chief composer of them. My great wonder is, how this man do to keep in memory so perfectly the music of the whole act, both for the voice and the instrument too. I confess I do admire it: but in recitative the sense much helps him, for there is but one proper way of discoursing and giving the accents. Having done our discourse, we all took coaches, my Lord's and T. Killigrew's, and to Mrs. Knipp's chamber, where this Italian is to teach her to sing her part. And so we all thither, and there she did sing an Italian song or two very fine, while he played the bass upon a harpsicon there; and exceedingly taken I am with her singing, and believe that she will do miracles at that and acting.

TRAVELLING

Pepys' DIARY

June 9, 1668.

9th (Tuesday). We came to Oxford, a very sweet place; paid our guide, £1 2. 6.; barber, 2s. 6d.; book *Stonehenge*, 4s.; boy that showed me the colleges before dinner, 1s. To dinner; and then out with my wife and people, and landlord; and to him that showed us the schools and library, 10s.; to him that showed us All Souls' College, and Chichly's picture, 5s. So to see Christ Church with my wife, I seeing several others very fine alone, before dinner, and did give the boy that went with me, 1s. Strawberries, 1s. 2d. Dinner and servants, £1 0s. 6d. After coming home from the schools, I out with the landlord to Brazenose College:—to the butteries, and in the cellar find the hand of the Child of Hales. . . . long Butler 2s. Thence with coach and people to Physic Garden, 1s. So to Friar Bacon's study: I up and saw it, and gave the man 1s. Bottle of sack for landlord, 2s. Oxford mighty fine place; and well seated, and cheap entertainment. At night came to Abingdon, where had been a fair of custard; and met many people and scholars going home; and there did get some pretty good music, and sang and danced till supper: 5s.

11th. (Thursday). So the three women behind W. Hewer, Murford, and our guide, and I single to Stonehenge, over the Plain and some great hills, even to fright us. Came thither, and find them as prodigious as any tales I ever heard of them, and worth going this journey to see. God knows what their use was! they are hard to tell, but yet may be told. Gave the shepherd-woman, for leading our horses, 4d. So back by Wilton, my Lord Pembroke's house, which we could not see, he being just coming to town; but the situation I do not like, nor the house promise much, it being in a low but rich valley. So back home: and there being 'light, we to the Church, and there find them at prayers again, so could not see the Choir; but I sent the women home, and I did go in, and saw very many fine tombs, and among the rest some very ancient, of the Montagus. So home to dinner; and, that being done, paid the reckoning, which was so exorbitant, and particular in rate of my horses, and 7s. 6d. for bread and beer, that I was mad, and resolve to trouble the master about it, and get something for the poor; and came away in that humour; £2 5. 6. Servants, 1s. 6d.; poor, 1s.; guide to the Stones, 2s.; poor woman in the street, 1s.; ribbons 9d.; washwoman, 1s.; sempstress for W. Hewer, 3s.; lent W. Hewer, 2s. Thence about six o'clock, and with a guide went over the smooth Plain indeed till night; and then by a happy mistake, and that looked like an adventure, we were carried out of our way to a town where we would lie, since we could not go so far as we would. And there with great difficulty came about ten at night to a little inn, where we were fain to go into a room where a pedlar was in bed, and made him rise; and there wife and I lay, and in a truckle-bed Betty Turner and Willet. But good beds, and the master of the house a sober understanding man, and I had good discourse with him about this country's matters, as wool, and corn, and other things. And he also merry, and made us mighty merry at supper about manning the new ship at Bristol with none but men whose wives do master them; and it seems it is in reproach to some men of estate that are such hereabouts, that this is become common talk. By and by to bed, glad of this mistake, because, it seems, had we gone on as we intended, we could not have passed with our coach, and must have lain on the Plain all night. This day from Salisbury I wrote by the post my excuse for not coming home, which I hope will do, for I am resolved to see the Bath, and, it may be, Bristol.

12th. (Friday). Up, finding our beds good, but lousy; which made us merry. We set out, the reckoning and servants coming to 9s. 6d.; my guide thither, 2s.; coachman, advanced, 10s. So rode a very good way, led to my great content by our landlord to Philips-Norton with great pleasure, being now come into Somersetshire; where my wife and Deb. mightily joyed thereat, I commending the country, as indeed it deserves. And the first town we came to was Brekington, where, stopping for something for the horses, we called two or three little boys to us, and pleased ourselves with their manner of speech. At Philips-Norton I walked to the Church, and there saw a very ancient tomb of some Knight Templar, I think; and here saw the tombstone whereon there were only two heads cut, which, the story goes, and credibly, were two sisters, called the Fair Maids of Foscott, that had two bodies upward and one belly, and there lie buried.

Here is also a very fine ring of six bells, and they mighty tuneable. Having dined very well, 10s., we came before night to the Bath; where I presently stepped out with my landlord, and saw the baths, with people in them. They are not so large as I expected, but yet pleasant; and the town most of stone and, clean, though the streets generally narrow. I home, and being weary, went to bed without supper; the rest supping.

13th. (Saturday). Up at four o'clock, being by appointment called up to the Cross Bath, where we were carried after one another, myself, and wife, and Betty Turner, Willet, and W. Hewer. And by and by, though we designed to have done, before company come, much company came; very fine ladies; and the manner pretty enough, only methinks it cannot be clean to go so many bodies together in the same water. Good conversation among them that are acquainted here, and stay together. Strange to see how hot the water is; and in some places, though this is the most temperate bath, the springs so hot as the feet not able to endure. But strange to see, when women and men here, that live all the season in these waters, cannot but be parboiled, and look like the creatures of the bath! Carried away, wrapped in a sheet, and in a chair, home; and there one after another thus carried, I stayed above two hours in the water, home to bed, sweating for an hour; and by and by, comes music to play to me, extraordinary good as ever I heard at London almost, or anywhere; 5s. Up, to go to Bristol, about eleven o'clock, and paying my landlord that was our guide from Chiltern, 10s., and the serjeant of the bath 10s., and the man that carried us in chairs, 3s. 6d., set out towards Bristol; and came thither, in a coach hired to spare our own horses, about two o'clock, the way bad, but country good, where set down at the Horseshoe; and there, being trimmed by a very handsome fellow, 2s. walked with my wife and people through the city, which is in every respect another London, that one can hardly know it to stand in the country, no more than that. No carts (it standing generally on vaults), only dog-carts. So to the Three Crowns Tavern I was directed; but, when I came in, the master told me that he had newly given over the selling of wine; it seems, grown rich; and so went to the Sun; and there Deb. going with W. Hewer and Betty Turner to see her uncle Butts, and leaving my wife with the mistress of the house, I to see the quay, where is a most large and noble place; and to see the new ship building by Bally, neither he nor Furzer being in town. It will be a fine ship. Spoke with the foreman, and did give the boys that kept the cabin 2s. Walked back to the Sun, where I find Deb. come back, and with her, her uncle, a sober merchant, very good company, and so like one of our sober, wealthy, London merchants, as pleased me mightily. Here we dined, and much good talk with him, 7s. 6d.; a messenger to Sir John Knight, who was not at home, 6d. Then walked with Butts and my wife and company round the quay, and to the ship; and he showed me the Custom-house, and made me understand many things of the place, and led us through Marsh Street, where our girl was born. But, Lord! the joy that was among the old poor people of the place, to see Mrs. Willet's daughter, it seems her mother being a brave woman and mightily beloved! And so brought us a back way by surprise to his house, where a substantial good house, and well furnished; and did give us good entertainment of strawberries, a whole venison-pasty, cold, and plenty of brave wine, and above all Bristol milk! where comes in another poor woman, who, hearing that Deb. was here, did come running hither, and with her eyes so full of tears, and heart so full of joy, that she could not speak when she came in, that it made me weep too; I protest that I was not able to speak to her, which I would have done, to have diverted her tears. Butt's wife a good woman, and so sober and substantial as I was never more pleased anywhere. Servant-maid, 2s. So thence took leave, and he with us through the city, where in walking I find the city pay him great respect, and he the like to the meanest, which pleased me mightily. He showed us the place where the merchants meet here, and a fine Cross yet standing, like Cheapside. And so to the Horseshoe, where paid the reckoning, 2s. 6d. We back, and by moonshine to the Bath again, about ten o'clock: bad way; and giving the coachman 1s., went all of us to bed.

14th. (Sunday). Up, and walked up and down the town, and saw a pretty good market-place, and many good streets, and very fair stone-houses. And so to the great Church, and there saw Bishop Montagu's tomb; and, when placed, did there see many brave people come, and, among others, two men brought in, in litters, and set down in the chancel to hear; but I did not know one face. Here a good organ; but a vain pragmatical fellow preached a ridiculous affected sermon, that made me angry, and some gentlemen that sat next me, and sang well. So home, walking round the walls of the city, which are good, and the battlements all whole. After dinner comes Mr. Butts again to see me, and he and I to church, where the same idle fellow preached; and I slept most of the sermon. To this church again, to see it, and look over the monuments, where, among others, Dr. Venner and Pelling, and a lady of Sir W. Wallers; he lying with his face broken. My landlord did give me a good account of the antiquity of this town and Wells; and of two heads, on two pillars, in Wells Church.

15th. (Monday). Looked into the baths, and find the King and Queen's full of a mixed sort, of good and bad, and the Cross only almost for the gentry. So home with my wife, and did pay my guides, two women, 5s.; one man, 2s. 6d.; poor, 6d.; woman to lay my foot-cloth, 1s. So to our inn, and there ate and paid reckoning, £1 8s. 6d. servants, 3s.; poor, 1s.; lent the coachman, 10s. Before I took coach, I went to make a boy dive in the King's bath, 1s. I paid also for my coach and a horse to Bristol, £1 1s. 6d. Took coach and away, without any of the company of the other stage-coaches that go out of this town to-day; and rode all day with some trouble, for fear of being out of our way, over the Downs, where the life of the shepherds is, in fair weather only, pretty.

A BET

Pepys' DIARY

19th May 1661.

19th. (Lord's day). I walked in the morning towards Westminster, and, seeing many people at York House, I went down and found them at mass, it being the Spanish ambassador's; and so I got into one of the galleries, and there heard two masses done, I think, not in so much state as I have seen them heretofore. After that, into the garden, and walked a turn or two; but found it not so fine a place as I always took it for by the outside. Captain Ferrers and Mr. Howe and myself to Mr. Wilkinson's at the Crown; then to my Lord's, where we went and sat talking and laughing in the drawing-room a great while. All our talk upon their going to sea this voyage, which Captain Ferrers is in some doubt whether he shall do or no, but swears that he would go, if he were sure never to come back again; and I, giving him some hopes, he grew so mad with joy that he fell a-dancing and leaping like a madman. Now it fell out that the balcony windows were open, and he went to the rail and made an offer to leap over, and asked what if he should leap over there. I told him I would give him £40 if he did not go to sea. With that thought, I shut the doors, and W. Howe hindered him all we could; yet he opened them again, and, with a vault, leaps down into the garden—the greatest and most desperate frolic that ever I saw in my life. I ran to see what was become of him, and we found him crawled upon his knees, but could not rise; so we went down into the garden, and dragged him to a bench, where he looked like a dead man, but could not stir; and, though he had broke nothing, yet the pain in his back was such as he could not endure. With this my Lord (who was in the little new room) come to us in amaze, and bid us carry him up, which, by our strength, we did, and so laid him in East's bedroom, by the door, where he lay in great pain. We sent for a doctor and surgeon, but none to be found, till, by and by, by chance comes in Dr. Clerke, who is afraid of him. So we went for a lodging for him.

VALENTINES

Pepys' Diary

Feb. 14th, 1667. This morning came up to my wife's bedside, I being up dressing myself, little Will Mercer to be her Valentine; and brought her name writ upon blue paper in gold letters, done by himself, very pretty; but we were both well pleased with it. But I am also this year my wife's Valentine, and it will cost me £5; but that I must have laid out if we had not been Valentines.

16th. I find that Mrs. Pierce's little girl is my

Valentine, she having drawn me; which I was not sorry for, it easing me of something more that I must have given others. But here I do first observe the fashion of drawing of mottoes as well as names; so that Pierce, who drew my wife, did draw also a motto, and this girl drew another for me. What mine was I have forgot; but my wife's was, 'Most virtuous and most fair'; which, as it may be used, or an anagram made upon each name, might be very pretty. One wonder I observed to-day, that there was no music in the morning to call up our new-married people, which is very mean, methinks.

CHAPTER III

THE EIGHTEENTH CENTURY.—I

TOWN AND COUNTRY MODES
THE SPECTATOR

*Urbem quam dicunt Romam, Melibœe, putavi
Stultus ego huic nostræ similem*—VIRG.

THE first and most obvious reflections which arise in a man who changes the city for the country, are upon the different manners of the people whom he meets with in those two different scenes of life. By manners I do not mean morals, but behaviour and good-breeding, as they show themselves in the town and in the country.

Of Politeness

And here, in the first place, I must observe a very great revolution that has happened in this article of good-breeding. Several obliging deferences, condescensions, and submissions, with many outward forms and ceremonies that accompany them, were first of all brought up among the politer part of mankind, who lived in courts and cities, and distinguished themselves from the rustic part of the species (who on all occasions acted bluntly and naturally) by such a mutual complaisance and intercourse of civilities. These forms of conversation by degrees multiplied, and grew troublesome; the modish world found too great a constraint in them, and have therefore thrown most of them aside. Conversation, like the Romish religion, was so encumbered with show and ceremony, that it stood in need of a reformation to retrench its superfluities, and restore its natural good sense and beauty. At present, therefore, an unconstrained carriage, and a certain openness of behaviour, are the height of good-breeding. The fashionable world is grown free and easy; our manners sit more loose upon us: nothing is so modish as an agreeable negligence. In a word, good-breeding shows itself most, where to an ordinary eye it appears the least.

If after this we look on the people of mode in the country, we find in them the manners of the last age. They have no sooner fetched themselves up to the fashions of a polite world, but the town has dropped them, and are nearer to the first state of nature, than to those refinements which formerly reigned in the court, and still prevail in the country. One may now know a man that never conversed in the world by his excess of good-breeding. A polite country squire shall make you as many bows in half an hour, as would serve a courtier for a week. There is infinitely more to do about place and precedency in a meeting of justices' wives, than in an assembly of duchesses.

This rural politeness is very troublesome to a man of my temper, who generally takes the chair that is next me, and walk first or last, in the front or in the rear, as chance directs. I have known my friend Sir Roger's dinner almost cold before the company could adjust the ceremonial, and be prevailed upon to sit down; and have heartily pitied my old friend, when I have seen him forced to pick and cull his guests, as they sat at the several parts of his table, that he might drink their healths according to their respective ranks and qualities. Honest Will. Wimble, who I should have thought had been altogether uninfected with ceremony, gives me abundance of trouble in this particular. Though he has been fishing all the morning, he will not help himself at dinner till I am served. When we are going out of the hall, he runs behind me ; and last night, as we were walking in the fields, stopped short at a stile till I came up to it, and upon my making signs to him to get over, told me, with a serious smile, that sure I believed they had no manners in the country.

There has happened another revolution in the point of good-breeding, which relates to the conversation among men of mode, and which I cannot but look upon as very extraordinary. It was certainly one of the first distinctions of a well-bred man, to express everything that had the most remote appearance of being obscene in modest terms and distant phrases ; whilst the clown, who had no such delicacy of conception and expression, clothed his ideas in those plain homely terms that are the most obvious and natural. This kind of good manners was perhaps carried to an excess, so as to make conversation too stiff, formal, and precise ; for which reason (as hypocrisy in one age is generally succeeded by atheism in another) conversation is in a great measure relapsed into the first extreme ; so that at present several of our men of the town, and particularly those who have been polished in France, make use of the most coarse, uncivilized words in our language, and utter themselves often in such a manner as a clown would blush to hear.

This infamous piece of good-breeding, which reigns among the coxcombs of the town, has not yet made its way into the country ; and as it is impossible for such an irrational way of conversation to last long among a people that makes any profession of religion, or show of modesty, if the country gentlemen get into it, they will certainly be left in the lurch. Their good-breeding will come too late to them, and they will be thought a parcel of lewd clowns, while they fancy themselves talking together like men of wit and pleasure.

As the two points of good-breeding, which I have hitherto insisted upon, regard behaviour and conversation, there is a third which turns upon dress. In this too the country are very much behindhand. The rural beaus are not yet got out of the fashion that took place at the time of the Revolution, but ride about the country in red coats and laced hats; while the women in many parts are still trying to outvie one another in the height of their head-dresses.

AT LEAST, BE HALF POLITE
Lord Chesterfield's LETTERS

Isleworth, July 8. 1739. I am afraid, my dear child, that you think my letters too grave, for I know you love to joke, and in that you are right; I too like cheerfulness, and we shall often joke together. Sometimes, however, we must think seriously, but in general one ought to be gay and lively. I would not wish such a jolly fellow as you should put up for a philosopher. When one is learning, one ought to apply, afterwards one should play and divert oneself.

In my last, I wrote to you concerning the politeness of people of fashion, such as are used to courts, the elegant part of mankind. Their politeness is easy and natural; and you must distinguish it from the civilities of inferior people, and rustics, which are always constraining and troublesome. These sort o people are full of ceremony, and overwhelm us with compliments.

For example, if you dine with a person in an ordinary sphere of life, instead of civilly offering to help you, he will press you to eat and drink whether you will or not, will heap things on your plate; and to

PHILIP DORMER STANHOPE, EARL OF CHESTERFIELD
From the painting by Gainsborough.

prove that you are welcome, he crams you till you are ready to burst.

A country 'squire stifles you with hearty embraces, and endeavouring to make you go before, throws you down. But a well-bred man shows a constant desire of pleasing, and takes care that his attentions for you be not troublesome. Few English are thoroughly polite; either they are shame-faced or impudent, whereas most French people are easy and polite in their manners, and, as by the better half you are a little Frenchman, so I hope you will at least be half polite. You will be the more distinguished in a country where politeness is not very common.

I have already mentioned to you, that, if there should be any words in my letters which you do not understand, you are to desire your Mamma to explain them.

OF "MILDNESS" TO INFERIORS
Lord Chesterfield's LETTERS

Isleworth, 1739. The politeness which I mentioned, my dear child, in my former letters, regards only your equals and your superiors. There is also a certain politeness due to your inferiors, of a different kind, 'tis true; but whoever is without it, is without good nature. We do not need to compliment those beneath us, nor to talk of their doing us the honour, etc. but we ought to treat them with benevolence and mildness. We are all of the same species, and no distinction whatever is between us, except that which arises from fortune. For example, your footman and Lisette would be your equals were they as rich as you. Being poor, they are obliged to serve you. Therefore you must not add to their misfortunes by insulting or by ill-treating them. If your situation is preferable to theirs, be thankful to God, without either despising them, or being vain of your better fortune. You must, therefore, treat all your inferiors with affability and good manners, and not speak to them in a surly tone, nor with harsh expression, as if they were of a different species. A good heart never reminds people of their misfortune, but endeavours to alleviate, or, if possible, to make them forget it.

I am persuaded you will always act in that manner, otherwise I should not love you so much as I do. Adieu.

"AN AWKWARD FELLOW"

Lord Chesterfield's LETTERS

Spa, July 25, 1741. When an awkward fellow first comes into a room, it is highly probable that his sword gets between his legs, and throws him down, or makes him stumble, at least; when he has recovered this accident, he goes and places himself in the very place of the whole room where he should not; there he soon lets his hat fall down, and, in taking it up again, throws down his cane; in recovering his cane, his hat falls a second time, so that he is a quarter of an hour before he is in order again. If he drinks tea or coffee, he certainly scalds his mouth, and lets either the cup or the saucer fall, and spills either the tea or coffee in his breeches. At dinner, his awkwardness distinguishes itself particularly, as he has more to do; there he holds his knife, fork and spoon differently from other people, eats with his knife, to the great danger of his mouth, picks his teeth with his fork, and puts his spoon, which has been in his throat twenty times, into the dishes again. If he is to carve, he can never hit the joint; but, in his vain efforts to cut through the bone, scatters the sauce in everybody's face. He generally daubs himself with soup and grease, though his napkin is commonly stuck through a button-hole, and tickles his chin. When he drinks, he infallibly coughs in his glass, and besprinkles the company. Besides all this, he has strange tricks and gestures; such as snuffing up his nose, making faces, putting his fingers in his nose, or blowing it and looking afterwards in his handkerchief, so as to make the company sick. His hands are troublesome to him, when he has not something in them, and he does not know where to put them; but they are in perpetual motion between his bosom and his breeches; he does not wear his clothes, and in short does nothing, like other people.

AFFECTATION

Lord Chesterfield's LETTERS

London, 31 Dec., 1748. Any affectation whatsoever in dress implies, in my mind, a flaw in the understanding. Most of our young fellows here display some character or other by their dress; some affect the tremendous, and wear a great and fiercely cocked hat, an enormous sword, a short waistcoat and a black cravat; these I should be almost tempted to swear the peace against, in my own defence, if I were not convinced that they are but meek asses in lions' skins. Others go in brown frocks, leather breeches, great oaken cudgels in their hands, their hats uncocked, and their hair unpowdered; and imitate grooms, stage-coachmen, and country bumpkins so well, in their outsides, that I do not make the least doubt of their resembling them equally in their insides. A man of sense carefully avoids any particular character in his dress; he is accurately clean for his own sake; but all the rest is for other people's.

"FRENCH FOPPERIES"

THE SPECTATOR

Natio Comœda est—JUV.

There is nothing which I more desire than a safe and honourable peace, though at the same time I am very apprehensive of many ill consequences that may attend it. I do not mean in regard to our politics, but to our manners. What an inundation of ribbons and brocades will break in upon us! What peals of laughter and impertinence shall we be exposed to! For the prevention of these great evils, I could heartily wish that there was an act of parliament for prohibiting the importation of French fopperies.

The female inhabitants of our island have already received very strong impressions from this ludicrous nation, though by the length of the war (as there is no evil which has not some good attending it) they are pretty well worn out and forgotten. I remember the time when some of our well-bred country-women kept their *valet de chambre*, because forsooth, a man was much more handy about them than one of their own sex. I myself have seen one of these male Abigails tripping about the room with a looking-glass in his hand, and combing his lady's hair a whole morning together. Whether or no there was any truth in the story of a lady's being got with child by one of these her handmaids, I cannot tell; but I think at present the whole race of them is extinct in our own country.

About the time that several of our sex were taken into this kind of service, the ladies likewise brought up the fashion of receiving visits in their beds. It was then looked upon as a piece of ill-breeding for a woman to refuse to see a man because she was not stirring; and a porter would have been thought unfit for his place, that could have made so awkward an excuse. As I love to see everything that is new, I once prevailed upon my friend Will. Honeycomb to carry me along with him to one of these travelled ladies, desiring him, at the same time, to present me as a foreigner who could not speak English, that so I might not be obliged to bear a part in the discourse. The lady, though willing to appear undrest, had put on her best looks, and painted herself for our reception. Her hair appeared in a very nice disorder, as the nightgown which was thrown upon her shoulders was ruffled with great care. For my part, I am so shocked with everything which looks immodest in the fair sex, that I could not forbear taking off my eye from her when she moved in her bed, and was in the greatest confusion imaginable every time she stirred a leg or an arm. As the coquets, who introduced this custom, grew old, they left it off by degrees; well knowing that a woman of threescore may kick and tumble her heart out, without making any impressions.

Sempronia is at present the most profest admirer of the French nation, but is so modest as to admit her visitants no further than her toilet. It is a very odd sight that beautiful creature makes, when she is talking politics with her tresses flowing about her shoulders, and examining that face in the glass, which does such execution upon all the male standers-by. How prettily does she divide her discourse between her woman and her visitants! What sprightly transitions does she make from an opera or a sermon, to an ivory comb or a pincushion! How have I been pleased to see her interrupted in an account of her travels by a message to her footman! and holding her tongue in the midst of a moral reflection by applying the tip of it to a patch!

There is nothing which exposes a woman to greater dangers, than that gaiety and airiness of temper, which are natural to most of the sex. It should be therefore the concern of every wise and virtuous woman, to keep this sprightliness from degenerating into levity. On the contrary, the whole discourse and behaviour of the French is to make the sex more fantastical, or (as they are pleased to term it) more awakened, than is consistent either with virtue or discretion. To speak loud in public assemblies, to let every one hear you talk of things that should only be mentioned in private, or in whisper, are looked upon as parts of a refined education. At the same time, a blush is unfashionable, and silence more ill-bred than anything that can be spoken. In short, discretion and modesty, which in all other ages and countries have been regarded as the greatest ornaments of the fair sex, are considered as the ingredients of narrow conversation and family behaviour.

Some years ago I was at the tragedy of Macbeth, and unfortunately placed myself under a woman of quality that is since dead; who, as I found by the noise she made, was newly returned from France. A little before the rising of the curtain, she broke out into a loud soliloquy, "When will the dear witches enter?" and immediately upon their first appearance, asked a lady that sat three boxes from her, on her right hand, if those witches were not charming creatures. A little after, as Betterton was in one of the finest speeches of the play, she shook her fan at another lady, who sat as far on the left hand, and told her with a whisper, that might be heard all over the pit, we must not expect to see Balloon to-night. Not long after, calling out to a young baronet by his name, who sat three seats before me, she asked him whether Macbeth's wife was still alive; and before he could give an answer, fell a talking of the ghost of Banquo. She had by this time formed a little audience to herself, and fixed the attention of all about her. But as I had a mind to hear the play, I got out of the sphere of her impertinence, and planted myself in one of the remotest corners of the pit.

This pretty childishness of behaviour is one of the most refined parts of coquetry, and is not to be attained in perfection by ladies that do not travel for their improvement. A natural and unconstrained behaviour has something in it so agreeable, that it is no wonder to see people endeavouring after it. But at the same time, it is so very hard to hit, when it is not born with us, that people often make themselves ridiculous in attempting it.

A very ingenious French author tells us, that the ladies of the court of France, in his time, thought it ill-breeding, and a kind of female pedantry, to pronounce an hard word right; for which reason they took frequent occasion to use hard words, that they might show a politeness in murdering them. He further adds, that a lady of some quality at court, having accidentally made use of an hard word in a proper place, and pronounced it right, the whole assembly was out of countenance for her.

I must, however, be so just to own, that there are many ladies who have travelled several thousands of miles without being the worse for it, and have brought home with them all the modesty, discretion, and good sense, that they went abroad with. As, on the contrary, there are great numbers of travelled ladies, who have lived all their days within the smoke of London. I have known a woman that never was out of the parish of St. James's betray as many foreign fopperies in her carriage, as she could have gleaned up in half the countries of Europe.

OF DANCING

Lord Chesterfield's LETTERS

Dublin Castle, 29 Nov. 1745. Now that the Christmas breaking-up draws near, I have ordered Mr. Desnoyers to go to you, during that time, to teach you to dance. I desire you will particularly attend to the graceful motion of your arms; which, with the manner of putting on your hat, and giving your hand, is all that a gentleman need attend to. Dancing is in itself a very trifling, silly thing; but it is one of those established follies to which people of sense are sometimes obliged to conform; and then they should be able to do it well. And though I would not have you a dancer, yet, when you do dance, I would have you dance well, as I would have you do everything you do well. There is not one thing so trifling, but which (if it is to be done at all) ought to be done well; and I have often told you, that I wished you even played at pitch, and cricket, better than any boy at Westminster. For instance, dress is a very foolish thing, and yet it is a very foolish thing for a man not to be well dressed, according to his rank and way of life; and it is so far from being a disparagement to any man's understanding, that it is rather a proof of it, to be as well dressed as those whom he lives with: the difference in this case between a man of taste and a fop is, that the fop values himself upon his dress, and the man of sense laughs at it, at the same time that he knows he must not neglect it. There are a thousand foolish customs of this kind, which, not being criminal, must be complied with, and even cheerfully, by men of sense. Diogenes the Cynic was a wise man for despising them; but a fool for showing it. Be wiser than other people, if you can; but do not tell them so.

A DANCING MASTER

The Tatler

I was this morning awakened by a sudden shake of the house; and as soon as I had got a little out of my consternation, I felt another, which was followed by two or three repetitions of the same convulsion. I got up as fast as possible, girt on my rapier, and snatched up my hat, when my landlady came up to me, and told me that the gentlewoman of the next house begged me to step thither; for that a lodger she had taken in was run mad, and she desired my advice; as indeed everybody in the whole lane does upon important occasions. I am not, like some artists, saucy, because I can be beneficial, but went immediately. Our neighbour told us, she had the day before let her second floor to a very genteel, youngish man, who told her he kept extraordinary good hours, and was generally at home most part of the morning and evening at study; but that this morning he had for an hour together made this extravagant noise which we then heard. I went upstairs with my hand upon the hilt of my rapier, and approached this new lodger's door. I looked in at the key-hole, and there I saw a well-made man look with great attention on a book, and on a sudden jump into the air so high, that his head almost touched the ceiling. He came down safe on his right foot, and again flew up, alighting on his left; then looked again at his book, and holding out his right leg, put it into such a quivering motion, that I thought he would have shaked it off. He used the left after the same manner; when on a sudden, to my great surprise, he stooped himself incredibly low, and turned gently on his toes. After this circular motion, he continued bent in that humble posture for some time, looking on his book. After this he recovered himself by a sudden spring, and flew round the room in all the violence and disorder imaginable, till he made a full pause for want of breath. In this interim my woman asked what I thought: I whispered, that I thought this learned person an enthusiast, who possibly had his first education in the peripatetic way, which was a sect of philosophers who always studied when walking. But observing him much out of breath, I thought it the best time to master him if he were disordered, and knocked at his door. I was surprised to find him open it, and say, with great civility and good mien, " That he hoped he had not disturbed us." I believed him in a lucid interval, and desired he would please to let me see the book. He did so, smiling. I could not make anything of it, and therefore asked in which language it was writ. He said, " It was one he studied with great application; but it was his profession to teach it, and could not communicate his knowledge without a consideration." I answered, " That I hoped he would hereafter keep his thoughts to himself; for his meditation this morning had cost me three coffee dishes, and a clean pipe." He seemed concerned at that, and told me he was a dancing-master, and had been reading a dance or two before he went out, which had been written by one who taught at an academy in France. He observed me at a stand, and went on to inform me, " That now articulate motions, as well as sounds, were expressed by proper characters; and that there is nothing so common as to communicate a dance by a letter." I beseeched him hereafter to meditate in a ground-room, for that otherwise it would be impossible for an artist of any other kind to live near him; and that I was sure, several of his thoughts this morning would have shaken my spectacles off my nose, had I been myself at study.

I then took my leave of this virtuoso, and returned

to my chamber, meditating on the various occupations of rational creatures.

LAUGHING

Lord Chesterfield's LETTERS

Bath, March 9, 1748. Having mentioned laughing, I must particularly warn you against it; and I could heartily wish, that you may often be seen to smile, but never be heard to laugh while you live. Frequent and loud laughter is the characteristic of folly and ill manners; it is the manner in which the mob express their silly joy at silly things; and they call it being merry. In my mind, there is nothing so illiberal, and so ill bred, as audible laughter. True wit, or sense, never yet made anybody laugh; they are above it: they please the mind, and give a cheerfulness to the countenance. But it is low buffoonery, or silly accidents, that always excite laughter, and that is what people of sense and breeding should show them selves above. A man's going to sit down, in the supposition that he has a chair behind him, and falling down upon his breech for want of one, sets a whole company a laughing, when all the wit in the world would not do it; a plain proof, in my mind, how low and unbecoming a thing laughter is: not to mention the disagreeable noise that it makes and the shocking distortion of the face that it occasions. Laughter is easily restrained by a very little reflection; but as it is generally connected with the idea of gaiety, people do not enough attend to its absurdity. I am neither of a melancholy nor a cynical disposition, and am as willing and as apt to be pleased as anybody; but I am sure that since I have had the full use of my reason, nobody has ever heard me laugh.

ON WOMEN

Lord Chesterfield's LETTERS

London, Sept. 5, 1748. Women, then, are only children of a larger growth; they have an entertaining tattle, and sometimes wit; but for solid reasoning, good sense, I never knew in my life one that had it, or who reasoned or acted consequentially too four and twenty hours together. Some little passion or humour always breaks in upon their best resolutions. Their beauty neglected or controverted, their age increased or their supposed understandings depreciated, instantly kindles their little passions, and overturns any system of consequential conduct, that in their most reasonable moments they might have been capable of forming. A man of sense only trifles with them, plays with them, humours and flatters them, as he does with a sprightly forward child; but he neither consults them about, nor trusts them with serious matters; though he often makes them believe that he does both; which is the thing in the world that they are proud of; for they love mightily to be dabbling in business (which, by the way, they always spoil); and being justly distrustful, that men in general look upon them in a trifling light, they almost adore that man who talks more seriously to them, and who seems to consult and trust them; I say, who seems; for weak men really do, but wise men only seem to do it. No flattery is either too high or too low for them. They will greedily swallow the highest, and gratefully accept of the lowest; and you may safely flatter any woman from her understanding down to the exquisite taste of her fan.

DR. JOHNSON IN THE ANTE-ROOM OF LORD CHESTERFIELD
After a painting by E. M. Ward, R.A.

THE EIGHTEENTH CENTURY 155

ON HOOPS
The Spectator

Of Dress

"Mr. Spectator, You have diverted the town almost a whole month at the expense of the country; it is now high time that you should give the country their revenge. Since your withdrawing from this place, the fair sex are run into great extravagancies. Their petticoats, which began to heave and swell before you left us, are now blown up into a most enormous concave, and rise every day more and more: in short, sir, since our women know themselves to be out of the eye of the Spectator, they will be kept within no compass. You praised them a little too soon for the modesty of their head-dresses; for as the humour of a sick person is often driven out of one limb into another, their superfluity of ornaments, instead of being entirely banished, seems only fallen from their heads upon their lower parts. What they have lost in height they make up in breadth, and contrary to all rules of architecture, widen the foundations at the same time that they shorten the superstructure. Were they, like Spanish jennets, to impregnate by the wind, they could not have thought on a more proper invention. But as we do not yet hear any particular use in this petticoat, or that it contains anything more than what was supposed to be in those of scantier make, we are wonderfully at a loss about it.

"The women give out, in defence of these wide bottoms, that they are airy, and very proper for the season; but this I look upon to be only a pretence, and a piece of art; for it is well known, we have not had a more moderate summer these many years; so that it is certain the heat they complain of cannot be in the weather: besides, I would fain ask these tender-constitutioned ladies, why they should require more cooling than their mothers before them.

"I find several speculative persons are of opinion, that our sex has of late years been very saucy, and that the hoop-petticoat is made use of to keep us at a distance. It is most certain that a woman's honour cannot be better entrenched than after this manner, in circle within circle, amidst such a variety of outworks and lines of circumvallation. A female who is thus invested in whalebone, is sufficiently secured against the approaches of an ill-bred fellow, who might as well think of Sir George Etheridges' way of making love in a tub as in the midst of so many hoops.

"Among these various conjectures there are men of superstitious tempers, who look upon the hoop-petticoat as a kind of prodigy. Some will have it that it portends the downfall of the French king, and observe that the farthingale appeared in England a little before the ruin of the Spanish monarchy. Others are of opinion, that it foretells battle and bloodshed, and believe it of the same prognostication as the tail of a blazing star. For my part, I am apt to think it is a sign that multitudes are coming into the world, rather than going out of it.

"The first time I saw a lady dressed in one of these petticoats, I could not forbear blaming her in my own thoughts, for walking abroad when she was so near her time; but soon recovered myself out of my error, when I found all the modish part of the sex as far gone as herself. It is generally thought some crafty women have thus betrayed their companions into hoops, that they might make them accessory to their own concealments, and by that means escape the censure of the world; as wary generals have sometimes dressed two or three dozen of their own friends in their own habit, that they might not draw upon themselves any particular attacks from the enemy. The strutting petticoat smooths all distinctions, levels the mother with the daughter, and sets maids and matrons, wives and widows, upon the same bottom. In the mean while, I cannot but be troubled to see so many well-shaped, innocent virgins bloated up, and wadling up and down like big-bellied women.

Should this fashion get among the ordinary people, our public ways would be so crowded that we should want street-room. Several congregations of the best fashion find themselves already very much straitened, and if the mode increase, I wish it may not drive many ordinary women into meetings and conventicles. Should our sex at the same time take it into their heads to wear trunk breeches (as who knows what their indignation at this female treatment may drive them to), a man and his wife would fill a whole pew.

"You know, sir, it is recorded of Alexander the Great, that in his Indian expedition he buried several suits of armour, which by his directions were made much too big for any of his soldiers, in order to give posterity an extraordinary idea of him, and make them believe he had commanded an army of giants. I am persuaded that if one of the present petticoats happens to be hung up in any repository of curiosities, it will lead into the same error the generations that lie some removes from us; unless we can believe our posterity will think so disrespectfully of their great-grandmothers, that they made themselves monstrous to appear amiable.

"When I survey this new-fashioned rotunda in all its parts, I cannot but think of the old philosopher, who, after having entered into an Egyptian temple, and looked about for the idol of the place, at length discovered a little black monkey enshrined in the midst of it; upon which he could not forbear crying out, (to the great scandal of the worshippers). 'What a magnificent palace is here for such a ridiculous inhabitant!'

"Though you have taken a resolution, in one of

your papers, to avoid descending to particularities of dress, I believe you will not think it below you on so extraordinary an occasion, to unhoop the fair sex, and cure this fashionable tympany that is got among them. I am apt to think the petticoat will shrink of its own accord at your first coming to town; at least a touch of your pen will make it contract itself, like the sensitive plant, and by that means oblige several who are either terrified or astonished at this portentous novelty, and among the rest.

"Your humble servant, &c."

ON HOODS

The Spectator

... The ladies have been for some time in a kind of moulting season, with regard to that part of their dress, having cast great quantities of ribbon, lace, and cambric, and in some measure reduced that part of the human figure to the beautiful globular form which is natural to it. We have for a great while expected what kind of ornament would be substituted in the place of those antiquated commodes. But our female projectors were all the last summer so taken up with the improvement of their petticoats that they had not time to attend to anything else: but having at length sufficiently adorned their lower parts, they now begin to turn their thoughts upon the other extremity as well remembering the old kitchen proverb, That if you light a fire at both ends, the middle will shift for itself.

I am engaged in this speculation by a sight which I lately met with at the opera. As I was standing in the hinder part of the box, I took notice of a little cluster of women sitting together in the prettiest-coloured hoods that I ever saw, One of them was blue, another yellow, and another philomot; the fourth was of a pink colour, and the fifth of a pale green. I looked with as much pleasure upon this little party-coloured assembly, as upon a bed of tulips, and did not know at first whether it might not be an embassy of Indian queens; but upon my going about into the pit, and taking them in front, I was immediately undeceived, and saw so much beauty in every face, that I found them all to be English. Such eyes and lips, cheeks and foreheads, could be the growth of no other country. The complexion of their faces hindered me from observing any further the colour of their hoods, though I could easily perceive by that unspeakable satisfaction which appeared in their looks, that their own thoughts were wholly taken up on those pretty ornaments they wore upon their heads.

I am informed that this fashion spreads daily, insomuch that the Whig and Tory ladies begin already to hang out different colours, and to show their principles by their head-dress. Nay, if I may believe my friend Will Honeycomb, there is a certain old coquette of his acquaintance, who intends to appear very suddenly in a rainbow hood, like the Iris in Dryden's Virgil, not questioning but that among such a variety of colours she shall have a charm for every heart.

My friend Will; who very much values himself upon his great insights into gallantry, tells me, that he can already guess at the humour a lady is in by her hood, as the courtiers of Morocco know the disposition of their present emperor by the colour of the dress which he puts on. When Melisinda wraps her head in flame colour, her heart is set upon execution. When she covers it with purple, I would not, says he, advise her lover to approach her; but if she appears in white, it is peace, and he may hand her out of her box with safety.

Will. informs me likewise, that these hoods may be used as signals. Why else, says he, does Cornelia always put on a black hood when her husband is gone into the country.

Such are my friend Honeycomb's dreams of gallantry. For my own part, I impute this diversity of colours in the hoods to the diversity of complexion in the faces of my pretty country-women. Ovid, in his Art of Love, has given some precepts as to this particular, though I find they are different from those which prevail among the moderns. He recommends a red striped silk to the pale complexion, white to the brown, and dark to the fair. On the contrary, my friend Will, who pretends to be a greater master in this art than Ovid, tells me, that the palest features look the most agreeable in white sarcenet, that a face which is over-flushed appears to advantage in the deepest scarlet, and that the darkest complexion is not a little alleviated by a black hood. In short, he is for losing the colour of the face in that of the hood, as a fire burns dimly, and a candle goes half out, in the light of the sun. This, says he, your Ovid himself has hinted, where he treats of these matters, when he tells us that the Blue Water-nymphs are dressed in sky-coloured garments; and that Aurora, who always appears in the light of the rising sun, is robed in saffron.

THE HEAD-DRESS

The Spectator

Tanta est quærendi cura decoris. Juv.

There is not so variable a thing in nature as a lady's head-dress: within my own memory I have known it rise and fall above thirty degrees. About ten years ago it shot up to a very great height, insomuch that the female part of our species were much taller than the men. The women were of such an enormous stature, that " we appeared as grasshoppers before them :" at present the whole sex is in a manner dwarfed and shrunk into a race of beauties that seems almost another species. I remember several ladies, who were once very near seven foot high, that at present want some inches of five ; how they came to be thus curtailed I cannot learn ; whether the whole sex be at present under any penance which we know nothing of, or whether they have cast their head-dresses in order to surprise us with something in that kind which shall be entirely new ; or whether some of the tallest of the sex, being too cunning for the rest, have contrived this method to make themselves appear sizeable, is still a secret ; though I find most are of opinion, they are at present like trees new lopped and pruned, that will certainly sprout up and flourish with greater heads than before. For my own part, as I do not love to be insulted by women who are taller than myself, I admire the sex much more in their present humiliation, which has reduced them to their natural dimensions, than when they had extended their persons, and lengthened themselves out into formidable and gigantic figures. I am not for adding to the beautiful edifice of nature, nor for raising any whimsical superstructure upon her plans : I must, therefore, repeat it, that I am highly pleased with the coiffure now in fashion, and think it shows the good sense which at present very much reigns among the valuable part of the sex. One may observe, that women in all ages have taken more pains than men to adorn the outside of their heads ; and, indeed, I very much admire, that those female architects, who raise such wonderful structures out of ribbons, lace, and wire, have not been recorded for their respective inventions. It is certain there have been as many orders in these kinds of building, as in those which have been made of marble; sometimes they rise in the shape of a pyramid, sometimes like a tower, and sometimes like a steeple. In Juvenal's time the building grew by several orders and stories, as he has very humourously described it.

> *Tot premit ordinibus, tot adhuc compagibus altum*
> *Ædificat caput* : *Andromachen a fronte videbis* ;
> *Post minor est* : *aliam credas.*   Juv.

But I do not remember, in any part of my reading, that the head-dress aspired to so great an extravagance as in the fourteenth century; when it was built up in a couple of cones or spires, which stood so excessively high on each side of the head, that a woman who was but a Pigmy without her head-dress, appeared like a Colossus upon putting it on. Monsieur Paradin says, "That these old-fashioned fontanges rose an ell above the head; that they were pointed like steeples, and had long loose pieces of crape fastened to the tops of them, which were curiously fringed, and hung down their backs like streamers."

The women might possibly have carried this Gothic building much higher, had not a famous monk, Thomas Connecte by name, attacked it with great zeal and resolution. This holy man travelled from place to place to preach down this monstrous commode; and succeeded so well in it, that as the magicians sacrificed their books to the flames upon the preaching of an apostle, many of the women threw down their head-dresses in the middle of his sermon, and made a bonfire of them within sight of the pulpit. He was so renowned for the sanctity of his life as his manner of preaching, that he had often a congregation of twenty thousand people; the men placing themselves on the one side of his pulpit, and the women on the other, that appeared (to use the similtude of an ingenious writer) like a forest of cedars with their heads reaching to the clouds. He so warmed and animated the people against this monstrous ornament, that it lay under a kind of persecution; and whenever it appeared in public, was pelted down by the rabble, who flung stones at the persons that wore it. But notwithstanding, this prodigy vanished while the peacher was among them, it began to appear again some months after his departure; or, to tell it in Monsieur Paradin's own words, "The women that, like snails in a fright, had drawn in their horns, shot them out again as soon as the danger was over." This extravagance of the women's head-dresses in that age is taken notice of by Monsieur D'Argentre in his History of Butagne, and by other historians as well as the person I have here quoted.

It is usually observed, that a good reign is the only time for the making of laws against the exorbitance of power; in the same manner, an excessive head-dress may be attacked the most effectually when the fashion is against it. I do, therefore, recommend this paper to my female readers by way of precention.

I would desire the fair sex to consider how impossible it is for them to add anything that can be ornamental to what is already the master-piece of nature. The head has the most beautiful appearance, as well as the highest station, in a human figure. Nature has laid out all her art in beautifying the face; she has touched it with vermilion, planted in it a double row of ivory, made it the seat of smiles and blushes, lighted it up and enlivened it with the brightness of the eyes; hung it on each side with curious organs of sense, given it airs and graces that cannot be described, and surrounded it with such a flowing shade of hair as sets all its beauties in the most agreeable light, in short, she seems to have designed the head as tne cupola to the most glorious of her works; and when we load it with such a pile of supernumerary ornaments, we destroy the symmetry of the human figure, and foolishly continue to call off the eye from great and real beauties, to childish gew-gaws, ribbons, and bone-lace.

MY LITTLE REPUBLIC

THE VICAR OF WAKEFIELD
Goldsmith

Domestic Economies Our little habitation was situated at the foot of a sloping hill, sheltered with a beautiful underwood behind, and a prattling river before; on the one side a meadow, on the other a green. My farm consisted of about twenty acres of excellent land, having given an hundred pound for my predecessor's good-will. Nothing could exceed the neatness of my little enclosures, the elms and hedgerows appearing with inexpressible beauty. My house consisted of but one story, and was covered with thatch, which gave it an air of great snugness; the walls on the inside were nicely whitewashed, and my daughters undertook to adorn them with pictures of their own designing. Though the same room served us for parlour and kitchen, that only made it the warmer. Besides, as it was kept with the utmost neatness, the dishes, plates, and coppers being well scoured, and all disposed in bright rows on the shelves, the eye was agreeably relieved, and did not want richer furniture. There were three other apartments; one for my wife and me, another for our two daughters within our own, and the third, with two beds, for the rest of the children.

The little republic to which I gave laws, was regulated in the following manner: By sunrise we all assembled in our common apartment, the fire being previously kindled by the servant. After we had saluted each other with proper ceremony—for I always thought fit to keep up some mechanical forms of good breeding, without which freedom ever destroys friendship—we all bent in gratitude to that Being who gave us another day. This duty being performed, my son and I went to pursue our usual industry abroad, while my wife and daughters employed themselves in providing breakfast, which was always ready at a certain time. I allowed half an hour for this meal, and an hour for dinner; which time was taken up in innocent mirth between my wife and daughters, and in philosophical arguments between my son and me.

RUSHES FOR CANDLES

NATURAL HISTORY OF SELBORNE
White

To Thomas Pennant

Selborne, Nov. 1st, 1775

" Hic . . . *tædæ pingues, hic plurimus ignis
Semper, et assiduâ postes fuligine nigri.*"

Dear Sir, I shall make no apology for troubling you with the detail of a very simple piece of domestic economy, being satisfied that you think nothing beneath your attention that tends to utility; the matter alluded to is the use of rushes instead of candles, which I am well aware prevails in many districts besides this; but as I know there are countries also where it does not obtain, and as I have considered the subject with some degree of exactness, I shall proceed in my humble story, and leave you to judge of the expediency.

The proper species of rush for this purpose seems to be the *juneus conglomeratus*, or common soft rush, which is to be found in most moist pastures, by the sides of streams, and under hedges. These rushes are in best condition in the height of summer; but may be gathered, so as to serve the purpose well, quite on to autumn. It would be needless to add that the largest and longest are best. Decayed labourers, women, and children, make it their business to procure and prepare them. As soon as they are cut, they must be flung into water, and kept there, for otherwise they will dry and shrink, and the peel will not run. At first a person would find it no easy matter to divest a rush of its peel or rind, so as to leave one regular, narrow, even rib from top to bottom that may support the pith; but this like other feats, soon becomes familiar even to children; and we have seen an old woman, stone blind, performing this business with great despatch, and seldom failing to strip them with the nicest regularity. When these *junci* are thus far prepared they must lie out on the grass to be bleached, and take the dew for some nights, and afterwards be dried in the sun.

Some address is required in dipping these rushes in scalding fat or grease; but this knack also is to be attained by practice. The careful wife of an industrious Hampshire labourer obtains all her fat for nothing; for she saves the scummings of her bacon-pot for this use: and, if the grease abounds with salt, she causes the salt to precipitate to the bottom, by setting the scummings in a warm oven. Where hogs are not much in use, and especially by the seaside, the coarser animal-oils will come very cheap. A pound of common grease, may be procured for fourpence, and about six pounds of grease will dip a pound of rushes, and one pound of rushes may be bought for one shilling; so that a pound of rushes, medicated and ready for use, will cost three shillings. If men that keep bees will mix a little wax with the grease, it will give it a consistency, and render it more

THE EIGHTEENTH CENTURY

cleanly, and make the rushes burn longer; mutton-suet would have the same effect.

A good rush, which measured in length two feet four inches and a half, being minuted, burnt only three minutes short of an hour; and a rush still of greater length has been known to burn one hour and a quarter.

These rushes give a good clear light. Watch-lights (coated with tallow), it is true, shed a dismal one, "darkness visible"; but then the wick of those have two ribs of the rind, or peel, to support the pith, while the wick of the dipped rush has but one. The two ribs are intended to impede the progress of the flame and make the candle last.

In a pound of dry rushes, avoirdupois, which I caused to be weighed and numbered, we found upwards of one thousand six hundred individuals. Now suppose each of these burns, one with another, only half an hour, then a poor man will purchase eight hundred hours of light, a time exceeding thirty-three entire days, for three shillings. According to this account each rush, before dipping, costs 1/33 of a farthing 1/11 afterwards. Thus a poor family will enjoy five and a half hours of comfortable light for a farthing. An experienced old housekeeper assures me that one pound and a half of rushes completely supplies his family the year round, since working people burn no candles in the long days, because they rise and go to bed by daylight.

Little farmers use rushes much in the short days both morning and evening, in the dairy and kitchen; but the very poor, who are always the worst economists, and therefore must continue very poor, buy a halfpenny candle every evening, which in their blowing open rooms, does not burn much more than two hours. Thus they have only two hours light for their money instead of eleven.

While on the subject of rural economy, it may not be improper to mention a pretty implement of housewifery that we have seen nowhere else; that is, little neat besoms which our foresters make from the stalks of the *polytricum commune*, or great golden maiden hair, which they call silk-wood, and find plenty in the bogs. When this moss is well combed and dressed, and divested of its outer skin, it becomes of a beautiful bright chestnut colour; and, being soft and pliant, is very proper for the dusting of beds, curtains, carpets, hangings, etc. If these besoms were known to the brush-makers in town, it is probable they might come much in use for the purpose above-mentioned.

I am, &c.

THE OPERA

The Spectator

The Diversions   I immediately bought the opera, by which means I perceived the sparrows were to act the part of singing birds in a delightful grove; though upon a nearer inquiry, I found the sparrows put the same trick upon the audience, that Sir Martin Mar-all practised upon his mistress; for, though they flew in sight, the music proceeded from a concert of flagelets and bird-calls which were planted behind the scenes. At the same time I made this discovery, I found, by the discourse of the actors, that there were great designs on foot for the improvement of the opera; that it had been proposed to break down a part of the wall, and to surprise the audience with a party of an hundred horse; and that there was actually a project of bringing the New River into the house, to be employed in jetteaus and water-works. This project, as I have since heard, is postponed till the summer season; when it is thought the coolness that proceeds from fountains and cascades will be more acceptable and refreshing to people of quality. In the mean time, to find out a more agreeable entertainment for the winter season, the opera of Rinaldo is filled with thunder and lightning, illuminations and fireworks; which the audience may look upon without catching cold, and indeed without much danger of being burnt; for there are several engines filled with water, and ready to play at a minutes warning, in case any such accident should happen.

A MIDNIGHT MASK

The Spectator

" The midnight mask, which has of late been very frequently held in one of the most conspicuous parts of the town, and which I hear will be continued with additions and improvements. As all the persons who compose this lawless assembly are masked, we dare not attack any of them in our way, lest we should send a woman of quality to Bridewell, or a peer of Great Britain to the Counter; besides their numbers are so very great, that I am afraid they would be able to rout our whole fraternity, though we were accompanied with all our guard of constables. Both these reasons, which secure them from our authority, make them obnoxious to yours; as both their disguise and their numbers will give no particular person reason to think himself affronted by you.

" If we are rightly informed, the rules that are observed by this new society, are wonderfully contrived for the advancement of cuckoldom. The women either come by themselves, or are introduced by friends, who are obliged to quit them, upon their first entrance, to the conversation of anybody that addresses himself to them. These are several rooms where the parties may retire, and, if they please, show their faces by consent.

"Whispers, squeezes, nods, and embraces, are the innocent freedoms of the place. In short, the whole design of this libidinous assembly, seems to terminate in assignations and intrigues; and I hope you will take effectual methods, by your public advice and admonitions, to prevent such a promiscuous multitude of both sexes from meeting together in so clandestine a manner. I am

Your humble servant, and fellow-labourer
T.B."

Not long after the perusal of this letter, I received another upon the same subject, which by the date and style of it, I take to be written by some young Templar.

Middle Temple 1710-11

" Sir,

When a man has been guilty of any vice or folly, I think the best atonement he can make for it is to warn others not to fall into the like. In order to this, I must acquaint you, that some time in February last, I went to the Tuesday's masquerade. Upon my first going in, I was attacked by half a dozen female Quakers, who seemed willing to adopt me for a brother; but, upon a nearer examination, I found they were a sisterhood of coquettes disguised in that precise habit. I was soon after taken out to dance, and, as I fancied, by a woman of the first quality, for she was very tall, and moved gracefully. As soon as the minuet was over, we ogled one another through our masques; and as I am very well read in Waller, I repeated to her the four following verses out of his poem of Vandyke.

THE EIGHTEENTH CENTURY

> The heedless lover does not know
> Whose eyes they are that wound him so;
> But, confounded with thy art,
> Inquires her name that has his heart.

"I pronounced these words with such a languishing air, that I had some reason to conclude that I had made a conquest. She told me that she hoped my face was not akin to my tongue; and looking upon her watch, I accidentally discovered the figure of a coronet on the back part of it. I was so transported with the thought of such an amour, that I plied her, from one room to another with all the gallantries I could invent; and at length brought things to so happy an issue, that she gave me a private meeting the next day, without page or footman, coach or equipage. My heart danced in raptures; but I had not lived in this golden dream above three days, before I found good reason to wish that I had continued true to my laundress. I have since heard, by a very great accident, that this fine lady does not live far from Covent Garden, and that I am not the first cully whom she has passed herself upon for a countess.

"Thus, sir, you see how I have mistaken a cloud for a Juno; and if you can make any use of this adventure, for the benefit of those who may possibly be as vain young coxcombs as myself, I do most heartily give you leave.
I am, Sir,
Your most humble admirer,
B.L."

A PARTY

THE VICAR OF WAKEFIELD
Goldsmith

Michaelmas-Eve happening on the next day, we were invited to burn nuts and play tricks at neighbour

Flamborough's. Our late mortifications had humbled us a little, or it is probable we might have rejected such an invitation with contempt: however, we suffered ourselves to be happy. Our honest neighbour's goose and dumplings were fine, and the lamb's-wool, even in the opinion of my wife, who was a connoisseur, was excellent. It is true, his manner of telling stories was not quite so well. They were very long, and very dull, and all about himself, and we had laughed at them ten times before: however, we were kind enough to laugh at them once more.

Mr. Burchell, who was of the party, was always fond of seeing some innocent amusement going forward, and set the boys and girls to blind-man's buff. My wife, too, was persuaded to join in the diversion, and it gave me pleasure to think she was not yet too old. In the meantime, my neighbour and I looked on, laughed at every feat, and praised our own dexterity when we were young. Hot cockles succeeded next, questions and commands followed that, and, last of all, they sat down to hunt the slipper. As every person may not be acquainted with this primeval pastime, it may be necessary to observe, that the company at this play plant themselves in a ring upon the ground, all except one who stands in the middle, whose business it is to catch a shoe, which the company shove about under their hams from one to another, something like a weaver's shuttle. As it is impossible, in this case, for the lady who is up to face all the company at once, the great beauty of the play lies in hitting her a thump with the heel of the shoe on that side least capable of making a defence. It was in this manner that my eldest daughter was hemmed in, and thumped about, all blowzed in spirits, and bawling for fair play, fair play, with a voice that might deafen a ballad-singer, when, confusion on confusion! who should enter the room but our two great acquaintances from

From an illustration by Thomas Rowlandson to "The Vicar of Wakefield," an edition of 1786,

town, Lady Blarney and Miss Carolina Wilelmina Amelia Skeggs!

ON CLUBS

The Spectator

*Tigris agit rabidâ cum tigride pacem
Perpetuam, sævis inter se convenit ursis.* Juv.

Man is said to be a sociable animal, and as an instance of it, we may observe, that we take all occasions and pretences of forming ourselves into those little nocturnal assemblies, which are commonly known by the name of clubs. When a set of men find themselves agree in any particular, though never so trivial, they establish themselves into a kind of fraternity, and meet once or twice a week, upon the account of such a fantastic resemblance. I know a considerable market town, in which there was a club of fat men, that did not come together (as you may well suppose) to entertain one another with sprightliness and wit, but to keep one another in countenance; the room where the club met was something of the largest, and had two entrances, the one by a door of a moderate size, and the other by a pair of folding doors. If a candidate for this corpulent club could make his entrance through the first, he was looked upon as unqualified; but if he stuck in the passage, and could not force his way through it, the folding doors were immediately thrown open for his reception, and he was saluted as a brother. I have heard that this club, though it consisted but of fifteen persons, weighed above three ton.

In opposition to this society, there sprung up another, composed of scarecrows and skeletons, who being very meagre and envious, did all they could to thwart the designs of their bulky brethren, whom they represented as men of dangerous principles; till at length they worked them out of the favour of the people, and consequently out of the magistracy. These factions tore the corporation in pieces for several years, till at length they came to this accommodation ; that the two bailiffs of the town should be annually chosen out of the two clubs ; by which means the principal magistrates are at this day coupled like rabbits, one fat and one lean.

Every one has heard of the club, or rather the confederacy, of the Kings. This grand alliance was formed a little after the return of King Charles the Second, and admitted into it men of all qualities and professions, provided they agreed in this surname of King, which, as they imagined, sufficiently declared the owners of it to be altogether untainted with republican and anti-monarchical principles.

A Christian name has likewise been often used as a badge of distinction, and made the occasion of a club. That of the Georges, which used to meet at the sign of the George on St. George's day, and swear " Before George," is still fresh in every one's memory.

There are at present in several parts of this city what they call Street Clubs, in which the chief inhabitants of the street converse together every night. I remember upon my inquiring after lodgings in Ormond Street, the landlord, to recommend that quarter of the town, told me, there was at that time a very good club in it : he also told me, upon further discourse with him, that two or three noisy country squires, who were settled there the year before, had considerably sunk the price of house rent ; and that the club (to prevent the like inconveniences for the future) had thoughts of taking every house that became vacant into their own hands, till they found a tenant for it of a sociable nature and good conversation.

The Hum-Drum Club, of which I was formerly an unworthy member, was made up of very honest

THE EIGHTEENTH CENTURY 175

gentlemen, of peaceable dispositions, that used to sit together, smoke their pipes, and say nothing till midnight. The Mum Club (as I am informed) is an institution of the same nature, and as great an enemy to noise.

After these two innocent societies, I cannot forbear mentioning a very mischievous one, that was erected in the reign of King Charles the Second. I mean, the Club of Duellists, in which none was to be admitted that had not fought his man. The president of it was said to have killed half a dozen in single combat; and as for the other members, they took their seats according to the number of their slain. There was likewise a side-table for such as had only drawn blood, and shown a laudable ambition of taking the first opportunity to qualify themselves for the first table. This club, consisting only of men of honour, did not continue long, most of the members of it being put to the sword, or hanged, a little after its institution.

Our modern celebrated clubs are founded upon eating and drinking, which are points wherein most men agree, and in which the learned and illiterate, the dull and the airy, the philosopher and the buffoon, can all of them bear a part. The Kit-Cat itself is said to have taken its original from a mutton-pie. The Beef-steak and October Clubs are neither of them averse to eating and drinking, if we may form a judgment of them from their respective titles.

When men are thus knit together by a love of society, not a spirit of faction, and do not meet to censure or annoy those that are absent, but to enjoy one another; when they are thus combined for their own improvement, or for the good of others, or at least to relax themselves from the business of the day, by an innocent and cheerful conversation; there may be something very useful in these little institutions and establishments.

I cannot forbear concluding this paper with a scheme of laws that I met with upon a wall in a little ale-house: how I came thither, I may inform my reader at a more convenient time. These laws were enacted by a knot of artisans and mechanics, who used to meet every night; and as there is something in them which gives us a pretty picture of low life, I shall transcribe them word for word.

RULES to be observed in the TWO-PENNY CLUB, *erected in this place, for the preservation of friendship and good neighbourhood.*

i. Every member at his first coming in shall lay down his two-pence.

ii. Every member shall fill his pipe out of his own box.

iii. If any member absents himself, he shall forfeit a penny for the use of the club, unless in case of sickness or imprisonment.

iv. If any member swears or curses, his neighbour may give him a kick upon the shins.

v. If any member tells stories in the club that are not true, he shall forfeit for every third lie an halfpenny.

vi. If any member strikes another wrongfully, he shall pay his club for him.

vii. If any member brings his wife into the club, he shall pay for whatever she drinks or smokes.

viii. If any member's wife come to fetch him home from the club, she shall speak to him without the door.

ix. If any member calls another cuckold, he shall be turned out of the club.

x. None shall be admitted into the club that is of the same trade with any member of it.

xi. None of the club shall have his clothes or shoes made or mended, but by a brother member.

xii. No conjuror shall be capable of being a member.

The morality of this little club is guarded by such wholesome laws and penalties, that I question not but my reader will be as well pleased with them, as he would have been with the Liges Convivales of Ben Jonson, the regulations of an old Roman club cited by Lipsius, or the rules of a Symposium in an ancient Greek author.

CHAPTER IV

THE EIGHTEENTH CENTURY II

FANCY DRESS

SIR CHARLES GRANDISON
Richardson

Letter X.

Our dresses are ready. Mr. Reeves is to be a *Good* hermit; Mrs. Reeves a nun; Lady Betty, a lady *Society* abbess; but I by no means like mine, because of its gaudiness: the very *thing* I was afraid of. They call it the dress of an Arcadian princess, but it falls not in with any of my notions of the pastoral dress of Arcadia. A white Paris net sort of cap, glittering with spangles, and encircled by a chaplet of artificial flowers, with a little white feather perking from the left ear, is to be my head-dress. My mask is Venetian. My hair is to be complimented with an appearance, because of its natural ringlets, as they call my curls, and to shade my neck. Tucker and ruffles, blonde lace. My shape is also said to be consulted in this dress. A kind of waistcoat, of blue satin, trimmed with silver Point d'Espagne, the skirts edged with silver fringe, is made to sit close to my waist by double clasps, a small silver tassel at the end of each clasp; all set off with bugles and spangles, which make a mighty glitter. But I am to be allowed a kind of scarf, of white Persian silk, which, gathered at the top, is to be fastened to my shoulders, and fly loose behind me.

Bracelets on my arms. They would have given me a crook, but I would not submit to that. It would give me, I said, an air of confidence to aim to manage it with any tolerable freedom; and I was apprehensive that I should not be thought to want *that* from the dress itself. A large Indian fan was not improper for the expected warmth of the place, and that contented me. My petticoat is of blue satin, trimmed and fringed as my waistcoat. I am not to have a hoop that is perceivable. They wore not hoops in Arcadia. What a sparkling figure shall I make! Had the ball been what they call a subscription ball, at which people dress with more glare than at a common one, this dress would have been more tolerable. But they all say that I shall be kept in countenance by masks as extravagant, and even more ridiculous. Be that as it may, I wish the night were over. I dare say it will be the last diversion of this kind I shall ever be at, for I never had any notion of masquerades.

Expect particulars of all in my next. I reckon you will be impatient for them. But pray, my Lucy, be fanciful, as I sometimes am, and let me know how you think everything will be beforehand, and how many pretty fellows you imagine, in this dress, will be slain by *your*

HARRIET BYRON.

THE "EXQUISITES"

RODERICK RANDOM
Smollett

Our new commander came on board in a ten-oared barge, overshadowed with a vast umbrella, and appeared in everything the reverse of Oakum, being a tall thin young man, dressed in this manner: a white hat, garnished with a red feather, adorned his head, from whence his hair flowed upon his shoulders, in ringlets tied behind with a ribbon. His coat, consisting of pink-coloured silk, lined with white, by the elegance of the cut retired backward, as it were, to discover a white satin waistcoat embroidered with gold, unbuttoned at the upper part to display a brooch set with garnets, that glittered in the breast of his shirt, which was of the finest cambric, edged with right Mechlin: the knees of his crimson velvet breeches scarce descended so low as to meet his silk stockings, which rose without spot or wrinkle on his meagre legs, from shoes of blue Meroquin, studded with diamond buckles, that flamed forth rivals to the sun! A steel-hilted sword, inlaid with gold, and decked with a knot of ribbon which fell down in a rich tassel, equipped his side; and an amber-headed cane hung dangling from his wrist. But the most remarkable parts of his furniture were, a mask on his face, and white gloves on his hands, which did not seem to be put on with an intention to be pulled off occasionally, but were fixed with a curious ring on the little finger of each hand.

In this garb, Captain Whiffle, for that was his name, took possession of the ship, surrounded with a crowd of attendants, all of whom, in their different degrees, seemed to be of their patron's disposition; and the air was so impregnated with perfumes, that one may venture to affirm the climate of Arabia Felix was not half so sweet-scented. My fellowmate, observing no surgeon among his train, thought he had found an occasion too favourable for himself to be neglected; and, remembering the old proverb, 'Spare to speek, and spare to speed,' resolved to solicit the new captain's interest immediately, before any other surgeon could be appointed for the ship. With this view he repaired to the cabin in his ordinary dress, consisting of a check shirt and trousers, a brown linen waistcoat, and a nightcap of the same (neither of them very clean), which, for his further misfortune, happened to smell strong of tobacco. Entering without any ceremony into this sacred place, he found Captain Whiffle reposing upon a couch, with a wrapper of fine chintz about his body, and a muslin cap bordered with lace about his head; and after several low congées began in this manner: 'Sir, I hope you will forgive, and excuse, and pardon, the presumption of one who has not the honour of being known unto you, but who is, nevertheless, a shentleman porn and pred, and moreover, has had misfortunes, Cot help me, in the world.'

Here he was interrupted by the captain, who, on seeing him, had started up with great amazement at the novelty of the apparition; and, having recollected himself, pronounced with a look and tone signifying disdain, curiosity, and surprise, 'Zauns! who art thou?' 'I am surgeon's first mate on board of this ship,' replied Morgan: 'and I most vehemently desire and beseech you, with all submission, to be pleased to condescend and vouchsafe to inquire into my character, and my pehaviour, and my deserts, which, under Cot, I hope, will entitle me to the vacancy of surgeon.' As he proceeded in his speech, he continued advancing towards the captain, whose nostrils were no sooner saluted with the aromatic flavour that exhaled from him, than he cried with great emotion, 'Heaven preserve! I am suffocated! Fellow, fellow, away with thee! Curse thee, fellow! get thee gone! I shall be stunk to death!' At the noise of his outcries, his servants ran into his apartment, and he accosted them thus: 'Villains! cut-throats! traitors! I am betrayed! I am sacrificed! Will you not carry that monster away? or must I be stifled with the stench of him? Oh! Oh! With these interjections he sank down upon his settee in a fit : his valet-de-chambre plied him with a smelling-bottle, one footman chafed his temples with Hungary water, another sprinkled the floor with spirits of lavender, a third pushed Morgan out of the cabin; who coming to the place where I was, sat down with a demure countenance, and, according to his custom, when he received any indignity which he durst not revenge, began to sing a Welsh ditty . . .

My wardrobe consisted of five fashionable coats full mounted, two of which were plain, one of cut velvet, one trimmed with gold, and another with silver lace ; two frocks, one of white drab, with large plate buttons, the other of blue, with gold binding; one waistcoat of gold brocade ; one of blue satin, embroidered with silver ; one of green silk, trimmed with broad figured gold lace ; one of black silk, with fringes ; one of white satin, one of black cloth, and one of scarlet ; six pair of cloth breeches ; one pair of crimson, and another of black velvet : twelve pair of white silk stockings, as many of black silk, and the same number of white cotton ; one hat, laced with gold *point d'Espagne*, another with silver lace scolloped, a third with gold binding, and a fourth plain ; three dozen of fine ruffled shirts, as many neckcloths ; one dozen of cambric handkerchiefs, and the like number of silk. The other moveables, which I possessed by the generosity and friendship of Strap, were a gold watch with a chased case, two valuable diamond rings, two mourning swords, one with a silver handle, and a fourth, cut steel, inlaid with gold, a diamond stock-buckle, and a set of stone buckles for the knees and shoes ; a pair of silver-mounted pistols with rich housings ; a gold-headed cane, and a snuff-box of tortoiseshell, mounted with gold, having the picture of a lady in the top. The gentleman left many other things of value, which my friend had converted into cash before I met with him; so that, over and above these particulars, our stock in ready money amounted to something more than two hundred pounds.

Thus equipped, I put on the gentleman of figure, and, attended by my honest friend, who was contented with the station of my valet, visited the Louvre, examined the gallery of Luxembourg, and appeared at Versailles, where I had the honour of seeing his Most Christian Majesty eat a considerable quantity of olives. During the month I spent at Paris, I went several times to court, the Italian comedy, opera, and playhouse, danced at a masquerade, and, in short, saw everything remarkable in and about that capital. Then we set out for England by way of Flanders, passed through Brussels, Ghent, and Bruges, and took shipping at Ostend, from whence, in fourteen hours, we arrived at Deal, hired a postchaise, and in twelve hours more got safe to London, having disposed of our heavy baggage in the waggon.

CHAP. XLV

As soon as we alighted at the inn, I dispatched Strap to inquire for my uncle at the Union Flag in Wapping; and he returned in a little time, with an account of Mr. Bowling's having gone to sea, mate of a merchant ship, after a long and unsuccessful application and attendance at the Admiralty; where, it seems, the interest he depended upon was not sufficient to reinstate him, or recover the pay that was due to him when he quitted the Thunder.

Next day I hired very handsome lodgings not far from Charing Cross; and in the evening dressed myself in a plain suit of true Paris cut, and appeared in a front box at the play, where I saw a good deal of company, and was vain enough to believe that I was observed with an uncommon degree of attention and applause. This silly conceit intoxicated me so much, that I was guilty of a thousand ridiculous coquetries; and I dare say, how favourable soever the thoughts of the company might be at my first appearance, they were soon changed by my absurd behaviour into pity or contempt. I rose and sat down, covered and uncovered my head twenty times between the acts; pulled out my watch, clapped it to my ear, wound it up, set it, gave it the hearing again; displayed my snuff-box, affected to take snuff, that I might have an opportunity of showing my brilliant, and wiped my nose with a perfumed handkerchief; then dangled my cane, and adjusted my sword-knot, and acted many more fooleries of the same kind, in hopes of obtaining the character of a pretty fellow, in the acquiring of which I found two considerable obstructions in my disposition—namely, a natural reserve and jealous sensibility. Fain would I have entered into conversation with the people around me; but I was restrained by the fear of being censured for my assurance, as well as by reflecting that I was more entitled to a compliment of this kind from them, than they to such condescension from a stranger like me. How often did I redden at the frequent whispers and loud laughter of my fellow beaux, which I imagined were excited by me; and how often did I envy the happy indifference of those choice spirits, who beheld the distress of the scene, without discovering the least symptom of approbation or concern. My attention was engaged in spite of myself, and I could not help weeping with the heroine of the stage, though I practised a great many shifts to conceal this piece of unpolite weakness.

"THERE'S NOTHING LIKE POLISH"

THE RIVALS
Sheridan

ACRES' *Lodgings*.

ACRES, *as just dressed, and* DAVID

Acres. Indeed, David—do you think I become it so?

Dav. You are quite another creature, believe me, master, by the mass! an' we've any luck we shall see the Devon monkeyrony in all the print-shops in Bath!

Acres. Dress does make a difference, David.

Dav. 'Tis all in all, I think.—Difference! why, an' you were to go now to Clod-Hall, I am certain the old lady wouldn't know you: master Butler wouldn't believe his own eyes, and Mrs. Pickle would cry, Lard presarve me! our dairy-maid would come giggling to the door, and I warrant Dolly Tester, your honour's favourite, would blush like my waistcoat,—Oons! I'll hold a gallon, there an't a dog in the house but would bark, and I question whether Phillis would wag a hair of her tail!

Acres. Ay, David, there's nothing like polishing.

Dav. So I says of your honour's boots; but the boy never heeds me!

Acres. But, David, has Mr. De-la-grace been here? I must rub up my balancing, and chasing, and boring.

Dav. I'll call again, sir.

Acres. Do--and see if there are any letters for me at the post-office.

Dav. I will. By the mass, I can't help looking at your head!—if I hadn't been by at the cooking, I wish I may die if I should have known the dish again myself!

[*Exit*

Acres. (Practising a dancing-step). Sink, slide—

coupee.—Confound the first inventors of cotillions! say I—they are as bad as algebra to us country gentlemen—I can walk a minuet easy enough when I am forced!—and I have been accounted a good stick in a country-dance.—Odd jigs and tabors! I never valued your cross-over to couple—figure in—right and left—and I'd foot it with e'er a captain in the country!—but these outlandish heathen allemandes and cotillions are quite beyond me!—I shall never prosper at 'em, that's sure—mine are true-born English legs—they don't understand their curst French lingo!—their *pas* this, and *pas* that, and *pas* t'other!—damn me! my feet don't like to be called paws! no, 'tis certain I have most Antigallican toes!

"MISSES OF THE TON"
CECILIA
Fanny Burney

"Are you, then, yet to learn," cried he, "that there are certain young ladies who make it a rule never to speak but to their own cronies? Of this class is Miss Leeson, and till you get into her particular coterie, you must never expect to hear from her a word of two syllables. The TON misses, as they are called, who now infest the town, are in two divisions, the SUPERCILIOUS, and the VOLUBLE. The SUPERCILIOUS, like Miss Leeson are silent, scornful, languid, and affected, and disdain all converse but with those of their own set: the VOLUBLE, like Miss Larolles, are flirting, communicative, restless and familiar, and attack without the smallest ceremony, every one they think worthy their notice. But this they have in common, that at home they think of nothing but dress, abroad, of nothing, but admiration, and that every where they hold in supreme contempt all but themselves."

"Probably, then," said Cecilia, "I have passed to-night, for one of the VOLUBLES; however, all the advantage has been with the SUPERCILIOUS, for I have suffered a total repulse."

"Are you sure, however, you have not talked too well for her?"

"O, a child of five years old ought to have been whipt for not talking better!"

"But it is not capacity alone you are to consult when you talk with Misses of the TON; were their understandings only to be considered, they would indeed be wonderfully easy of access! in order, therefore, to render their commerce somewhat difficult, they will only be pleased by an observance of their humours: which are ever most various and least exuberant where the intellects are weakest and least cultivated."

THE "ENNUYÉ"

CECILIA
Fanny Burney

"Do, pray, now," cried Miss Larolles, "observe Mr. Meadows! only just see where he has fixed himself! in the very best place in the room, and keeping the fire from everybody! I do assure you that's always his way, and it's monstrous provoking, for if one's ever so cold, he lollops so, that one's quite starved. But you must know there's another thing he does is quite as bad, for if he gets a seat, he never offers to move, if he sees one sinking with fatigue. And besides, if one is waiting for one's carriage two hours together, he makes it a rule never to stir a step to see for it. Only think how monstrous!"

"These are heavy complaints, indeed," said Cecilia, looking at him attentively; "I should have expected from his appearance a very different account of his gallantry, for he seems dressed with more studied elegance than anybody here."

" O yes," cried Miss Larolles, " he is the sweetest dresser in the world; he has the most delightful taste you can conceive, nobody has half so good a fancy. I assure you it's a great thing to be spoke to by him : we are all of us quite angry when he won't take any notice of us."

" Is your anger," said Cecilia, laughing, " in honour of himself or of his coat ?"

" Why, Lord, don't you know all this time that he is an *ennuyé* ?"

" I know, at least," answered Cecilia, " that he would soon make one of me."

" O, but one is never affronted with an *ennuyé*, if he is ever so provoking, because one always knows what it means."

" Is he agreeable ?"

" Why, to tell you the truth,—but pray now, don't mention it,—I think him most excessive disagreeable ! He yawns in one's face every time one looks at him. I assure you sometimes I expect to see him fall fast asleep while I am talking to him, for he is so immensely absent he don't hear one half that one says ; only conceive how horrid !

" But why, then, do you encourage him ? Why do you take any notice of him ?"

" O, every body does, I assure you, else I would not for the world ; but he is so courted you have no idea. However, of all things let me advise you never to dance with him ; I did once myself, and I declare I was quite distressed to death the whole time, for he was taken with such a fit of absence he knew nothing he was about, sometimes skipping and jumping with all the violence in the world, just as if he only danced for exercise, and sometimes standing quite still, or lolling against the wainscott and gaping, and taking no more notice of me than if he had never seen me in his life!"

"A VERY GREAT WRITER"
AMELIA
Fielding

"One of them sir," says Mr. Bondum, "is a very great writer, or author as they call him: he has been here these five weeks, at the suit of a bookseller, for eleven pounds odd money; but he expects to be discharged in a day or two; for he has writ out the debt. He is now writing for five or six booksellers, and he will get you sometimes, when he sits to it, a matter of fifteen shillings a day; for he is a very good pen, they say, but is apt to be idle. Some days he won't write above five hours; but at other times I have known him at it above sixteen." "Ay!" cries Booth: "pray, what are his productions? What does he write?"—"Why, sometimes," answered Bondum, "he writes your history books for your numbers, and sometimes your verses, your poems, what do you call them? and then again he writes news for your newspapers."—"Ay, indeed! he is a most extraordinary man, truly. How does he get his news here?"—"Why, he makes it, as he does your parliament speeches for your magazines. He reads them sometimes to us over a bowl of punch. To be sure, it is all one as if one was in the parliament-house; it is about liberty and freedom, and about the constitution of England. I say nothing for my part; for I will keep my neck out of a halter: but, faith, he makes it out plainly to me that all matters are not as they should be. I am all for liberty, for my part."—"Is that consistent with your calling?" cries Booth: "I thought, my friend, you had lived by depriving men of their liberty."—"That's another matter," cried the bailiff; "that's all according to law, and in the way of business. To be sure, men must be obliged to pay their debts, or else there would be an end of everything." Booth desired the bailiff to give him his opinion of liberty: upon which, he hesitated a moment, and then cried out. "O, it is a fine thing, it is a very fine thing, and the constitution of England." Booth told him, that by the old constitution of England, he had heard that men could not, be arrested for debt; to which the bailiff answered that must have been in very bad times: "because, as why," says he, "would it not be the hardest thing in the world if a man could not arrest another for a just and lawful debt? besides, sir, you must be mistaken; for, how could that ever be? Is not liberty the constitution of England? well, and is not the constitution, as a man may say, whereby the constitution, that is the law and liberty, and all that—"

Booth had a little mercy upon the poor bailiff, when he found him rounding in this manner, and told him he had made the matter very clear. Booth then proceeded to inquire after the other gentlemen, his fellows in affliction: upon which Bondum acquainted him, that one of the prisoners was a poor fellow. "He calls himself a gentleman," says Bondman; "but I am sure I never saw anything genteel about him. In a week that he has been in my house, he has drunk only part of one bottle of wine. I intend to carry him to Newgate within a day or two, if he cannot find bail, which, I suppose, he will not be able to do; for everyone says that he is an undone man. He has run out all he has by losses in business, and one way or other; and he has a wife and seven children. Here was the whole family here the other day, all howling together. I never saw such a beggarly crew:—I was almost ashamed to see them in my house: I thought they seemed fitter for Bridewell than any other place. To be sure, I do not reckon him as proper company for such as you, sir; but there is another prisoner in the house, that I dare say you will like very much. He is, indeed, very much of a gentleman, and spends his money like one: I have had him only three days, and I am afraid he won't stay much longer. They say, indeed, he is a gameſter; but what is that to me or any one, as long as a man appears as a gentleman? I always love to speak by people as I find: and, in my opinion, he is fit company for the greateſt lord in the land; for he has very good clothes and money enough. He is not here for debt, but upon a judge's warrant for assault and battery; for the tipſtaff locks up here."

MODERN EDUCATION

SIR CHARLES GRANDISON
Richardson

She has charming spirits. I daresay she sings well, from the airs she now and then warbles in the gaiety of her heart. She is very polite; yet has a vein of raillery, that, were she *not* polite, would give one too much apprehension for one's ease: but I am sure she is frank, easy, and good-humoured. She says she has but lately taken a very great liking to reading. She pretends that she was too volatile, too gay, too airy, to be confined to sedentary amusements. Her father, however, according to the genteeleſt and moſt laudable modern education for women, had given her a maſter who taught her history and geography, in both which she *acknowledges* she made some progress. In music she *owns* she has skill; but I am told by her maid, who attended me by her young lady's direction, and who delights to praise her mistress, that she reads and speaks French and Italian; that she writes finely;

and is greatly admired for her wit, prudence, and obligingness. "Nobody," said Jenny (who is a sensible young woman, a clergyman's daughter, well-educated, and very obliging), "can stand against her good-natured raillery, "Her brother, she says, is not spared; but he takes delight in her vivacity, and gives way to it, when it is easy to see that he could take her down if he pleased. "And then," added the good young woman, "she is an excellent manager in a family, finely as she is educated. She knows everything, and how to direct what should be done, from the private family dinner to a sumptuous entertainment; and every day inspects, and approves, or alters, the bill of fare." By the way, my Lucy, she is an early riser—do you mind that?—and so can do everything with ease, pleasure, and without hurry and confusion; for all her servants are early risers of course.

THE PRESS

THE SCHOOL FOR SCANDAL
Sheridan

LADY SNEERWELL'S *Dressing-room.*

LADY SNEERWELL *discovered at her toilet*;
SNAKE *drinking chocolate*

Lady Sneer. The paragraphs, you say, Mr. Snake, were all inserted?
Snake. They were, madam; and, as I copied them myself in a feigned hand, there can be no suspicion whence they came.
Lady Sneer. Did you circulate the report of Lady Brittle's intrigue with Captain Boastall?
Snake That's in as fine a train as your ladyship could wish. In the common course of things, I think it must reach Mrs. Clackitt's ears within four-and-

twenty hours; and then, you know, the business is as good as done.

Lady Sneer. Why, truly, Mrs. Clackitt has a very pretty talent, and a great deal of industry.

Snake. True, madam, and has been tolerably successful in her day. To my knowledge, she has been the cause of six matches being broken off, and three sons being disinherited; of four forced elopements, and as many close confinements; nine separate maintenances, and two divorces. Nay, I have more than once traced her causing a *tête-à-tête* in the "Town and Country Magazine," when the parties perhaps, had never seen each other's face before in the course of their lives.

Lady Sneer. She certainly has talents, but her manner is gross.

Snake. 'Tis very true. She generally designs well, has a free tongue and a bold invention; but her colouring is too dark, and her outlines often extravagant. She wants that delicacy of tint, and mellowness of sneer, which distinguish your ladyship's scandal.

Lady Sneer. You are partial, Snake.

Snake. Not in the least; everybody allows that Lady Sneerwell can do more with a word or look than many can with the most laboured detail, even when they happen to have a little truth on their side to support it.

Lady Sneer. Yes, my dear Snake; and I am no hypocrite to deny the satisfaction I reap from the success of my efforts. Wounded myself, in the early part of my life, by the envenomed tongue of slander, I confess I have since known no pleasure equal to the reducing others to the level of my own reputation.

THE COUNTESS'S DRESSING ROOM
From a painting by Hogarth in the Tate Gallery.

"A CLASS OF FEMALES"

SIR CHARLES GRANDISON
Richardson

I believe there are more bachelors now in England, by many thousands, than were a few years ago : and, probably, the numbers of them (and of single women, of course), will every year increase. The luxury of the age will account a good deal for this ; and the turn our sex take in *un*-domesticating themselves, for a good deal more. But let not those worthy young women, who may think themselves destined to a single life, repine over-much at their lot ; since possibly, if they have had no lovers, or, having had one, two, or three, have not found a husband, they have had rather a miss than a loss, as men go. And let me here add, that I think, as matters stand in this age, or indeed ever did stand, that those women who have joined with the men in their insolent ridicule of old maids, ought never to be forgiven : no, though Miss Grandison should be one of the ridiculers. An old maid *may be* an odious character, if they will tell us, that the bad qualities of the persons, not the maiden state, are what they mean to expose : but they must allow that there are old maids of twenty, and even that there are widows and wives of all ages and complexions, who, in the abusive sense of the words, are as much old maids as the most particular of that class of females.

THE PROPOSAL

SIR CHARLES GRANDISON
Richardson

My uncle, Mr. Deane, and my cousin James, were too much taken with Sir Charles to think of withdrawing, as it might have been expected they would ;

and, after some general conversation, which succeeded our playing, Sir Charles drew his chair between my grandmamma and aunt, and taking my grandmamma's hand, " May I not be allowed a quarter of an hour's conversation with Miss Byron in your presence, ladies ?" said he, speaking low. " We have, indeed, only friends and relations present; but it will be most agreeable, I believe, to the dear lady that what I have to say to her, and to you, may be rather reported *to* the gentlemen than heard *by* them."

The moment Sir Charles applied himself in this particular manner to them, my heart, without hearing what he said, was at my mouth. I arose, and withdrew to the cedar parlour, followed by Lucy and Nancy. The gentlemen, seeming to recollect themselves, withdrew likewise to another apartment. My aunt came to me—" Love!—But ah! my dear, how you tremble!—You must come with *me.*" And then she told me what he had said to my Grandmamma and her.

" I have no courage—None at all," said I. " If apprehension, if timidity, be signs of love, I have them all, Sir Charles Grandison has not one."

" Don't be silly, Harriet," said my aunt.

My aunt led me in to Sir Charles and my grandmamma. He met me at my entrance into the room, and conducted me to a chair which happened to be vacant between my aunt and my grandmother. He took no notice of my emotion, and I the sooner recovered myself, as he himself seemed to be in some little confusion. However, he sat down, and with a manly, yet respectful air, his voice gaining strength as he proceeded, thus delivered himself—

But I cannot tell you all he said, for I should neither do it justice, nor need you know. It is sufficient to say that he explained all that was needful regarding his peculiar position with the Italian lady—which we all know—and finally kissed our hands, and understood our tearful eyes, and said—

"You have seen Clementina's constant adherence to the step she so greatly took. In this letter, received but last Wednesday" [taking one out of his bosom], "you will see that I am urged by all her family, for the sake of setting *her* an example, to address myself to a lady of my own country—This *impels* me, as I may say, to *accelerate* the humble tender of my vows to you, madam. However hasty the step may be thought, in my situation, would not an inexcusable neglect, or seeming indifference, as if I were balancing as to the person, have been attributable to me, had I, for *dull* and *cold* form's sake, been capable of postponing the declaration of my affection to Miss Byron? And if, madam, you can so far get over observances, which perhaps, on consideration, will be found to be punctilious only, as to give your heart, with your hand, to a man who himself has been perplexed by what some would call a *double love*, you will lay him under obligation to your goodness, which all the affectionate tenderness of my life to come will never enable me to discharge."

He then put the letter into my hand. "I have already answered it, madam," said he, "and acquainted my friend that I have actually tendered myself to the acceptance of a lady worthy of a sisterly relation to their Clementina, and have not been rejected. Your goodness must enable me (I humbly hope it will) to give them still stronger assurances of your favour."

Not well before, I was more than once apprehensive of fainting as he talked, agreeable as was his talk, and engaging as was his manner. My grandmamma and aunt saw my complexion change in the last part of his speech. Each put her kind hand on one of mine, and held it. At the same moment that he ceased speaking, he took our triply-united hands in both his, and in the most respectful manner pressed each of the three with his lips, mine twice. I could not speak. "I have, perhaps," said he, with some emotion, "taken up too much of Miss Byron's attention on this my first personal declaration: I will now return to the company below. To-morrow I will do myself the honour to dine with you. We will for this evening postpone the important subject. Miss Byron, I presume, will be best pleased to have it so. I shall to-morrow be favoured with the result of your deliberations. Meantime, may I meet with an interceding friend in every one I have had the pleasure to see this day!" He withdrew, with a grace which was all his own. . . . .

After breakfast, first one, then another, dropped away, and left only Sir Charles and me together. Lucy was the last that went, and the moment she was withdrawn, while I was thinking to retire to dress, he placed himself by me: "Think me not abrupt, my dearest Miss Byron," said he, "that I take almost the only opportunity which has offered of entering upon a subject that is next my heart." I found my face glow. I was silent. "You have given me hope, madam: all your friends encourage that hope. I love, I revere your friends. What I have now to petition for, is a confirmation of the hope I have presumed upon. *Can* you, madam. CAN you say, that the man before you is the man whom you *can*, whom you *do* prefer to any other?"

He stopped, expecting my answer.

Although my cheeks were crimson I answered with a calmness which astonished myself: "Sir—I CAN, I DO."

He kissed my hand with fervour; dropped down on one knee; again kissed it. "You have laid me, madam, under everlasting obligation: and will you permit me before I rise to beg an early day? I have many affairs on my hands; many more in design, now I am come, as I hope, to settle in my native country for the rest of my life. My chief glory will be to behave commendably in *private* life. I wish not to be a *public* man, and it must be a very particular call, for the service of my King and country united, that shall draw me out into public notice. Make me, madam, soon the happy *husband* I hope to be. I prescribe not to you the time: but you are above empty forms. May I presume to hope it will be before the end of a month to come?"

He had forgot himself. He said he would not prescribe to me.

" Rise, sir, I beseech you! I cannot answer you in this attitude."

" I will, madam, and rise as well as kneel to thank you, when you have answered a question so very important to my happiness."

" I hope, sir, you will not be displeased," said I, " but I did not think you would so *soon* be so *very* earnest. But this, sir, I say, let me have reason to think, that my happiness will not be the misfortune of a more excellent woman, and it shall be my endeavour to make the man happy who *only* can make me so."

He clasped me in his arms with an ardour that displeased me not, though at the time it startled me. He then thanked me again on one knee. I held out the hand he had not in his, with intent to raise him, for I could not speak. He received it as a token of favour; kissed it with ardour; arose; again pressed my cheek with his lips.

Sir Charles, on my making towards the door that led to the stairs, withdrew with such a grace, as showed he was capable of recollection.

Sir Charles, my uncle, and Mr. Deane, took a little walk, and returned just as dinner was ready. My uncle took me aside, and whispered to me—" I am glad at my heart and soul the ice is broken. This is the man of true spirit—*Ods-heart*, Harriet, you will be Lady Grandison in a fortnight, at furthest, I hope. You have had a charming *confabulation*, I doubt not. I can guess you have, by Sir Charles's declaring himself more and more delighted with you. And he owns, that he put the question to you.—Hay, Harriet!" —Smiling in my face.

Every one's eyes were upon me. Sir Charles, I believe, saw me look as if I were apprehensive of my uncle's raillery. He came up to us—" My dear Miss Byron," said he, in my uncle's hearing, " I have owned to Mr. Selby the request I presumed to make you. I am afraid that he, as well as you, think me too bold, and forward. If, madam, *you* do, I ask your pardon: my hopes shall always be controlled by your pleasure."

This made my uncle complaisant to me. I was reassured. I was pleased to be so seasonably relieved.

"DAMNS HAVE HAD THEIR DAY"
THE RIVALS
Sheridan

Abs. ' But pray, Bob, I observe you have got an odd kind of a new method of swearing—

Acres. Ha! ha! you've taken notice of it—'tis genteel, isn't it!—I didn't invent it myself though; but a commander in our militia, a great scholar, I assure you, says that there is no meaning in the common oaths, and that nothing but their antiquity makes them respectable;—because, he says, the ancients would never stick to an oath or two, but would say by Jove! or by Bacchus! or by Mars! or by Venus! or by Pallas, according to the sentiment: so that to swear with propriety, says my little major, the oath should be an echo to the sense; and this we call the *oath referential* or *sentimental swearing*—ha! ha! 'tis genteel, isn't it?

    Abs. Very genteel, and very new, indeed!—and I dare say will supplant all other figures of imprecation.

    Acres. Ay, ay, the best terms will grow obsolete.—Damns have had their day.

THE VICAR

THE BOROUGH
Crabbe

Yet our good priest to Joseph's praise aspired,   *The*
As once rejecting what his heart desired;   *Parish*
'I am escaped,' he said, when none pursued;
When none attacked him, 'I am unsubdued';
'Oh pleasing pangs of love,' he sang again,
Cold to the joy, and stranger to the pain.
Ev'n in his age would he address the young,
'I too have felt these fires, and they are strong;'
But from the time he left his favourite maid,
To ancient females his devoirs were paid;
And still they miss him after morning prayer;
Nor yet successor fills the Vicar's chair,
Where kindred spirits in his praise agree,
A happy few, as mild and cool as he;
The easy followers in the female train,
Led without love, and captives without chain.
    Ye lilies male! think (as your tea you sip,
While the town small-talk flows from lip to lip;
Intrigues half-gather'd, conversation-scraps,
Kitchen-cabals, and nursery-mishaps,)
If the vast world may not some scene produce,
Some state where your small talents might have use;
Within seraglios you might harmless move,

'Mid ranks of beauty, and in haunts of love;
There from too daring man the treasures guard,
An easy duty, and its own reward;
Nature's soft substitutes, you there might save
From crime the tyrant, and from wrong the slave.
 But let applause be dealt in all we may,
Our priest was cheerful, and in season gay;
His frequent visits seldom fail'd to please;
Easy himself, he sought his neighbour's ease:
To a small garden with delight he came,
And gave successive flowers a summer's fame;
These he presented with a grace his own
To his fair friends, and made their beauties known,
Not without moral compliment; how they
' Like flowers were sweet, and must like flowers decay.'
 Simple he was, and loved the simple truth,
Yet had some useful cunning from his youth;
A cunning never to dishonour lent,
And rather for defence than conquest meant;
'Twas fear of power, with some desire to rise,
But not enough to make him enemies;
He ever aim'd to please; and to offend
Was ever cautious; for he sought a friend;
Yet for the friendship never much would pay,
Content to bow, be silent, and obey,
And by a soothing suffr'ance find his way.
 Fiddling and fishing were his arts; at times
He alter'd sermons, and he aim'd at rhymes;
And his fair friends, not yet intent on cards,
Oft he amused with riddles and charades.

THE PARSON

THE VILLAGE
Crabbe

A jovial youth, who thinks his Sunday's task
As much as God or man can fairly ask;

The rest he gives to loves and labours light,
To fields the morning, and to feasts the night;
None better skill'd the noisy pack to guide,
To urge their chase, to cheer them or to chide;
A sportsman keen, he shoots through half the day,
And, skill'd at whist, devotes the night to play :
Then, while such honours bloom around his head,
Shall he sit sadly by the sick man's bed,
To raise the hope he feels not, or with zeal
To combat fears that e'en the pious feel ?

A WISE LADY
THE PARISH REGISTER
Crabbe

There lived a Lady, wise, austere, and nice,
Who show'd her virtue by her scorn of vice;
In the dear fashions of her youth she dress'd,
A pea-green Joseph was her favourite vest;
Erect she stood, she walked with stately mien,
Tight was her length of stays, and she was tall and lean.
 There long she lived in maiden-state immured,
From looks of love and treacherous man secured;
Though evil fame—(but that was long before)
Had blown her dubious blast at Catherine's door :
A Captain thither, rich from India came,
And though a cousin call'd, it touch'd her fame :
Her annual stipend rose from his behest,
And all the long-prized treasures she possess'd :—
If aught like joy awhile appear'd to stay
In that stern face, and chase those frowns away;
'Twas when her treasures she disposed, for view,
And heard the praises to their splendour due;
Silks beyond price, so rich, they'd stand alone,
And diamonds blazing on the buckled zone;
Rows of rare pearls by curious workmen set,

And bracelets fair in box of glossy jet;
Bright polish'd amber precious from its size,
Of forms the fairest fancy could devise:
Her drawers of cedar, shut with secret springs,
Conceal'd the watch of gold and rubied rings;
Letters, long proofs of love, and verses fine
Round the pink'd rims of crisped Valentine.
Her china-closet, cause of daily care,
For woman's wonder held her pencill'd ware;
That pictured wealth of China and Japan,
Like its cold mistress, shunn'd the eye of man.
   Her neat small room, adorn'd with maiden-taste,
A clipp'd French puppy, first of favourites, graced;
A parrot next, but dead and stuff'd with art;
(For Poll, when living, lost the Lady's heart,
And then his life; for he was heard to speak
Such frightful words as tinged his Lady's cheek :)
Unhappy bird! who had no power to prove,
Save by such speech, his gratitude and love.
A grey old cat his whiskers lick'd beside;
A type of sadness in the house of pride.
The polish'd surface of an India chest,
A glassy globe, in frame of ivory, press'd;
Where swam two finny creatures; one of gold,
Of silver one; both beauteous to behold :—
All these were form'd the guiding taste to suit;
The beasts well-manner'd and the fishes mute.
A widow'd Aunt was there, compell'd by need
The nymph to flatter and her tribe to feed;
Who, veiling well her scorn, endured the clog,
Mute as the fish and fawning as the dog.

THE FARMER'S WIFE

THE PARISH REGISTER
Crabbe

Our farmers too, what though they fail to prove,
In Hymen's bonds, the tenderest slaves of love,
(Nor, like those pairs whom sentiment unites,
Feel they the fervour of the mind's delights;)
Yet coarsely kind and comfortably gay,
They heap the board, and hail the happy day:
And though the bride, now freed from school, admits,
Of pride implanted there, some transient fits;
Yet soon she casts her girlish flights aside,
And in substantial blessings rest her pride.
No more she moves in measured steps, no more
Runs, with bewilder'd ear, her music o'er;
No more recites her French the hinds among,
But chides her maidens in her mother-tongue;
Her tambour-frame she leaves and diet spare,
Plain work and plenty with her house to share;
Till, all her varnish lost, in few short years,
In all her worth, the farmer's wife appears.

THE DOCTOR

THE VILLAGE
Crabbe

But soon a loud and hasty summons calls,
Shakes the thin roof, and echoes round the walls;
Anon, a figure enters, quaintly neat,
All pride and business, bustle and conceit;
With looks unalter'd by these scenes of wo,
With speed that, entering, speaks his haste to go,
He bids the gazing throng around him fly,
And carries fate and physic in his eye:
A potent quack, long versed in human ills,

Who first insults the victim whom he kills;
Whose murd'rous hand a drowsy Bench protect,
And whose most tender mercy is neglect.
   Paid by the parish for attendance here,
He wears contempt upon his sapient sneer;
In haste he seeks the bed where Misery lies,
Impatience mark'd in his averted eyes;
And, some habitual queries hurried o'er,
Without reply, he rushes on the door:
His drooping patient, long inured to pain,
And long unheeded, knows remonstrance vain;
He ceases now the feeble help to crave
Of man; and silent sinks into the grave.

CARD PLAYER

THE BOROUGH
Crabbe

   ' Poor Dolly Murray!—I might live to see
My hundredth year, but no such lass as she.
Easy by nature, in her humour gay,
She chose her comforts, ratafia and play:
She loved the social game, the decent glass;
And was a jovial, friendly, laughing lass;
We sat not then at Whist demure and still,
But pass'd the pleasant hours at gay Quadrille;
Lame in her side, we placed her in her seat,
Her hands were free, she cared not for her feet;
As the game ended, came the glass around,
(So was the loser cheer'd, the winner crown'd.)
Mistress of secrets, both the young and old
In her confided—not a tale she told;
Love never made impression on her mind,
She held him weak, and all his captives blind;
She suffer'd no man her free soul to vex,
Free from the weakness of her gentle sex;

One with whom ours unmoved conversing sate,
In cool discussion or in free debate.
  ' Once in her chair we'd placed the good old lass,
Where first she took her preparation-glass ;
By lucky thought she'd been that day at prayers,
And long before had fix'd her small affairs ;
So all was easy—on her cards she cast
A smiling look ; I saw the thought that pass'd :
" A king," she call'd—though conscious of her skill,
" Do more," I answer'd—" More," she said, " I will;"
And more she did—cards answer'd to her call,
She saw the mighty to her mightier fall :
" A vole ! a vole !" she cried, " 'tis fairly won,
My game is ended and my work is done :"—
This said, she gently, with a single sigh,
Died as one taught and practised how to die.'

THE POOR HOUSE

THE BOROUGH
Crabbe

  Your plan I love not ;—with a number you
Have placed your poor, your pitiable few ;
There, in one house, throughout their lives to be,
The pauper-palace which they hate to see :
That giant-building, that high-bounding wall,
Those bare-worn walks, that lofty thund'ring hall !
That large loud clock, which tolls each dreaded hour,
Those gates and locks, and all those signs of power :
It is a prison, with a milder name,
Which few inhabit without dread or shame.
  Be it agreed—the poor who thither come
Partake of plenty, seldom found at home ;
That airy rooms and decent beds are meant
To give the poor by day, by night, content ;
That none are frighten'd, once admitted here,
By the stern looks of lordly overseer :

Grant that the guardians of the place attend,
And ready ear to each petition lend ;
That they desire the grieving poor to show
What ills they feel, what partial acts they know,
Not without promise, nay desire to heal
Each wrong they suffer and each wo they feel.

Alas ! their sorrows in their bosoms dwell ;
They've much to suffer, but have nought to tell ;
They have no evil in the place to state,
And dare not say, it is the house they hate :
They own there's granted all such place can give,
But live repining, for 'tis there they live.

A MASQUERADE
CECILIA
Fanny Burney

The Diversions

Mean time Cecilia, delighted at being released, hurried into a corner, where she hoped to breathe and look on in quiet; and the white domino having exhorted Harlequin to torment the tormentor, and keep him at bay, followed her with congratulations upon her recovered freedom.

"It is you," answered she, "I ought to thank for it, which indeed I do most heartily. I was so tired of confinement, that my mind seemed almost as little at liberty as my person."

"Your persecutor, I presume," said the domino, "is not known to you."

"I hope so," answered she, "because there is one man I suspect, and I should be sorry to find there was another equally disagreeable."

"O, depend upon it," cried he, "there are many who would be happy to confine you in the same manner; neither have you much cause for complaint; you have, doubtless, been the aggressor, and played this game yourself without mercy, for I read in your face the captivity of thousands : have you, then, any right to be offended at the spirit of retaliation which one, out of such numbers, has courage to exert in return ?"

"I protest," cried Cecilia, "I took you for my defender ! whence is it that you are become my accuser?"

"From seeing the danger to which my incautious knight-errantry has exposed me ; I begin, indeed, to take you for a very mischievous sort of person, and I fear the poor devil from whom I rescued you will be amply revenged for his disgrace, by finding that the first use you make of your freedom is to doom your deliverer to bondage."

Here they were disturbed by the extreme loquacity of two opposite parties : and listening attentively, they heard from one side, "My angel ! fairest of creatures ! goddess of my heart !" uttered in accents of rapture ; while from the other, the vociferation was so violent they could distinctly hear nothing.

The white domino satisfied his curiosity by going to both parties ; and then, returning to Cecilia, said, "Can you conjecture who was making those soft speeches ? a Shylock ! his knife all the while in his hand, and his design, doubtless, to *cut as near the heart as possible* ! while the loud cackling from the other side is owing to the riotous merriment of a noisy Mentor ! when next I hear a disturbance, I shall expect to see some simpering Pythagoras stunned by his talkative disciples."

"To own the truth," said Cecilia, "the almost universal neglect of the characters assumed by these masquers has been the chief source of my entertainment this evening ; for at a place of this sort, the next best thing to a character well supported is a character ridiculously burlesqued."

"You cannot, then, have wanted amusement," returned the domino, "for among all the persons assembled in these apartments, I have seen only three who have seemed conscious that any change but that of dress was necessary to disguise them."

" And pray who are those ?"

" A Don Quixote, a schoolmaster, and your friend the devil."

" O, call him not my friend," exclaimed Cecilia, " for indeed in or out of that garb he is particularly my aversion."

" *My* friend, then, I will call him," said the domino, " for so, were he ten devils, I must think him, since I owe to him the honour of conversing with you. And, after all, to give him his due, to which, you know, he is even proverbially entitled, he has shewn such abilities in the performance of his part, so much skill in the display of malice, and so much perseverance in the art of tormenting, that I cannot but respect his ingenuity and capacity. And, indeed, if instead of an evil genius, he had represented a guardian angel, he could not have shewn a more refined taste in his choice of an object to hover about."

Just then they were approached by a young haymaker, to whom the white domino called out, " You look as gay and brisk as if fresh from the hay-field after only half a day's work. Pray, how is it you pretty lasses find employment for the winter ?"

" How ?" cried she, pertly, " why, the same as for the summer !" And pleased with her own readiness at repartee, without feeling the ignorance it betrayed, she tript lightly on.

Immediately after the schoolmaster mentioned by the white domino advanced to Cecilia. His dress was merely a long wrapping gown of green stuff, a pair of red slippers, and a woollen night-cap of the same colour ; while, as the symbol of his profession, he held a rod in his hand.

" Ah, fair lady," he cried, " how soothing were it

to the austerity of my life, how softening to the rigidity of my manners, might I—without a *breaking out of bounds*, which I ought to be the first to discourage, and a " confusion to all order " for which the schoolboy should himself chastise his master—be permitted to cast at your feet this emblem of my authority ! and to forget, in the softness of your conversation, all the roughness of discipline !"

" No, no," cried Cecilia, " I will not be answerable for such corruption of taste !"

" This repulse," answered he, " is just what I feared ; for alas ! under what pretence could a poor miserable country pedagogue presume to approach you ? Should I examine you in the dead languages, would not your living accents charm from me all power of reproof ? Could I look at you, and hear a false concord ? Should I doom you to water-gruel as a dunce, would not my subsequent remorse make me want it myself as a madman ? Were your fair hand spread out to me for correction, should I help applying my lips to it, instead of my rat-tan ? If I ordered you to be *called up*, should I ever remember to have you sent back ? And if I commanded you to stand in a corner, how should I forbear following you thither myself ?"

Cecilia, who had no difficulty in knowing this pretended schoolmaster for Mr. Gosport, was readily beginning to propose conditions for according him her favour, when their ears were assailed by a forced phthisical cough, which they found proceeded from an apparent old woman, who was a young man in disguise, and whose hobbling gait, grunting voice, and most grievous asthmatic complaints, seemed greatly enjoyed and applauded by the company.

" How true is it, yet how inconsistent," cried the white domino, " that while we all desire to live long, we have all a horror of being old ! The figure now passing is not meant to ridicule any particular person, nor to stigmatize any particular absurdity; its sole view is to expose to contempt and derision the general and natural infirmities of age! and the design is not more disgusting than impolitic; for why, while so carefully we guard from all approaches of death, should we close the only avenues to happiness in long life, respect and tenderness?"

Cecilia, once again freed from her persecutor, instantly quitted her place, almost equally desirous to escape the haughty Turk, who was peculiarly her aversion, and the facetious chimney-sweeper, whose vicinity, either on account of his dress or his conversation, was by no means desirable. She was not, however, displeased that the white domino and the schoolmaster still continued to attend her.

"Pray, look," said the white domino, as they entered another apartment, "at that figure of Hope; is there any in the room half so expressive of despondency?"

"The reason, however," answered the schoolmaster," is obvious; that light and beautiful silver anchor upon which she reclines presents an occasion irresistible for an attitude of elegant dejection; and the assumed character is always given up where an opportunity offers to display any beauty, or manifest any perfection in the dear proper person!"

"But why," said Cecilia, "should she assume the character of *Hope*? Could she not have been equally dejected and equally elegant as Niobe, or some tragedy queen?"

"But she does not assume the character," answered the schoolmaster, "she does not even think of it: the dress is her object, and that alone fills up all her ideas. Enquire of almost any body in the room concerning the persons they seem to represent, and you will find their ignorance more gross than you can imagine ; they have not once thought upon the subject ; accident, or convenience, or caprice has alone directed their choice."

A tall and elegant youth now approached them, whose laurels and harp announced Apollo. The white domino immediately enquired of him if the noise and turbulence of the company had any chance of being stilled into silence and rapture by the divine music of the inspired god ?

"No," answered he, pointing to the room in which was erected the new gallery, and whence, as he spoke, issued the sound of a *hautboy*, " there is a flute playing there already."

"O for a Midas," cried the white domino, " to return to this leather-eared god the disgrace he received from him !"

They now proceeded to the apartment which had been lately fitted up for refreshments, and which was so full of company that they entered it with difficulty. And here they were again joined by Minerva, who, taking Cecilia's head, said, " Lord, how glad I am you've got away from that frightful black mask ! I can't conceive who he is ; nobody can find out ; it's monstrous odd, but he has not spoke a word all night, and he makes such a shocking noise when people touch him, that I assure you it's enough to put one in a fright."

" And pray," cried the schoolmaster, disguising his voice, " how camest thou to take the helmet of Minerva for a fool's cap ?"

" Lord, I have not," cried she, innocently, " why, the whole dress is Minerva's ; don't you see ?"

" My dear child," answered he, " thou could'st as well with that little figure pass for a Goliath, as with that little wit for a Pallas."

Their attention was now drawn from the goddess of wisdom to a mad Edgar, who so vehemently ran about the room calling out " Poor Tom's a cold !" that, in a short time, he was obliged to take off his mask, from an effect, not very delicate, of the heat !

Soon after, a gentleman desiring some lemonade whose toga spoke the consular dignity, though his broken English betrayed a native of France, the schoolmaster followed him, and, with reverence the most profound, began to address him in Latin; but, turning quick towards him, he gaily said, " *Monsieur, j'ai l'honneur de representer Ciceron, le grand Ciceron, père de sa patrie ! mais quoique j'ai cet honneur-ıâ, je ne suis pas pedant !—mon dieu, Monsieur, je ne parle que le Francois dans la bonne campagnie !*" And, politely bowing, he went on.

A PRIVATE BALL

EVELINA
Fanny Burney

Queen-Ann-Street, April 5, Tuesday morning.

I have a vast deal to say, and shall give all this morning to my pen. As to my plan of writing every day the adventures of the day, I find it impracticable; for the diversions here are so very late, that if I begin my letters after them, I could not go to bed at all.

We past a most extraordinary evening. A *private* ball this was called, so I expected to have seen about four or five couple; but Lord ! my dear Sir, I believe I saw half the world ! Two very large rooms were full of company; in one, were cards for the elderly ladies, and in the other, were the dancers. My mamma Mirvan, for she always calls me her child, said she would sit with Maria and me till we were provided with partners, and then join the card-players.

THE EIGHTEENTH CENTURY

The gentlemen, as they passed and repassed, looked as if they thought we were quite at their disposal, and only waiting for the honour of their commands; and they sauntered about, in a careless indolent manner, as if with a view to keep us in suspense. I don't speak of this in regard to Miss Mirvan and myself only, but to the ladies in general; and I thought it so provoking, that I determined, in my own mind, that, far from humouring such airs, I would rather not dance at all, than with any one who should seem to think me ready to accept the first partner who would condescend to take me.

Not long after, a young man, who had for some time looked at us with a kind of negligent impertinence, advanced, on tiptoe, towards me; he had a set smile on his face, and his dress was so foppish, that I really believe he even wished to be stared at; and yet he was very ugly.

Bowing almost to the ground, with a sort of swing and waving his hand with the greatest conceit, after a short and silly pause, he said, " Madam—may I presume?"—and stopt, offering to take my hand. I drew it back, but could scarce forbear laughing. " Allow me, madam," (continued he, affectedly breaking off every half moment) " the honour and happiness —if I am not so unhappy as to address you too late— to have the happiness and honour—"

Again he would have taken my hand, but, bowing my head, I begged to be excused, and turned to Miss Mirvan to conceal my laughter. He then desired to know if I had already engaged myself to some more fortunate man? I said No, and that I believed I should not dance at all. He would keep himself, he told me, disengaged, in hopes I should relent; and then, uttering some ridiculous speeches of sorrow and disappointment, though his face still wore the same invariable smile, he retreated.

It so happened, as we have since recollected, that during this little dialogue, Mrs. Mirvan was conversing with the lady of the house. And very soon after another gentleman, who seemed about six-and-twenty years old, gayly, but not foppishly, dressed, and indeed extremely handsome, with an air of mixed politeness and gallantry, desired to know if I was engaged, or would honour him with my hand. So he was pleased to say, though I am sure I know not what honour he could receive from me; but these sort of expressions, I find, are used as words of course, without any distinction of persons, or study of propriety.

Well, I bowed, and I am sure I coloured; for indeed I was frightened at the thoughts of dancing before so many people, all strangers, and, which was worse, *with* a stranger; however, that was unavoidable, for though I looked round the room several times, I could not see one person that I knew. And so, he took my hand, and led me to join in the dance.

The minuets were over before we arrived, for we were kept late by the milliners making us wait for our things.

He seemed very desirous of entering into conversation with me; but I was seized with such a panic, that I could hardly speak a word, and nothing but the shame of so soon changing my mind, prevented my returning to my seat, and declining to dance at all.

He appeared to be surprised at my terror, which I believe was but too apparent: however, he asked no questions, though I fear he must think it very strange; for I did not choose to tell him it was owing to my never before dancing but with a schoolgirl.

His conversation was sensible and spirited; his air and address were open and noble; his manners

"ADIEU"
From an engraving by J. M. Moreau.

gentle, attentive, and infinitely engaging; his person is all elegance, and his countenance, the most animated and expressive I have ever seen.

In a short time we were joined by Miss Mirvan, who stood next couple to us. But how was I startled, when she whispered me that my partner was a nobleman! This gave me a new alarm; how will he be provoked, thought I, when he finds what a simple rustic he has honoured with his choice! one whose ignorance of the world makes her perpetually fear doing something wrong!

That he should be so much my superior every way quite disconcerted me; and you will suppose my spirits were not much raised, when I heard a lady, in passing us, say, "This is the most difficult dance I ever saw."

"O dear, then," cried Maria to her partner, "with your leave, I'll sit down till the next."

"So will I too, then," cried I, "for I am sure I can hardly stand."

"But you must speak to your partner first," answered she; for he had turned aside to talk with some gentlemen. However, I had not sufficient courage to address him, and so away we three all tript, and seated ourselves at another end of the room. But, unfortunately for me, Miss Mirvan soon after suffered herself to be prevailed upon to attempt the dance; and just as she rose to go, she cried, "My dear, yonder is your partner, Lord Orville, walking about the room in search of you."

"Don't leave me then, dear girl!" cried I; but she was obliged to go. And now I was more uneasy than ever, I would have given the world to have seen Mrs. Mirvan, and begged of her to make my apologies; for what, thought I, can I possibly say to him in excuse for running away? he must either conclude me a fool, or half mad; for anyone brought up in the great world, and accustomed to its ways, can have no idea of such sort of fears as mine.

My confusion increased when I observed that he was every where seeking me, with apparent perplexity and surprise; but when, at last I saw him move towards the place where I sat, I was ready to sink with shame and distress. I found it absolutely impossible to keep my seat, because I could not think of a word to say for myself, and so I rose, and walked hastily towards the card-room, resolving to stay with Mrs. Mirvan the rest of the evening, and not to dance at all. But before I could find her, Lord Orville saw and approached me.

He begged to know if I was not well? You may easily imagine how much I was embarrassed. I made no answer, but hung my head, like a fool, and looked on my fan.

He then, with an air the most respectfully serious, asked if he had been so unhappy as to offend me?

"No, indeed!" cried I: and, in hopes of changing the discourse, and preventing his further inquiries, I desired to know if he had seen the young lady who had been conversing with me?

No;—but would I honour him with any commands to her?

"O, by no means!"

Was there any other person with whom I wished to speak?

I said *no*, before I knew I had answered at all.

Should he have the pleasure of bringing me any refreshments?

I bowed, almost involuntarily. And away he flew.

I was quite ashamed of being so troublesome, and so much *above* myself as these seeming airs made me appear; but indeed I was too much confused to think or act with any consistency.

If he had not been swift as lightning, I don't know

whether I should not have stolen away again; but he returned in a moment. When I had drunk a glass of lemonade, he hoped, he said, that I would again honour him with my hand as a new dance was just begun. I had not the presence of mind to say a single word, and so I let him once more lead me to the place I had left.

Shocked to find how silly, how childish a part I had acted, my former fears of dancing before such a company, and with such a partner, returned more forcibly than ever. I suppose he perceived my uneasiness, for he intreated me to sit down again, if dancing was disagreeable to me. But I was quite satisfied with the folly I had already shewn, and therefore declined his offer, tho' I was really scarce able to stand.

Under such conscious disadvantages, you may easily imagine, my dear Sir, how ill I acquitted myself. But, though I both expected and deserved to find him very much mortified and displeased at his ill fortune in the choice he had made, yet, to my very great relief, he appeared to be even contented, and very much assisted and encouraged me. These people in high life have too much presence of mind, I believe, to *seem* disconcerted, or out of humour, however they may feel: for had I been the person of the most consequence in the room, I could not have met with more attention and respect.

When the dance was over, seeing me still very much flurried, he led me to a seat, saying that he would not suffer me to fatigue myself from politeness.

And then, if my capacity, or even if my spirits had been better, in how animated a conversation might I have been engaged! It was then I saw that the rank of Lord Orville was his least recommendation, his understanding and his manners being far more distinguished. His remarks upon the company in general were so apt, so just, so lively, I am almost surprised myself that they did not re-animate me; but indeed I was too well convinced of the ridiculous part I had myself played before so nice an observer, to be able to enjoy his pleasantry: so self-compassion gave me feeling for others. Yet I had not the courage to attempt either to defend them, or to rally in my turn, but listened to him in silent embarrassment.

When he found this, he changed the subject, and talked of public places, and public performers; but he soon discovered that I was totally ignorant of them.

He then, very ingeniously, turned the discourse to the amusements and occupations of the country.

It now struck me, that he was resolved to try whether or not I was capable of talking upon *any* subject. This put so great a constraint upon my thoughts, that I was unable to go further than a monosyllable, and not even so far, when I could possibly avoid it

We were sitting in this manner, he conversing with all gaiety, I looking down with all foolishness, when that fop who had first asked me to dance, with a most ridiculous solemnity, approached, and after a profound bow or two, said, "I humbly beg pardon, Madam—and of you too, my Lord,—for breaking in upon such agreeable conversation—which must, doubtless, be much more delectable—than what I have the honour to offer—but—"

I interrupted him—I blush for my folly,—with laughing; yet I could not help it, for added to the man's stately foppishness, (and he actually took snuff between every three words) when I looked round at Lord Orville, I saw such extreme surprise in his face,—the cause of which appeared so absurd, that I could not for my life preserve my gravity.

I had not laughed before from the time I had left Miss Mirvan, and I had much better have cried then;

Lord Orville actually stared at me; the beau, I know not his name, looked quite enraged. "Refrain—Madam," (said he, with an important air), "a few moments refrain!—I have but a sentence to trouble you with.—May I know to what accident I must attribute not having the honour of your hand?"

"Accident, Sir!" repeated I, much astonished.

"Yes, accident, Madam—for surely,—I must take the liberty to observe—pardon me, Madam,—it ought to be no common one—that should tempt a lady —so young a one too,—to be guilty of ill-manners."

A confused idea now for the first time entered my head, of something I had heard of the rules of an assembly; but I was never at one before,—I have only danced at school,—and so giddy and heedless I was, that I had not once considered the impropriety of refusing one partner, and afterwards accepting another. I was thunderstruck at the recollection: but while these thoughts were rushing into my head, Lord Orville, with some warmth, said, "This lady, Sir, is incapable of meriting such an accusation!"

The creature—for I am very angry with him—made a low bow, and with a grin the most malicious I ever saw, "My Lord," said he, "far be it from me to *accuse* the lady, for having the discernment to distinguish and prefer—the superior attractions of your Lordship."

Again he bowed, and walked off.

Was ever anything so provoking? I was ready to die with shame. "What a coxcomb!" exclaimed Lord Orville; while I, without knowing what I did, rose hastily, and moving off, "I can't imagine," cried I, "where Mrs. Mirvan has hid herself!"

"Give me leave to see," answered he. I bowed and sat down again, not daring to meet his eyes; for what must he think of me, between my blunder, and the supposed preference?

He returned in a moment, and told me that Mrs. Mirvan was at cards, but would be glad to see me; and I went immediately. There was but one chair vacant, so, to my great relief, Lord Orville presently left us. I then told Mrs. Mirvan my disasters, and she good-naturedly blamed herself for not having better instructed me, but said she had taken it for granted that I must know such common customs. However, the man may, I think, be satisfied with his pretty speech, and carry his resentment no farther.

In a short time, Lord Orville returned. I consented, with the best grace I could, to go down another dance, for I had had time to recollect myself, and therefore resolved to use some exertion, and, if possible, appear less a fool than I had hitherto done; for it occurred to me that, insignificant as I was, compared to a man of his rank and figure, yet, since he had been so unfortunate as to make choice of me for a partner, why I should endeavour to make the best of it.

The dance, however was short, and he spoke very little; so I had no opportunity of putting my resolution in practice. He was satisfied, I suppose, with his former successless efforts to draw me out; or rather, I fancied, he had been inquiring *who I was*. This again disconcerted me, and the spirits I had determined to exert, again failed me. Tired, ashamed and mortified, I begged to sit down till we returned home, which I did soon after. Lord Orville did me the honour to hand me to the coach, talking all the way of the honour *I* had done *him*! O these fashionable people!

Well, my dear Sir, was it not a strange evening? I could not help being thus particular, because, to me, everything is so new. But it is now time to conclude.

I am, with all love and duty, your

EVELINA

"TWO WAYS OF EATING"

RODERICK RANDOM
Smollett

About dinner-time, our landlord asked how we proposed to live? to which interrogation we answered, that we would be directed by him. 'Well, then,' says he, 'there are two ways of eating in this town for people of your condition—the one more creditable and expensive than the other: the first is to dine at an eating-house frequented by well-dressed people only; and the other is called diving, practised by those who are either obliged or inclined to live frugally.' I gave him to understand that provided the last was not infamous, it would suit much better with our circumstances than the other. 'Infamous!' cried he, 'not at all; there are many creditable people, rich people, ay, and fine people, that dive every day. I have seen many a pretty gentleman with a laced waistcoat dine in that manner very comfortably for three pence halfpenny, and go afterwards to the coffee house, where he made a figure with the best lord in the land; but your own eyes shall bear witness—I will go along with you to-day and introduce you.'

He accordingly conducted us to a certain lane, where stopping, he bade us observe him, and do as he did, and, walking a few paces, dived into a cellar, and disappeared in an instant. I followed his example, and descending very successfully, found myself in the middle of a cook's shop, almost suffocated with the steams of boiled beef, and surrounded by a company of hackney coachmen, chairmen, draymen, and a few footmen out of place or on board-wages; who sat eating shin of beef, tripe, cow-heel, or sausages, at separate boards, covered with cloths which turned my stomach. While I stood in amaze, undetermined whether to sit down or walk upwards again, Strap, in his descent, missing one of the steps, tumbled headlong into this infernal ordinary, and overturned the cook as she carried a porringer of soup to one of the guests. In her fall, she dashed the whole mess against the legs of a drummer belonging to the footguards, who happened to be in her way, and scalded him so miserably, that he started up, and danced up and down, uttering a volley of execrations that made my hair stand on end.

While he entertained the company in this manner, with an eloquence peculiar to himself, the cook got up, and after a hearty curse on the poor author of this mischance, who lay under the table scratching his rump with a woful countenance, emptied a salt-cellar in her hand, and stripping down the patients' stocking, which brought the skin along with it, applied the contents to the sore. This poultice was scarce laid on, when the drummer, who had begun to abate of his exclamation, broke forth into such a hideous yell as made the whole company tremble; then, seizing a pewter pint pot that stood by him, squeezed the sides of it together, as if it had been made of pliant leather, grinding his teeth at the same time with a most horrible grin. Guessing the cause of this violent transport, I bade the woman wash off the salt, and bathe the part with oil, which she did, and procured him immediate ease. But here another difficulty occurred, which was no other than the landlady's insisting on his paying for the pot he had rendered useless. He said, he would pay for nothing but what he had eaten, and bade her be thankful for his moderation, or else he would prosecute her for damages. Strap, foreseeing the whole affair would lie at his door, promised to satisfy the cook, and called for a dram of gin to treat the drummer, which entirely appeased him, and composed all animosities. After this accommodation, our landlord and we sat down at a board, and dined upon shin of beef most deliciously;

our reckoning amounting to twopence halfpenny each, bread and small beer included.

SHOPS AND HAIR-DRESSING

EVELINA
Fanny Burney

We have been *a shopping*, as Mrs. Mirvan calls it, all this morning, to buy silks, caps, gauzes and so forth.

The shops are really very entertaining, especially the mercers ; there seem to be six or seven men belonging to each shop, and every one took care, by bowing and smirking, to be noticed ; we were conducted from one to another, and carried from room to room, with so much ceremony, that at first I was almost afraid to go on.

I thought I should never have chosen a silk, for they produced so many, I knew not which to fix upon, and they recommended them all so strongly, that I fancy they thought I only wanted persuasion to buy everything they shewed me. And, indeed, they took so much trouble, that I was almost ashamed I could not.

At the milliners, the ladies we met were so much dressed, that I should rather have imagined they were making visits than purchases. But what most diverted [me] was, that we were more frequently served by men than by women ; and such men ! so finical, so affected ! they seemed to understand every part of a woman's dress better than we do ourselves ; and they recommended caps and ribbands with an air of so much importance, that I wished to ask them how long they had left off wearing them !

The dispatch with which they work in these great shops is amazing, for they have promised me a compleat suit of linen against the evening.

I have just had my hair dressed. You can't think how oddly my head feels; full of powder and black pins, and a great *cushion* on the top of it. I believe you would hardly know me, for my face looks quite different to what it did before my hair was dressed. When I shall be able to make use of a comb for myself I cannot tell, for my hair is so much entangled, *frizled* they call it, that I fear it will be very difficult.

AT VAUXHALL

AMELIA
Fielding

The coaches being come to the water-side they all alighted, and getting into one boat, proceeded to Vauxhall.

The extreme beauty and elegance of this place is well known to almost every one of my readers: and happy is it for me that it is so; since to give an adequate idea of it would exceed my power of description. To delineate the particular beauties of these gardens, would, indeed, require as much pains, and as much paper too, as to rehearse all the good actions of their master; whose life proves the truth of an observation which I have read in some ethic writer, that a truly elegant taste is generally accompanied with an excellency of heart; or, in other words, that true virtue is, indeed, nothing else but true taste.

Here our company diverted themselves with walking an hour or two before the music began. Of all the seven, Booth alone had been here before; so that, to all the rest, the place, with its other charms, had that of novelty. When the music played, Amelia, who stood next the doctor, said to him in a whisper, " I hope I am not guilty of profaneness; but in pursuance of that cheerful train of thoughts, with which you have inspired me this afternoon, I was just now lost in a reverie; and fancied myself in those blissful mansions which we hope to enjoy hereafter. The delicious sweetness of the place, the enchanting charms of the music, and the satisfaction which appears in every one's countenance, carried my soul almost to heaven in its ideas. I could not have, indeed, imagined there had been anything like this in the world."

The doctor smiled, and said, " You see, dear madam, there may be pleasures, of which you could conceive no idea, till you actually enjoyed them."

And now the little boy, who had long withstood the attractions of several cheesecakes that passed to and fro, could contain no longer; but asked his mother to give him one, saying, " I am sure my sister would be glad of another, though she is ashamed to ask." The doctor, overhearing the child, proposed that they should all retire to some place, where they might sit down and refresh themselves; which they accordingly did. Amelia now missed her husband, but, as she had three men in her company, and one of them was the doctor, she concluded herself and her children to be safe, and doubted not but that Booth would soon find her out.

They now sat down, and the doctor very gallantly desired Amelia to call for what she liked. Upon which the children were supplied with cakes; and some ham and chicken were provided for the rest of the company, with which, while they were regaling themselves with the highest satisfaction, two young fellows walking arm in arm came up; and when they came opposite to Amelia, they stood still, staring Amelia full in the face; and one of them cried aloud to the other. " D—n me, my lord, if she is not an angel !"

My lord stood still, staring likewise at her, without

speaking a word; when two others of the same gang came up, and one of them cried, " Come along, Jack, I have seen her before; but she is too well manned already. Three—are enough for one woman, or the devil is in it."

" D—n me, " says he that spoke first, and whom they called Jack, " I will have a brush at her, if she belonged to the whole convocation." And so saying, he went up to the young clergyman, and cried,— " Doctor, sit up a little, if you please ; and don't take up more room in a bed than belongs to you." At which words he gave the young man a push, and seated himself down directly over against Amelia ; and leaning both his elbows on the table, he fixed his eyes on her in a manner, with which modesty can neither look, nor bear to be looked at.

Amelia seemed greatly shocked at this treatment ; upon which the doctor removed her within him, and then facing the gentleman, asked him what he meant by this rude behaviour. Upon which my lord stepped up and said, " Don't be impertinent, old gentleman. Do you think such fellows as you are to keep, d—n me, such fine wenches, d—n me, to yourselves, d—n me ?"

" No, no," cries Jack, " the old gentleman is more reasonable. Here's the fellow that eats up the tithe-pig. Don't you see how his mouth waters at her ? Where's your slabbering-bib ?" for though the gentleman had rightly guessed he was a clergyman ; yet he had not any of those insignia on, with which it would have been improper to have appeared there.

" Such boys as you," cries the young clergyman, " ought to be well whipped at school, instead of being suffered to become nuisances in society."

" Boys, sir ?" says Jack : " I believe I am as good a man as yourself, Mr.———, and as good a scholar too. *Bos fur sus quotque sacerdos.* Tell me what's next.

A NIGHT SCENE AT RANELAGH, ON WEDNESDAY, 6TH MAY, 1752
"Thus I bore my point, six rogues let drive at me."
From a print in the British Museum.

D—n me, I'll hold you fifty pounds you don't tell me what's next."

"You have him, Jack," cries my lord: "it is over with him, d—n me: he can't strike another blow."

"If I had you in a proper place," cries the clergyman, "you should find I would strike a blow, and a pretty hard one too."

"There," cries my lord, "there is the meekness of the clergyman. There spoke the wolf in sheep's clothing. D—n me, how big he looks! You must be civil to him, faith! or else he will burst with pride."

"Ay, ay," cries Jack: "let the clergy alone for pride; there's not a lord in the kingdom now has half the pride of that fellow."

"Pray, sir," cries the doctor, turning to the other, "are you a lord?"

"Yes, Mr—," cries he, "I have that honour, indeed."

"And I suppose you have pride too," said the doctor.

"I hope I have, sir," answered he, "at your service."

"If such a one as you, sir," cries the doctor, "who are not only a scandal to the title you bear as a lord, but even as a man, can pretend to pride, why will you not allow it to a clergyman? I suppose, sir, by your dress, you are in the army; and by the ribbon in your hat, you seem to be proud of that too. How much greater and more honourable is the service in which that gentleman is enlisted than yours! Why, then, should you object to the pride of the clergy, since the lowest of the function is in reality every way so much your superior?"

"Tida, tidu, tidum," cries my lord.

"However, gentlemen," cries the doctor, "if you have the least pretension to that name, I beg you will put an end to your frolic; since you see it gives so much uneasiness to the lady. Nay, I intreat you, for your own sakes; for here is one coming who will talk to you in a very different style from ours."

"One coming," cries my lord; "what care I who is coming?"

"I suppose it is the devil," cries Jack; "for here are two of his livery servants already."

"Let the devil come as soon as he will," cries my lord; "d—n me if I have not a kiss."

Amelia now fell a-trembling; and her children, perceiving her fright, both hung on her and began to cry, when Booth and Captain Trent both came up.

Booth, seeing his wife disordered, asked eagerly, what was the matter. At the same time, the lord and his companion seeing Captain Trent, whom they well knew, said both together, "What, does this company belong to you?" when the doctor, with great presence of mind, as he was apprehensive of some fatal consequence if Booth should know what had passed, said, "So, Mr. Booth, I am glad you are returned: your poor lady here began to be frightened out of her wits; but now you have him again," said he to Amelia, "I hope you will be easy."

Amelia, frightened as she was, presently took the hint, and greatly chid her husband for leaving her; but the little boy was not so quick-sighted, and cried, "Indeed, papa, those naughty men there have frighmy mamma out of her wits."

"How!" cries Booth, a little moved; "frightened? Has any one frightened you, my dear?"

"No, my love," answered she, "nothing. I know not what the child means. Everything is well, now I see you safe."

Trent had been all the while talking aside with the young sparks; and now, addressing himself to Booth, said, "Here has been some little mistake; I believe my lord mistook Mrs. Booth for some other lady."

"It is impossible," cries my lord, " to know everyone. I am sure, if I had known the lady to be a woman of fashion, and an acquaintance of Captain Trent, I should have said nothing disagreeable to her; but if I have, I ask her pardon, and the company's."

"I am in the dark," cries Booth. "Pray, what is all this matter?"

"Nothing of any consequence," cries the doctor, "nor worth your inquiring into. You hear it was a mistake of the person : and I really believe his lordship, that all proceeded from his not knowing to whom the lady belonged."

"Come, come," says Trent, "there is nothing in the matter I assure you. I will tell you the whole another time."

"Very well; since you say so," cries Booth, "I am contented." So ended the affair, and the two sparks made their congee, and sneaked off.

"Now they are gone," said the young gentleman, "I must say I never saw two worse-bred jackanapes, nor fellows that deserved to be kicked more. If I had had them in another place, I would have taught them a little more respect to the church."

"You took rather a better way," answered the doctor, "to teach them that respect."

Booth now desired his friend Trent to sit down with them, and proposed to call for a fresh bottle of wine; but Amelia's spirits were too much disconcerted to give her any prospect of pleasure that evening. She therefore laid hold of the pretence of her children, for whom she said the hour was already too late, with which the doctor agreed. So they paid their reckoning and departed leaving to the two rakes the triumph of having totally dissipated the mirth of this little innocent company, who were before enjoying complete satisfaction.

BATH

THE RIVALS
Sheridan

Thos. But pray, Mr. Fag, what kind of a place is this Bath?—I ha' heard a deal of it—here's mort o' merry-making, hey?

Fag. Pretty well, Thomas, pretty well—'tis a good lounge; in the morning we go to the pump-room (though neither my master nor I drink the waters); after breakfast we saunter on the parades, or play a game at billiards; at night we dance; but damn the place, I'm tired of it: their regular hours stupify me—not a fiddle nor a card after eleven!—However, Mr. Faulkland's gentleman and I keep it up a little in private parties;—I'll introduce you there, Thomas—you'll like him much.

Thos. Sure I know Mr. Du-Peigne—you know his master is to marry Madam Julia.

Fag. I had forgot.—But, Thomas, you must polish a little—indeed you must.—Here now—this wig!—What the devil do you do with a wig, Thomas?—None of the London whips of any degreee of *ton* wear wigs now.

Thos. More's the pity! more's the pity! I say.—Odd's life! when I heard how the lawyers and doctors had took to their own hair, I thought how 'twould go next:—odd rabbit it! when the fashion had got foot on the bar, I guessed 'twould mount to the box!—but 'tis all out of character, believe me, Mr. Fag: and look'ee, I'll never gi' up mine—the lawyers and doctors may do as they will.

CHAPTER V

THE NINETEENTH CENTURY—I

MODERN GALLANTRY

ESSAYS OF ELIA
Lamb

In comparing modern with ancient manners, we are *Gentility* pleased to compliment ourselves upon the point of gallantry; a certain obsequiousness, or deferential respect, which we are supposed to pay to females, as females.

I shall believe that this principle actuates our conduct, when I can forget, that in the nineteenth century of the era from which we date our civility, we are but just beginning to leave off the very frequent practice of whipping females in public, in common with the coarsest male offenders.

I shall believe it to be influential, when I can shut my eyes to the fact that in England women are still occasionally—hanged.

I shall believe in it, when actresses are no longer subject to be hissed off a stage by gentlemen.

I shall believe in it, when Dorimant hands a fishwife across the kennel; or assists the apple-woman to pick up her wandering fruit, which some unlucky dray has just dissipated.

I shall believe in it, when the Dorimants in humbler life, who would be thought in their way notable adepts in this refinement, shall act upon it in places where they are not known, or think themselves not observed—when I shall see the traveller for some rich tradesman part with his admired box-coat, to spread it over the defenceless shoulders of the poor woman, who is passing to her parish on the roof of the same stage-coach with him, drenched in the rain—when I shall no longer see a woman standing up in the pit of a London theatre, till she is sick and faint with the exertion, with men about her, seated at their ease, and jeering at her distress; till one, that seems to have more manners or conscience than the rest, significantly declares " she should be welcome to his seat, if she were a little younger and handsomer." Place this dapper warehouseman, or that rider, in a circle of their own female acquaintance, and you shall confess you have not seen a politer-bred man in Lothbury.

Lastly, I shall begin to believe that there is some such principle influencing our conduct, when more than one-half of the drudgery and coarse servitude of the world shall cease to be performed by women.

Until that day comes I shall never believe this boasted point to be anything more than a conventional fiction; a pageant got up between the sexes, in a certain rank, and at a certain time of life, in which both find their account equally.

I shall be even disposed to rank it among the salutary fictions of life, when in polite circles I shall see the same attentions paid to age as to youth, to homely features as to handsome, to coarse complexions as to clear—to the woman, as she is a woman, not as she is beauty, a fortune, or a title.

I shall believe it to be something more than a name, when a well-dressed gentleman in a well-dressed company can advert to the topic of *female old age* without exciting, and intending to excite, a sneer:—when the phrases " antiquated virginity," and such a one has " overstood her market," pronounced in good company, shall raise immediate offence in man, or woman, that shall hear them spoken.

Joseph Paice, of Bread-street-hill, merchant, and one of the Directors of the South Sea company—the same to whom Edwards, the Shakspeare commentator, has addressed a fine sonnet—was the only pattern of consistent gallantry I have met with. He took me under his shelter at an early age, and bestowed some pains upon me. I owe to his precepts and example whatever there is of the man of business (and that is not much) in my composition. It was not his fault that I did not profit more. Though bred a Presbyterian, and brought up a merchant, he was the finest gentleman of his time. He had not *one* system of attention to females in the drawing-room, and *another* in the shop, or at the stall. I do not mean that he made no distinction. But he never lost sight of sex, or overlooked it in the casualties of a disadvantageous situation. I have seen him stand bareheaded—smile if you please—to a poor servant-girl, while she has been inquiring of him the way to some street—in such a posture of unforced civility, as neither to embarrass her in the acceptance, nor himself in the offer, of it. He was no dangler, in the common acceptation of the word, after women; but he reverenced and upheld, in every form in which it came before him, *womanhood*. I have seen him—nay, smile not—tenderly escorting a market-woman, whom he had encountered in a shower, exalting his umbrella over her poor basket of fruit, that it might receive no damage, with as much carefulness as if she had been a Countess. To the reverend form of Female Eld he would yield the wall (though it were to an ancient beggar-woman) with more ceremony than we can afford to show our grandams. He was the Preux Chevalier of Age; the Sir Calidore, or Sir Tristan, to those who have no Calidores or Tristans to defend them. The roses, that had long faded thence, still bloomed for him in those withered and yellow cheeks.

He was never married, but in his youth he paid his addresses to the beautiful Susan Winstanley—old Winstanley's daughter of Clapton—who dying in the early days of their courtship, confirmed in him the resolution of perpetual bachelorship. It was during their short courtship, he told me, that he had been one day treating his mistress with a profusion of civil speeches—the common gallantries—to which kind of thing she had hitherto manifested no repugnance— but in this instance with no effect. He could not obtain from her a decent acknowledgement in return. She rather seemed to resent his compliments. He could not set it down to caprice, for the lady had always shown herself above that littleness. When he ventured on the following day, finding her a little better humoured, to expostulate with her on her coldness of yesterday, she confessed, with her usual frankness, that she had no sort of dislike to his attentions; that she could even endure some high-flown compliments; that a young woman placed in her situation had a right to expect all sorts of civil things said to her; that she hoped she could digest a dose of adulation, short of insincerity, with as little injury to her humility as most young women; but that—a little before he had commenced his compliments—she had overheard him by accident, in rather rough language, rating a young woman, who had not brought home his cravats quite to the appointed time, and she thought to herself, " As I am Miss Susan Winstanley, and a young lady— a reputed beauty, and known to be a fortune—I can have my choice of the finest speeches from the mouth of this very fine gentleman who is courting me— but if I had been poor Mary Such-a-one (*naming the milliner*),—and had failed of bringing home the cravats to the appointed hour—though perhaps I had sat up half the night to forward them—what sort of compliments should I have received then?—And my woman's pride came to my assistance; and I thought, that if it were only to do *me* honour, a female, like myself, might have received handsomer usage; and I was determined not to accept any fine speeches to the compromise of that sex, the belonging to which was after all my strongest claim and title to them."

I think the lady discovered both generosity and a just way of thinking, in this rebuke which she gave her lover; and I have sometimes imagined, that the uncommon strain of courtesy, which through life regulated the actions and behaviour of my friend towards all of womankind indiscriminately, owed its happy origin to the seasonable lesson from the lips of his lamented mistress.

I wish the whole female world would entertain the same notion of these things that Miss Winstanley showed. Then we should see something of the spirit of consistent gallantry; and no longer witness the anomaly of the same man—a pattern of true politeness to a wife—of cold contempt, or rudeness, to a sister—the idolater of his female mistress—the disparager and despiser of his no less female aunt, or unfortunate—still female—maiden cousin. Just so much respect as a woman derogates from her own sex, in whatever condition placed—her hand-maid, or dependent—she deserves to have diminished from herself on that score; and probably will feel the diminution, when youth, and beauty, and advantages, not inseparable from sex, shall lose of their attraction. What a woman should demand of a man in courtship, or after it, is first—respect for her as she is a woman;—and next to that—to be respected by him above all other women. But let her stand upon her female character as upon a foundation; and let the attentions, incident to individual preference, be so many pretty additaments and ornaments—as many, and as fanciful, as you please—to that main structure. Let her first lesson be—with sweet Susan Winstanley—to *reverence her sex.*

A MORNING CALL

PRIDE AND PREJUDICE
Jane Austen

Convinced as Elizabeth now was that Miss Bingley's dislike of her had originated in jealousy, she could not help feeling how very unwelcome her appearance at Pemberley must be to her, and was curious to know with how much civility on that lady's side the acquaintance would now be renewed.

On reaching the house, they were shown through the hall into the saloon, whose northern aspect rendered it delightful for summer. Its windows, opening to the ground, admitted a most refreshing view of the high woody hills behind the house, and of the beautiful oaks and Spanish chestnuts which were scattered over the intermediate lawn.

In this room they were received by Miss Darcy, who was sitting there with Mrs. Hurst and Miss Bingley and the lady with whom she lived in London. Georgiana's reception of them was very civil, but attended with all that embarrassment which, though proceeding from shyness and the fear of doing wrong, would easily give to those who felt themselves inferior the belief of her being proud and reserved. Mrs. Gardiner and her niece, however, did her justice, and pitied her.

By Mrs. Hurst and Miss Bingley they were noticed only by a curtsey; and, on their being seated, a pause, awkward as such pauses always must be, succeeded for a few moments. It was first broken by Mrs.

Annesley, a genteel, agreeable-looking woman, whose endeavour to introduce some kind of discourse proved her to be more truly well-bred than either of the others; and between her and Mrs. Gardiner, with occasional help from Elizabeth, the conversation was carried on. Miss Darcy looked as if she wished for courage enough to join in it; and sometimes did venture a short sentence when there was least danger of its being heard.

Elizabeth soon saw that she was herself closely watched by Miss Bingley, and that she could not speak a word, especially to Miss Darcy, without calling her attention. This observation would not have prevented her from trying to talk to the latter, had they not been seated at an inconvenient distance; but she was not sorry to be spared the necessity of saying much. Her own thoughts were employing her. She expected every moment that some of the gentlemen would enter the room. She wished, she feared, that the master of the house might be amongst them; and whether she wished or feared it most she could scarcely determine. After sitting in this manner a quarter of an hour without hearing Miss Bingley's voice, Elizabeth was roused by receiving from her a cold inquiry after the health of her family. She answered with equal indifference and brevity, and the other said no more.

The next variation which their visit afforded was produced by the entrance of servants with cold meat, cake, and a variety of all the finest fruits in season; but this did not take place till after many a significant look and smile from Mrs. Annesley to Miss Darcy had been given, to remind her of her post. There was now employment for the whole party—for though they could not all talk, they could all eat; and the beautiful pyramids of grapes, nectarines and peaches soon collected them round the table.

ON CALLING

CRANFORD
Mrs. Gaskell

Then there were rules and regulations for visiting and calls; and they were announced to any young people, who might be staying in the town, with all the solemnity with which the old Manx Laws were read once a year on the Tinwald Mount.

"Our friends have sent to inquire how you are after your journey to-night, my dear" (fifteen miles in a gentleman's carriage); "they will give you some rest to-morrow, but the next day, I have no doubt, they will call; so be at liberty after twelve—from twelve to three are our calling-hours."

Then, after they had called—

"It is the third day; I daresay your mamma has told you, my dear, never to let more than three days elapse between receiving a call and returning it; and also, that you are never to stay longer than a quarter of an hour."

"But am I to look at my watch? How am I to find out when a quarter of an hour was passed?"

"You must keep thinking about the time, my dear, and not allow yourself to forget it in conversation."

As everybody had this rule in their minds, whether they received or paid a call, of course no absorbing subject was ever spoken about. We kept ourselves to short sentences of small talk, and were punctual to our time.

FRIENDSHIP

NORTHANGER ABBEY
Jane Austen

Their conversation turned upon those subjects of which the free discussion has generally much to do in perfecting a sudden intimacy between two young ladies; such as dress, balls, flirtations, and quizzes. Miss Thorpe, however, being four years older than Miss Morland, and at least four years better informed, had a very decided advantage in discussing such points. She could compare the balls of Bath with those of Tunbridge; its fashions with the fashions of London; could rectify the opinions of her new friend in many articles of tasteful attire; could discover a flirtation between any gentleman and lady who only smiled on each other; and point out a quiz through the thickness of a crowd. These powers received due admiration from Catherine, to whom they were entirely new; and the respect which they naturally inspired might have been too great for familiarity, had not the easy gaiety of Miss Thorpe's manners, and her frequent expressions of delight on this acquaintance with her, softened down every feeling of awe, and left nothing but tender affection. Their increasing attachment was not to be satisfied with half a dozen turns in the Pump-room, but required, when they all quitted it together, that Miss Thorpe should accompany Miss Morland to the very door of Mr. Allen's house; and that they should there part with a most affectionate and lengthened shake of hands, after learning, to their mutual relief, that they should see each other across the theatre at night, and say their prayers in the same chapel the next morning. Catherine then ran directly upstairs, and watched Miss Thorpe's progress down the street from the drawing-room window; admired the graceful spirit of her walk, the fashionable air of her figure and dress, and felt grateful, as well she might, for the chance which had procured her such a friend.

A YEOMAN FARMER

CRANFORD
Mrs. Gaskell

The aspect of the country was quiet and pastoral. Woodley stood among fields ; and there was an old-fashioned garden where roses and currant-bushes touched each other, and where the feathery asparagus formed a pretty background to the pinks and gilly-flowers ; there was no drive up to the door. We got out at a little gate, and walked up a straight box-edged path.

" My cousin might make a drive, I think," said Miss Pole, who was afraid of ear-ache, and had only her cap on.

" I think it is very pretty," said Miss Matty, with a soft plaintiveness in her voice, and almost in a whisper, for just then Mr. Holbrook appeared at the door, rubbing his hands in very effervescence of hospitality. He looked more like my idea of Don Quixote than ever, and yet the likeness was only external. His respectable housekeeper stood modestly at the door to bid us welcome ; and, while she led the elder ladies upstairs to a bedroom, I begged to look about the garden. My request evidently pleased the old gentleman, who took me all round the place, and showed me his six and twenty cows, named after the different letters of the alphabet. As we went along, he surprised me occasionally by repeating apt and beautiful quotations from the poets, ranging easily from Shakespeare and George Herbert to those of our own day. He did this as naturally as if he were thinking aloud, and their true and beautiful words were the best expression he could find for what he was thinking or feeling. To be sure he called Byron " My Lord Byrron," and pronounced the name of Goethe strictly in accordance with the English sound of the letters—" As Goethe says, ' Ye ever-verdant palaces,' " etc. Altogether, I never met with a man, before or since, who had spent so long a life in a secluded and not impressive country, with ever-increasing delight in the daily and yearly change of season and beauty.

When he and I went in, we found that dinner was nearly ready in the kitchen—for so I suppose the room ought to be called, as there were oak dressers and cupboards all round, all over by the side of the fireplace, and only a small Turkey carpet in the middle of the flag-floor. The room might have been easily made into a handsome dark oak dining-parlour by removing the oven and a few other appurtenances of a kitchen, which were evidently never used, the real cooking-place being at some distance. The room in which we were expected to sit was a stiffly-furnished, ugly apartment; but that in which we did sit was what Mr. Holbrook called the counting-house, when he paid his labourers their weekly wages at a great desk near the door. The rest of the pretty sitting-room—looking into the orchard, and all covered over with dancing tree-shadows—was filled with books. They lay on the ground, they covered the walls, they strewed the table. He was evidently half-ashamed and half-proud of his extravagance in this respect. They were of all kinds—poetry and wild weird tales prevailing. He evidently chose his books in accordance with his own tastes, not because such and such were classical or established favourites.

" Ah !" he said, " we farmers ought not to have much time for reading; yet somehow one can't help it."

" What a pretty room !" said Miss Matty, *sotto voce*.

" What a pleasant place !" said I aloud, almost simultaneously.

" Nay ! if you like it," replied he; " but can you

sit on these great black-leather three-cornered chairs ? I like it better than the best parlour; but I thought ladies would take that for the smarter place."

It was the smarter place, but, like most smart things, not at all pretty, or pleasant, or home-like; so, while we were at dinner, the servant-girl dusted and scrubbed the counting-house chairs, and we sat there all the rest of the day.

We had pudding before meat; and I thought Mr. Holbrook was going to make some apology for his old-fashioned ways, for he began—

" I don't know whether you like new-fangled ways."

" Oh, not at all !" said Miss Matty.

" No more do I," said he. " My housekeeper *will* have these in her new fashion; or else I tell her that, when I was a young man, we used to keep strictly to my father's rule, ' No broth, no ball; no ball, no beef' and always began dinner with broth. Then we had suet puddings, boiled in the broth with the beef; and then the meat itself. If we did not sup our broth, we had no ball, which we liked a deal better; and the beef came last of all, and only those had it who had done justice to the broth and the ball. Now folks begin with sweet things, and turn their dinners topsy-turvy."

When the ducks and green peas came, we looked at each other in dismay; we had only two-pronged black-handled forks. It is true the steel was as bright as silver; but what were we to do? Miss Matty picked up her peas, one by one, on the point of the prongs, much as Aminé ate her grains of rice after her previous feast with the Ghoul. Miss Pole sighed over her delicate young peas as she left them on one side of her plate untasted, for they *would* drop between the prongs. I looked at my host: the peas were going wholesale into his capacious mouth, shovelled up by his large round-ended knife. I saw, I imitated, I

THE JUBILEE BALL AT RANELAGH ON THE BIRTHDAY OF GEORGE, PRINCE OF WALES, MAY 24TH, 1759
From a print in the British Museum.

survived! My friends, in spite of my precedent, could not muster up courage enough to do an ungenteel thing; and, if Mr. Holbrook had not been so heartily hungry, he would probably have seen that the good peas went away almost untouched.

After dinner a clay pipe was brought in, and a spittoon; and, asking us to retire to another room, where he would soon join us, if we disliked tobacco-smoke, he presented his pipe to Miss Matty, and requested her to fill the bowl. This was a compliment to a lady in his youth; but it was rather inappropriate to propose it as an honour to Miss Matty, who had been trained by her sister to hold smoking of every kind in utter abhorrence. But if it was a shock to her refinement, it was also a gratification to her feelings to be thus selected; so she daintily stuffed the strong tobacco into the pipe, and then we withdrew.

It is very pleasant dining with a bachelor," said Miss Matty softly, as we settled ourselves in the counting-house. "I only hope it is not improper; so many pleasant things are!"

"What a number of books he has!" said Miss Pole, looking round the room. "And how dusty they are!"

"I think it must be like one of the great Dr. Johnson's rooms," said Miss Matty. "What a superior man your cousin must be!"

"Yes!" said Miss Pole, "he's a great reader; but I am afraid he has got into very uncouth habits with living alone."

"Oh! uncouth is too hard a word. I should call him eccentric; very clever people always are!" replied Miss Matty.

When Mr. Holbrook returned, he proposed a walk in the fields; but the two elder ladies were afraid of damp and dirt, and had only very unbecoming calashes to put on over their caps; so they declined, and I was again his companion in a turn which he said he was obliged to take to see after his men. He strode along, either wholly forgetting my existence, or soothed into silence by his pipe—and yet it was not silence exactly. He walked before me, with a stooping gait, his hands clasped behind him; and, as some tree or cloud, or glimpse of distant upland pastures, struck him, he quoted poetry to himself, saying it out loud in a grand sonorous voice, with just the emphasis that true feeling and appreciation give. We came upon an old cedar-tree, which stood at one end of the house—

"Capital term—' layers !' wonderful man !" I did not know whether he was speaking to me or not; but I put in an assenting "wonderful," although I knew nothing about it, just because I was tired of being forgotten, and of being consequently silent.

He turned sharp round. "Ay! you may say 'wonderful.' Why, when I saw the review of his poems in *Blackwood*, I set off within an hour, and walked seven miles to Misselton (for the horses were not in the way) and ordered them. Now, what colour are ash-buds in March?"

Is the man going mad? thought I. He is very like Don Quixote.

"What colour are they, I say?" repeated he vehemently.

"I am sure I don't know, sir," said I, with the meekness of ignorance.

"I knew you didn't. No more did I—an old fool that I am!—till this young man comes and tells me. Black as ash-buds in March. And I've lived all my life in the country; more shame for me not to know. Black: they are jet-black, madam." And he went off again, swinging along to the music of some rhyme he had got hold of.

"The cedar spreads his dark-green layers of shade."

"A GENTLEMANLY OILMAN"

ESSAYS OF ELIA
Lamb

We went [to my first play] with orders, which my godfather F. had sent us. He kept the oil-shop (now Davies's) at the corner of Featherstone-buildings, in Holborn. F. was a tall, grave person, lofty in speech, and had pretensions above his rank. He associated in those days with John Palmer, the comedian, whose gait and bearing he seemed to copy; if John (which is quite as likely) did not rather borrow somewhat of his manner from my godfather. He was also known to and visited by Sheridan. It was to his house in Holborn that young Brinsley brought his first wife on her elopement with him from a boarding-school at Bath—the beautiful Maria Linley. My parents were present (over a quadrille table) when he arrived in the evening with his harmonious charge. From either of these connections it may be inferred that my godfather could command an order for the then Drury-lane theatre at pleasure—and, indeed, a pretty liberal issue of those cheap billets, in Brinsley's easy autograph, I have heard him say was the sole remuneration which he had received for many years' nightly illumination of the orchestra and various avenues of that theatre—and he was content it should be so. The honour of Sheridan's familiarity—or supposed familiarity—was better to my godfather than money.

F. was the most gentlemanly of oilmen; grandiloquent, yet courteous. His delivery of the commonest matters of fact was Ciceronian. He had two Latin words almost constantly in his mouth (how odd sounds Latin from an oil-man's lips!), which my better knowledge since has enabled me to correct. In strict pronunciation they should have been sounded *vice versâ*—but in those young years they impressed me with more awe than they would now do, read aright from Seneca or Varro—in his own peculiar pronunciation, monosyllabically elaborated, or Anglicised, into something like *verse verse*. By an imposing manner, and the help of these distorted syllables, he climbed (but that was little) to the highest parochial honours which St. Andrew's has to bestow.

He is dead—and thus much I thought due to his memory, both for my first orders (little wondrous talismans!—slight keys, and insignificant to outward sight, but opening to me more than Arabian paradises!) and, moreover, that by his testamentary beneficence I came into possession of the only landed property which I could ever call my own—situate near the road-way village of pleasant Puckeridge, in Hertfordshire. When I journeyed down to take possession, and planted foot on my own ground, the stately habits of the donor descended upon me, and I strode (shall I confess the vanity?) with larger paces over my allotment of three quarters of an acre, with its commodious mansion in the midst, with the feeling of an English freeholder that all betwixt sky and centre was my own. The estate has passed into more prudent hands, and nothing but an agrarian can restore it.

In those days were pit orders. Beshrew the uncomfortable manager who abolished them!—with one of these we went. I remember the waiting at the door—not that which is left—but between that and an inner door in shelter—O when shall I be such an expectant again!—with the cry of non-pareils, an indispensable play-house accompaniment in those days. As near as I can recollect, the fashionable pronunciation of the theatrical fruiteresses then was, "Chase some oranges, chase some numparels, chase a bill of the play";—chase *pro* choose. But when we got in, and I beheld the green curtain that veiled a heaven to my imagination, which was soon to be disclosed—the breathless anticipations I endured! I had seen something like it in the plate prefixed to Troilus and Cressida, in Rowe's Shakspeare—the tent scene with Diomede—and a sight of that place can always bring back in a measure the feeling of that evening.—The boxes at that time, full of well-dressed women of quality, projected over the pit; and the pilasters reaching down were adorned with a glistening substance (I know not what) under glass (as it seemed), resembling—a homely fancy—but I judged it to be sugar-candy—yet to my raised imagination, divested of its homelier qualities, it appeared a glorified candy!—The orchestra lights at length rose, those " fair Auroras!" Once the bell sounded. It was to ring out yet once again—and, incapable of the anticipation, I reposed my shut eyes in a sort of resignation upon the maternal lap. It rang the second time. The curtain drew up—I was not past six years old, and the play was Artaxerxes!

PARTIES

CRANFORD
Mrs. Gaskell

I wondered what the Cranford ladies did with Captain Brown at their parties. We had often rejoiced, in former days, that there was no gentleman to be attended to, and to find conversation for, at the card-parties. We had congratulated ourselves upon the snugness of the evenings; and, in our love for gentility and distaste of mankind, we had almost persuaded ourselves that to be a man was to be " vulgar "; so that when I found my friend and hostess, Miss Jenkyns, was going to have a party in my honour and that Captain and the Miss Browns were invited, I wondered much what would be the course of the evening. Card-tables, with green-baize tops, were set out by daylight, just as usual; it was the third week in November, so the evenings closed in about four. Candles and clean packs of cards were arranged on each table. The fire was made up; the neat maid-servant had received her last directions; and there we stood, dressed in our best, each with a candle-lighter in our hands, ready to dart at the candles as soon as the first knock came. Parties in Cranford were solemn festivities, making the ladies feel gravely elated as they sat together in their best dresses. As soon as three had arrived, we sat down to " Preference," I being the unlucky fourth. The next four comers were put down immediately to another table; and presently the tea-trays, which I had seen set out in the storeroom as I passed in the morning, were placed each on the middle of a card-table. The china was delicate egg-shell; the old-fashioned silver glittered with polishing; but the eatables were of the slightest description. While the trays were yet on the tables, Captain and the Miss Browns came in; and I could see that, somehow or other, the Captain was a favourite with all the ladies present. Ruffled brows were smoothed, sharp voices lowered at his approach. Miss Brown looked ill, and depressed almost to gloom. Miss Jessie smiled as usual, and seemed nearly as popular as her father. He immediately and quietly assumed the man's place in the room; attended to every one's wants, lessened the pretty maidservant's labour by waiting on empty cups and bread-and-butterless ladies; and yet did it all in so easy and dignified a manner, and so much as if it were a matter of course for the strong to attend to the weak, that he was a true man throughout. He played for threepenny points with as grave an interest as if they had been pounds; and yet, in all his attention to strangers, he had an eye on his suffering daughter—for suffering I was sure she was, though to many eyes she might only appear to be irritable. Miss Jessie could not play cards, but she talked to the sitters-out, who, before her coming, had been rather inclined to be cross. She sang, too, to an old cracked piano, which I think had been a spinnet in its youth. Miss Jessie sang " Jock o' Hazeldean " a little out of tune ; but we were none of us musical, though Miss Jenkyns beat time, out of time, by way of appearing to be so.

It was very good of Miss Jenkyns to do this ; for I had seen that, a little before, she had been a good deal annoyed by Miss Jessie Brown's unguarded admission (*à propos* of Shetland wool) that she had an uncle, her mother's brother, who was a shopkeeper in Edinburgh. Miss Jenkyns tried to drown this confession by a terrible cough—for the Honourable Mrs. Jamieson was sitting at the card-table nearest Miss Jessie, and what would she say or think if she found out she was in the same room with a shopkeeper's niece ! But Miss Jessie Brown (who had no tact, as we all agreed the next morning) *would* repeat the information, and assure Miss Pole she could easily get her the identical Shetland wool required, " through my uncle, who has the best assortment of Shetland goods of any one in Edinboro'." It was to take the taste of this out of our mouths, and the sound of this out of our ears, that Miss Jenkyns proposed music ; so I say again, it was very good of her to beat time to the song.

When the trays reappeared with biscuits and wine, punctually at a quarter to nine, there was conversation, comparing of cards, and talking over tricks ; but by and by Captain Brown sported a bit of literature.

A GAME OF CARDS

ESSAYS OF ELIA
Lamb

"A clean fire, a clean hearth, and the rigour of the game." This was the celebrated *wish* of old Sarah Battle (now with God), who, next to her devotions, loved a good game of whist. She was none of your lukewarm gamesters, your half-and-half players, who have no objection to take a hand, if you want to make up a rubber; who affirm that they have no pleasure in winning; that they like to win one game and lose another; that they can while away an hour very agreeably at a card-table, but are indifferent whether they play or no; and will desire an adversary, who has slipped a wrong card to take it up and play another. These insufferable triflers are the curse of a table. One of these flies will spoil a whole pot. Of such it may be said that they do not play at cards, but only play at playing at them.

Sarah Battle was none of that breed. She detested them, as I do, from her heart and soul; and would not, save upon a striking emergency, willingly seat herself at the same table with them.

She loved a thorough-paced partner, a determined enemy. She took, and gave, no concessions. She hated favours. She never made a revoke, nor ever passed it over in her adversary without exacting the utmost forfeiture. She fought a good fight: cut and thrust. She held not her good sword (her cards) "like a dancer." She sate bolt upright; and neither showed you her cards, nor desired to see yours. All people have their blind side—their superstitions; and I have heard her declare, under the rose, that Hearts was her favourite suit.

I never in my life—and I knew Sarah Battle many of the best years of it—saw her take out her snuff-box when it was her turn to play; or snuff a candle in the middle of a game; or ring for a servant, till it was fairly over. She never introduced, or connived at, miscellaneous conversation during its process. As she emphatically observed, cards were cards; and if I ever saw unmingled distaste in her fine last-century countenance, it was at the airs of a young gentleman of a literary turn, who had been with difficulty persuaded to take a hand; and who, in his excess of candour, declared, that he thought there was no harm in unbending the mind now and then, after serious studies, in recreations of that kind! She could not bear to have her noble occupation, to which she wound up her faculties, considered in that light. It was her business, her duty, the thing she came into the world to do,—and she did it. She unbent her mind afterwards—over a book.

Pope was her favourite author: his Rape of the Lock her favourite work. She once did me the favour to play over with me (with the cards) his celebrated game of Ombre in that poem; and to explain to me how far it agreed with, and in what points it would be found to differ from, tradrille. Her illustrations were apposite and poignant; and I had the pleasure of sending the substance of them to Mr. Bowles; but I suppose they came too late to be inserted among his ingenious notes upon that author.

Quadrille, she has often told me, was her first love; but whist had engaged her maturer esteem. The former, she said, was showy and specious, and likely to allure young persons. The uncertainty and quick shifting of partners—a thing which the constancy of whist abhors; the dazzling supremacy and regal investiture of Spadrille—absurd, as she justly observed, in the pure aristocracy of whist, where his crown and garter give him no proper power above his brother-nobility of the Aces;—the giddy vanity so taking to the inexperienced, of playing alone; above all, the overpowering attractions of a *Sans Prendre Vole*,—to the triumph of which there is nothing parallel or approaching, in the contingencies of whist;—all these, she would say, make quadrille a game of captivation to the young and enthusiastic. But whist was the *solider* game: that was her word. It was a long meal; not like quadrille, a feast of snatches. One or two rubbers might co-extend in duration with an evening. They gave time to form rooted friendships, to cultivate steady enmities. She despised the chance-started, capricious, and ever-fluctuating alliances of the other. The skirmishes of quadrille, she would say, reminded her of the petty ephemeral embroilments of the little Italian states, depicted by Machiavel: perpetually changing postures and connexions; bitter foes to-day, sugared darlings to-morrow; kissing and scratching in a breath;—but the wars of whist were comparable to the long, steady, deep-rooted, rational antipathies of the great French and English nations.

A grave simplicity was what she chiefly admired in her favourite game. There was nothing silly in it, like the nob in cribbage—nothing superfluous. No *flushes*—that most irrational of all pleas that a reasonable being can set up:—that any one should claim four by virtue of holding cards of the same mark and colour, without reference to the playing of the game, or the individual worth or pretensions of the cards themselves! She held this to be a solecism; as pitiful an ambition at cards as alliteration is in authorship. She despised superficiality, and looked deeper than the colours of things.—Suits were soldiers, she would say, and must have a uniformity of array to distinguish them: but what should we say to a foolish squire, who should claim a merit from dressing up his tenantry in red jackets, that never were to be marshalled—never to take the field?—She even wished that whisT were more simple than it is; and, in my mind, would have stripped it of some appendages, which, in the state of human frailty, may be venially, and even commendably, allowed of. She saw no reason for the deciding of the trump by the turn of the card. Why not one suit always trumps ?—Why two colours, when the mark of the suit would have sufficiently distinguished them without it ?

"But the eye, my dear madam, is agreeably refreshed with the variety. Man is not a creature of pure reason—he must have his senses delightfully appealed to. We see it in Roman Catholic countries, where the music and the paintings draw in many to worship, whom your quaker spirit of unsensualising would have kept out.—You, yourself, have a pretty collection of paintings—but confess to me, whether, walking in your gallery at Sandham, among those clear Vandykes, or among the Paul Potters in the ante-room, you ever felt your bosom glow with an elegant delight, at all comparable to *that* you have it in your power to experience most evenings over a well-arranged assortment of the court-cards ?—the pretty antic habits, like heralds in procession—the gay triumph assuring-scarlets—the contrasting deadly-killing sables—the " hoary majesty of spades '—Pam in all his glory !—

"All these might be dispensed with; and with their naked names upon the drab pasteboard, the game might go on very well, pictureless; but the *beauty* of cards would be extinguished for ever. Stripped of all that is imaginative in them, they muSt degenerate into mere gambling. Imagine a dull deal board, or drum head, to spread them on, instead of that nice verdant carpet (next to nature's), fitteSt arena for those courtly combatants to play their gallant jouSts and turneys in !—Exchange those delicately-turned ivory markers—(work of Chinese artist, unconscious of their symbol,—or as profanely slighting their true application as the arrantest Ephesian journeyman that turned out those little shrines for the goddess)—exchange them for little bits of leather (our ancestors' money), or chalk and a slate!"—

The old lady, with a smile, confessed the soundness of my logic; and to her approbation of my arguments on her favourite topic that evening I have always fancied myself indebted for the legacy of a curious cribbage-board, made of the finest Sienna marble, which her maternal uncle (old Walter Plumer, whom I have elsewhere celebrated) brought with him from Florence:—this, and a trifle of five hundred pounds, came to me at her death.

The former bequest (which I do not least value) I have kept with religious care; though she herself, to confess a truth, was never greatly taken with cribbage. It was an essentially vulgar game, I have heard her say,—disputing with her uncle, who was very partial to it. She could never heartily bring her mouth to pronounce "*Go*," or "*That's a go*." She called it an ungrammatical game. The pegging teased her. I once knew her to forfeit a rubber (a five-dollar stake) because she would not take advantage of the turn-up knave, which would have given it her, but which she must have claimed by the disgraceful tenure of declaring "*two for his heels*." There is something extremely genteel in this sort of self-denial. Sarah Battle was a gentlewoman born.

Piquet she held the best game at the cards for two persons, though she would ridicule the pedantry of the terms—such as pique—repique—the capot—they savoured (she thought) of affectation. But games for two, or even three, she never greatly cared for. She loved the quadrate, or square. She would argue thus: —Cards are warfare: the ends are gain, with glory. But cards are war, in disguise of a sport: when single adversaries encounter, the ends proposed are too palpable. By themselves, it is too close a fight; with spectators, it is not much bettered. No looker-on can be interested, except for a bet, and then it is a mere affair of money; he cares not for your luck *sympathetically*, or for your play.—Three are still worse; a mere naked war of every man against every man, as in cribbage, without league or alliance; or a rotation of petty and contradictory interests, a succession of heartless leagues, and not much more hearty infractions of them, as in tradrille.—But in square games (*she meant whist*), all that is possible to be attained in card-playing is accomplished. There are the incentives of profit with honour, common to every species—though the *latter* can be but very imperfectly enjoyed in those other games, where the spectator is only feebly a participator. But the parties in whist are spectators and principals too. They are a theatre to themselves, and a looker-on is not wanted. He is rather worse than nothing, and an impertinence. Whist abhors neutrality, or interests beyond its sphere. You glory in some surprising stroke of skill or fortune, not because a cold—or even an interested—bystander witnesses it, but because your *partner* sympathises in the contingency. You win for two. You triumph for two. Two are exalted. Two again are mortified; which divides their disgrace, as the conjunction doubles (by taking off the invidiousness) your glories. Two losing to two are better reconciled, than one to one in that close butchery. The hostile feeling is weakened by multiplying the channels. War becomes a civil game. By such reasonings as these the old lady was accustomed to defend her favourite pastime.

"A RATTLE"

NORTHANGER ABBEY
Jane Austen

"You will not be frightened, Miss Morland," sad Thorpe, as he handed her in, "if my horse should dance about a little at first setting off. He will most likely give a plunge or two, and perhaps take the rest for a minute; but he will soon know his master. He is full of spirits, playful as can be, there is no vice in him."

Catherine did not think the portrait a very inviting one, but it was too late to retreat, and she was too young to own herself frightened; so, resigning herself to her fate, and trusting to the animal's boasted knowledge of its owner, she sat peaceably down, and saw Thorpe sit down by her. Everything being then arranged, the servant who stood at the horse's head was bid in an important voice to "let him go," and off they went in the quietest manner imaginable, without a plunge or a caper, or anything like one. . . . A silence of several minutes succeeded their first short dialogue. It was broken by Thorpe's saying very abruptly, "Old Allen is as rich as a Jew, is not he?" Catherine did not understand him, and he repeated his question, adding in explanation, "Old Allen, the man you are with."

"Oh! Mr. Allen you mean. Yes, I believe he is very rich."

"And no children at all?"

"No, not any."

"A famous thing for his next heirs. He is your godfather, is not he?"

"My godfather! No."

"But you are always very much with them?"

"Yes, very much."

"Aye, that is what I meant. He seems a good kind

of old fellow enough, and has lived very well in his time, I dare say; he is not gouty for nothing. Does he drink his bottle a-day now?"

"His bottle a-day! No. Why should you think of such a thing? He is a very temperate man, and you could not fancy him in liquor last night?"

"Lord help you! You women are always thinking of men being in liquor. Why, you do not suppose a man is overset by a bottle? I am sure of this, that if everybody was to drink their bottle a-day, there would not be half the disorders in the world there are now. It would be a famous good thing for us all."

"I cannot believe it."

"Oh! lord, it would be the saving of thousands. There is not the hundredth part of the wine consumed in this kingdom that there ought to be. Our foggy climate wants help."

"And yet I have heard that there is a great deal of wine drank in Oxford."

"Oxford! There is no drinking at Oxford now, I assure you. Nobody drinks there. You would hardly meet with a man who goes beyond his four pints at the utmost. Now, for instance, it was reckoned a remarkable thing at the last party in my rooms, that upon an average we cleared about five pints a head. It was looked upon as something out of the common way. Mine is famous good stuff, to be sure. You would not often meet with anything like it in Oxford, and that may account for it. But this will just give you a notion of the general rate of drinking there" . . .

"You do not really think, Mr. Thorpe," said Catherine, venturing after some time to consider the matter as entirely decided, and to offer some little variation on the subject, "that James's gig will break down?"

"Break down! Oh, Lord! Did you ever see such

a little tittuppy thing in your life? There is not a sound piece of iron about it. The wheels have been fairly worn out these ten years at least; and as for the body, upon my soul, you might shake it to pieces yourself with a touch. It is the most devilish little rickety business I ever beheld. Thank God! we have got a better. I would not be bound to go two miles in it for fifty thousand pounds."

"Good heavens!" cried Catherine, quite frightened, "then pray let us turn back; they will certainly meet with an accident if we go on. Do let us turn back, Mr. Thorpe; stop and speak to my brother, and tell him how very unsafe it is."

"Unsafe! Oh, lord! what is there in that? They will only get a roll if it does break down; and there is plenty of dirt, it will be excellent falling. Oh, curse it! the carriage is safe enough if a man knows how to drive it; a thing of that sort in good hands will last above twenty years after it is fairly worn out. Lord bless you! I would undertake for five pounds to drive it to York and back again without losing a nail."

CHARADES

EMMA
Jane Austen

It was much easier to chat than to study; much pleasanter to let her imagination range and work at Harriet's fortune, than to be labouring to enlarge her comprehension, or exercise it on sober facts; and the only literary pursuit which engaged Harriet at present, the only mental provision she was making for the evening of life, was the collecting and transcribing all the riddles of every sort that she could meet with, into a thin quarto of hot-pressed paper, made up by her friend, and ornamented with cyphers and trophies.

In this age of literature, such collections on a very grand scale are not uncommon. Miss Nash, head-teacher at Mrs. Goddard's, had written out at least three hundred; and Harriet, who had taken the first hint of it from her, hoped, with Miss Woodhouse's help, to get a great many more. Emma assisted with her invention, memory and taste; and as Harriet wrote a very pretty hand, it was likely to be an arrangement of the first order, in form as well as quantity.

HOOPS

BELINDA
Maria Edgworth

'The drawing-room has lasted an unconscionable time this morning,' said he, as he handed her ladyship out of her coach. ' Am not I the most virtuous of virtuous women,' said Lady Delacour, ' to go to court such a day as this? But,' whispered she, as she went upstairs, ' like all other amazingly good people, I have amazingly good reasons for being good. The queen is soon to give a charming breakfast at Frogmore, and I am paying my court with all my might, in hopes of being asked; for Belinda must see one of their galas before we leave town, *that* I'm determined upon.—But where is she?' ' Not at home,' said Clarence, smiling. ' Oh, not at home is nonsense, you know. Shine out, appear, be found, my lovely Zara!' cried Lady Delacour, opening the library door. ' Here she is—what doing I know not—studying Hervey's *Meditations on the Tombs*, I should guess, by the sanctification of her looks. If you be not totally above all sublunary considerations, admire my lilies of the valley, and let me give you a lecture, not upon heads or upon hearts, but on what is of much more consequence, upon hoops. Everybody wears hoops, but how few—'tis a melancholy consideration—how very few can manage them! There's my friend Lady C——; in an elegant undress she passes for very genteel, but put her into a hoop and she looks as pitiable a figure, as much a prisoner, and as little able to walk, as a child in a go-cart. She gets on I grant you, and so does the poor child; but getting on, you know, is not walking. Oh, Clarence, I wish you had seen the two Lady R's sticking close to one another, their father pushing them on together, like two decanters in a bottle-coaster, with such magnificent diamond labels round their necks!'

Encouraged by Clarence Hervey's laughter, Lady Delacour went on to mimic what she called the hoop awkwardness of all her acquaintance; and if these could have failed to divert Belinda, it was impossible for her to be serious when she heard Clarence Hervey declare that he was convinced he could manage a hoop as well as any woman in England, except Lady Delacour.

'Now here,' said he, 'is the purblind dowager, Lady Boucher, just at the door, Lady Delacour; she would not know my face, she would not see my beard, and I will bet fifty guineas that I come into a room in a hoop, and that she does not find me out by my air—that I do not betray myself, in short, by my masculine awkwardness.'

'I hold you to your word, Clarence,' cried Lady Delacour. 'They have let the purblind dowager in; I hear her on the stairs. Here—through this way you can go; as you do everything quicker than anybody else in the world, you will certainly be full dressed in a quarter of an hour; I'll engage to keep the dowager in scandal for that time. Go! Marriott has old hoops and old finery of mine, and you have all-powerful influence, I know, with Marriott: so go and use it, and let us see you in all your glory—though I vow I tremble for my fifty guineas.'

THE SUPPER-PARTY
From an engraving by J. M. Moreau.

Lady Delacour kept the dowager in scandal, according to her engagement, for a good quarter of an hour; then the dresses at the drawing-room took up another quarter; and, at last, the dowager began to give a account of sundry wonderful cures that had been performed, to her certain knowledge, by her favourite concentrated extract or anima of quassia. She entered into the history of the negro slave named Quassi, who discovered this medical wood, which he kept a close secret till Mr. Daghlberg, a magistrate of Surinam, wormed it out of him, brought a branch of the tree to Europe, and communicated it to the great Linnæus—when Clarence Hervey was announced by the title of ' The Countess de Pomenars.'

An *émigrée*—a charming woman!" whispered Lady Delacour; ' she was to have been at the drawing-room to-day but for a blunder of mine; ready dressed she was, and I didn't call for her! Ah, Mad. de Pomenars, I am actually ashamed to see you,' continued her ladyship; and she went forward to meet Clarence Hervey, who really made his *entreé* with very composed assurance and grace. He managed his hoop with such skill and dexterity, that he well deserved the praise of being a universal genius.

The Countess de Pomenars spoke French and broken English incomparably well, and she made out that she was descended from the Pomenars of the time of Mad. de Sévigné: she said that she had in her possession several original letters of Mad. de Sévigné,' and a lock of Mad. de Grignan's fine hair.

' I have sometimes fancied, but I believe it is only my fancy,' said Lady Delacour, ' that this young lady,' turning to Belinda, ' is not unlike your Mad. de Grignan. I have seen a picture of her at Strawberry Hill.'

Mad. de Pomenars acknowledged that there was a resemblance, but added, that it was flattery in the extreme to Mad. de Grignan to say so.

'It would be a sin, undoubtedly, to waste flattery upon the dead, my dear countess,' said Lady Delacour; 'but here, without flattery to the living, as you have a lock of Mad. de Grignan's hair, you can tell us whether *la belle chevelure*, of which Mad. de Sévigné talked so much, was anything to be compared to my Belinda's.' As she spoke, Lady Delacour, before Belinda was aware of her intentions, dexterously let down her beautiful tresses; and the Countess de Pomenars was so much struck at the sight, that she was incapable of paying the necessary compliments. 'Nay, touch it,' said Lady Delacour,—' it is so fine and so soft.'

At this dangerous moment her ladyship artfully let drop the comb. Clarence Hervey suddenly stooped to pick it up, totally forgetting his hoop and his character. He threw down the music-stand with his hoop. Lady Delacour exclaimed 'Bravissima!' and burst out a-laughing. Lady Boucher, in amazement, looked from one to another for an explanation, and was a considerable time before, as she said, she could believe her own eyes. Clarence Hervey acknowledged he had lost his bet, joined in the laugh, and declared that fifty guineas was too little to pay for the sight of the finest hair that he had ever beheld. 'I declare he deserves a lock of *la belle chevelure* for that speech, Miss Portman,' cried Lady Delacour; 'I'll appeal to all the world—Mad. de Pomenars must have a lock to measure with Mad. de Grignan's? Come, a second rape of the lock, Belinda.'

Fortunately for Belinda, 'the glittering forfex' was not immediately produced, as fine ladies do not now, as in former times, carry any such useless implements about with them.

Such was the modest graceful dignity of Miss Portman's manners, that she escaped without even the charge of prudery. She retired to her own apartment as soon as she could.

'She passes on in unblenched majesty,' said Lady Delacour.

'She is really a charming woman,' said Clarence Hervey, in a low voice to Lady Delacour, drawing her into a recessed window : he in the same low voice continued, 'Could I obtain a private audience of a few minutes when your ladyship is at leisure ? I have—'
'I am never at leisure,' interrupted Lady Delacour; 'but if you have anything particular to say to me as I guess you have, by my skill in human nature—come here to my concert to-night, before the rest of the world. Wait patiently in the music-room, and perhaps I may grant you a private audience, as you had the grace not to call it a *tete-a-tete*. In the meantime, my dear Countess de Pomenars, had we not better take off our hoops ? '

A VILLAGE

OUR VILLAGE
Mary Russell Mitford

OF all situations for a constant residence, that which appears to me most delightful is a little village far in the country ; a small neighbourhood, not of fine mansions finely peopled, but of cottager and cottage-like houses, ' messuages or tenements,' as a friend of mine calls such ignoble and nondescript dwellings, with inhabitants whose faces are as familiar to us as the flowers in our garden ; a little world of our own, close-packed and insulated like ants in an ant-hill, or bees in a hive, or sheep in a fold, or nuns in a convent, or sailors in a ship ; where we know every one, are known to every one, interested in every one, and authorised to hope that every one feels an interest in us. How pleasant it is to slide into these true-hearted feelings from the kindly and unconscious influence of

Town and Country

habit, and to learn to know and love the people about us, with all their peculiarities, just as we learn to know and to love the nooks and turns of the shady lanes and sunny commons that we pass every day. . . .

. . .And a small neighbourhood is as good in sober waking reality as in poetry or prose; a village neighbourhood, such as this Berkshire hamlet in which I write, a long, straggling, winding street at the bottom of a fine eminence, with a road through it, always abounding in carts, horsemen and carriages, and lately enlivened by a stage-coach from B—— to S——, which passed through about ten days ago, and will I suppose return some time or other. There are coaches of all varieties nowadays; perhaps this may be intended for a monthly diligence, or a fortnight fly. Will you walk with me through our village, courteous reader? The journey is not long. We will begin at the lower end, and proceed up the hill.

The tidy, square, red cottage on the right hand, with the long well-stocked garden by the side of the road, belongs to a retired publican from a neighbouring town; a substantial person with a comely wife; one who piques himself on independence and idleness, talks politics, reads newspapers, hates the minister and cries out for reform. He introduced into our peaceful vicinage the rebellious innovation of an illumination on the Queen's acquittal. Remonstrance and persuasion were in vain; he talked of liberty and broken windows—so we all lighted up. Oh! how he shone that night with candles, and laurel, and white bows, and gold paper, and a transparency (originally designed for a pocket-handkerchief) with a flaming portrait of her Majesty, hatted and feathered, in red ochre. He had no rival in the village, that we all acknowledged; the very bonfire was less splendid; the little boys reserved their best crackers to be expended in his honour, and he gave them full sixpence more than any one else. He would like an illumination once a month; for it must not be concealed that, in spite of gardening, of newspaper reading, of jaunting about in his little cart, and frequently both church and meeting, our worthy neighbour begins to feel the weariness of idleness. He hangs over his gate, and tries to entice passengers to stop and chat; he volunteers little jobs all round, smokes cherry trees to cure the blight, and traces and blows up all the wasp's-nests in the parish. I have seen a great many wasps in our garden to-day, and shall enchant him with the intelligence. He even assists his wife in her sweepings and dustings. Poor man! he is a very respectable person, and would be a very happy one, if he would add a little employment to his dignity. It would be the salt of life to him.

Next to his house, though parted from it by another long garden with a yew arbour at the end, is the pretty dwelling of the shoemaker, a pale, sickly-looking, black-haired man, the very model of sober industry. There he sits in his little shop from early morning till late at night. An earthquake would hardly stir him: the illumination did not. He stuck immovably to his last, from the first lighting up, through the long blaze and the slow decay, till his large solitary candle was the only light in the place. One cannot conceive anything more perfect than the contempt which the man of transparencies and the man of shoes must have felt for each other on that evening. There was at least as much vanity in the sturdy industry as in the strenuous idleness, for our shoemaker is a man of substance; he employs three journeymen, two lame, and one a dwarf, so that his shop looks like a hospital; he has purchased the lease of his commodious dwelling, some even say that he has bought it out and out; and he has only one pretty daughter, a light, delicate, fair-haired girl of fourteen, the champion, protectress and playfellow of every brat under three years old, whom she jumps, dances, dandles and feeds all day long. A very attractive person is that child-loving girl. I have never seen anyone in her station who possessed so thoroughly that undefinable charm, the lady-look. See her on a Sunday in her simplicity and her white frock, and she might pass for an earl's daughter. She likes flowers too, and has a profusion of white stocks under her window, as pure and delicate as herself.

The first house on the opposite side of the way is the blacksmith's; a gloomy dwelling, where the sun never seems to shine; dark and smoky within and without, like a forge. The blacksmith is a high officer in our little state, nothing less than a constable; but, alas! alas! when tumults arise, and the constable is called for, he will commonly be found in the thickest of the fray. Lucky would it be for his wife and her eight children if there were no public-house in the land : an inveterate inclination to enter those bewitching doors is Mr. Constable's only fault.

Next to this official dwelling is a spruce brick tenement, red, high, and narrow, boasting, one above another, three sash-windows, the only sash-windows in the village, with a clematis on one side and a rose on the other, tall and narrow like itself. That slender mansion has a fine, genteel look. The little parlour seems made for Hogarth's old maid and her stunted footboy; for tea and card parties,—it would just hold one table; for the rustle of faded silks, and the splendour of old china; for the delight of four by honours, and a little snug, quiet scandal between the deals; for affected gentility and real starvation. This should have been its destiny; but fate has been unpropitious : it belongs to a plump, merry, bustling dame, with four, fat, rosy, noisy children, the very essence of vulgarity and plenty.

Then comes the village shop, like other village shops, multifarious as a bazaar; a repository for bread, shoes, tea, cheese, tape, ribands and bacon; for everything, in short, except the one particular thing which you happen to want at the moment, and will be sure not to find. The people are civil and thriving, and frugal withal; they have let the upper part of their house to two young women (one of them is a pretty blue-eyed girl) who teach little children their A B C, and make caps and gowns for their mammas,—parcel school-mistress, parcel mantua-maker. I believe they find adorning the body a more profitable vocation than adorning the mind.

THE DECAY OF BEGGARS

ESSAYS OF ELIA
Lamb

The all-sweeping besom of societarian reformation—your only modern Alcides' club to rid the time of its abuses—is uplift with many-handed sway to extirpate the last fluttering tatters of the bugbear MENDICITY from the metropolis. Scrips, wallets, bags—staves, dogs and crutches—the whole mendicant fraternity, with all their baggage, are fast posting out of the purliens of this eleventh persecution. From the crowded crossing, from the corners of streets and turnings of alleys, the parting Genuis of Beggary is " with sighing sent."

I do not approve of this wholesale going to work, this impertinent crusado, or *bellum ad exterminationem*, proclaimed against a species. Much good might be sucked from these Beggars.

They were the oldest and the honourablest form of

pauperism. Their appeals were to our common nature; less revolting to an ingenious mind than to be a suppliant to the particular humours or caprice of any fellow-creature, or set of fellow-creatures, parochial or societarian. Theirs were the only rates uninvidious in the levy, ungrudged in the assessment.

There was a dignity springing from the very depth of their desolation; as to be naked is to be so much nearer to the being a man, than to go in livery.

The greatest spirits have felt this in their reverses; and when Dionysius from king turned schoolmaster, do we feel anything towards him but contempt? Could Vandyke have made a picture of him, swaying a ferula for a sceptre, which would have affected our minds with the same heroic pity, the same compassionate admiration, with which we regard his Belisarius begging for an *obolus*? Would the moral have been more graceful, more pathetic?

The Blind Beggar in the legend—the father of pretty Bessy—whose story doggerel rhymes and ale-house signs cannot so degrade or attenuate but that some sparks of a lustrous spirit will shine through the disguisements—this noble Earl of Cornwall (as indeed he was) and memorable sport of fortune, fleeing from the unjust sentence of his liege lord, stript of all, and seated on the flowering green of Bethnal, with his more fresh and springing daughter by his side, illuminating his rags and his beggary—would the child and parent have cut a better figure doing the honours of a counter, or expiating their fallen condition upon the three-foot eminence of some sempstering shop-board?

In tale or history your Beggar is ever the just antipode to your King. The poets and romancical writers (as dear Margaret Newcastle would call them), when they would most sharply and feelingly paint a reverse of fortune, never stop till they have brought down their hero in good earnest to rags and the wallet. The depth of the descent illustrates the height he falls from. There is no medium which can be presented to the imagination without offence. There is no breaking the fall. Liar, thrown from his palace, must divest him of his garments, till he answer "mere nature"; and Cresseid, fallen from a prince's love, must extend her pale arms, pale with other whiteness than of beauty, supplicating lazar alms with bell and clap-dish.

The Lucian wits knew this very well; and, with a converse policy, when they would express scorn of greatness without the pity, they show us an Alexander in the shades cobbling shoes, or a Semiramis getting up foul linen.

How would it sound in song, that a great monarch had declined his affections upon the daughter of a baker! yet do we feel the imagination at all violated when we read the " true ballad," where King Cophetua woos the beggar maid?

Pauperism, pauper, poor man, are expressions of pity, but pity alloyed with contempt. No one properly contemns a Beggar. Poverty is a comparative thing, and each degree of it is mocked by its " neighbour grice." Its poor rents and comings-in are soon summed up and told. Its pretences to property are almost ludicrous. Its pitiful attempts to save excite a smile. Every scornful companion can weigh his trifle-bigger purse against it. Poor man reproaches poor man in the streets with impolitic mention of his condition, his own being a shade better, while the rich pass by and jeer at both. No rascally comparative insults a Beggar, or thinks of weighing purses with him. He is not in the scale of comparison. He is not under the measure of property. He confessedly hath none, any more than a dog or a sheep. No one twitteth him with ostentation above his means. No one accuses him of pride, or upbraideth him with mock humility. None jostle with him for the wall, or pick quarrels for precedency. No wealthy neighbour seeketh to eject him from his tenement. No man sues him. No man goes to law with him. If I were not the independent gentleman that I am, rather than I would be a retainer to the great, a lid captain, or a poor relation, I would choose, out of the delicacy and true greatness of my mind, to be a Beggar.

Rags, which are the reproach of poverty, are the Beggar's robes, and graceful *insignia* of his profession, his tenure, his full dress, the suit in which he is expected to show himself in public. He is never out of the fashion, or limpeth awkwardly behind it. He is not required to put on court mourning. He weareth all colours, fearing none. His costume hath undergone less change than the Quaker's. He is the only man in the universe who is not obliged to study appearances. The ups and downs of the world concern him no longer. He alone continueth in one stay. The price of stock or land affecteth him not. The fluctuations of agricultural or commercial prosperity touch him not, or at worst but change his customers. He is not expected to become bail or surety for any one. No man troubleth him with questioning his religion or politics. He is the only free man in the universe.

A FARMER

EMMA
Jane Austen

The Martins of Abbey Mill Farm . . . occupied her thoughts a good deal : she had spent two very happy months with them, and now loved to talk of the pleasures of her visit, and describe the many comforts and wonders of the place. Emma encouraged her talkativeness, amused by such a picture of another set of beings, and enjoying the youthful simplicity which could speak with so much exultation of Mrs. Martin's having " *two* parlours, two very good parlours, indeed: one of them quite as large as Mrs. Goddard's drawing-room ; and of her having an upper maid who had lived five-and-twenty years with her ; and of their having eight cows, two of them Alderneys, and one a little Welsh cow, a very pretty little Welsh cow, indeed, and of Mrs. Martin's saying, as she was so fond of it, it should be called *her* cow ; and of their having a very handsome summer-house in their garden, where some day next year they were all to drink tea ; a very handsome summer-house, large enough to hold a dozen people."

For some time she was amused, without thinking beyond the immediate cause ; but as she came to understand the family better, other feelings arose. She had taken up a wrong idea, fancying it was a mother and daughter, a son and son's wife, who all lived together ; but when it appeared that the Mr. Martin, who bore a part in the narrative, and was always mentioned with approbation for his great good-nature in doing something or other, was a single man ; that there was no young Mrs. Martin, no wife in the case ; she did suspect danger to her poor little friend from all this hospitality and kindness, —and that, if she were not taken care of, she might be required to sink herself for ever.

With this inspiring notion, her questions increased in number and meaning ; and she particularly led Harriet to talk more of Mr. Martin, and there was evidently no dislike to it. Harriet was very ready to speak of the share he had had in their moonlight walks and merry evening games ; and dwelt a good deal upon his being so very good-humoured and obliging. "He had gone three miles round one day in order to bring her some walnuts, because she had said how fond she was of them, and in everything else he was so very obliging. He had his shepherd's son into the parlour one night on purpose to sing to her. She was very fond of singing. He could sing a little himself. She believed he was very clever, and understood everything. He had a very fine flock; and, while she was with them, he had been bid more for his wool than anybody in the country. She believed everybody spoke well of him. His mother and sisters were very fond of him. Mrs. Martin had told her one day (and there was a blush as she said it) that it was impossible for anybody to be a better son; and therefore she was sure, whenever he married, he would make a good husband. Not that she *wanted* him to marry. She was in no hurry at all."

"Well done, Mrs. Martin!" thought Emma. "You know what you are about."

"And when she had come away, Mrs. Martin was so very kind as to send Mrs. Goddard a beautiful goose: the finest goose Mrs. Goddard had ever seen. Mrs. Goddard had dressed it on a Sunday, and asked all the three teachers, Miss Nash, and Miss Prince, and Miss Richardson, to sup with her."

"Mr. Martin, I suppose, is not a man of information beyond the line of his own business? He does not read?"

"Oh yes!—that is, no—I do not know—but I believe he has read a good deal—but not what you would think anything of. He reads the Agricultural Reports, and some other books that lay in one of the window seats—but he reads all *them* to himself. But sometimes of an evening, before we went to cards, he would read something aloud out of the 'Elegant Extracts,' very entertaining. And I know e has read the 'Vicar of Wakefield.' He never read the 'Romance of the Forest,' nor the 'Children of the Abbey.' He had never heard of such books before I mentioned them, but he is determined to get them now as soon as ever he can."

The next question was—

"What sort of looking man is Mr. Martin?"

"Oh! not handsome—not at all handsome. I thought him very plain at first, but I do not think him so plain now. One does not, you know, after a time. But did you never see him? He is in Highbury every now and then, and he is sure to ride through every week on his way to Kingston. He has passed you very often."

"That may be, and I may have seen him fifty times, but without having any idea of his name. A young farmer, whether on horseback or on foot, is the very last sort of person to raise my curiosity. The yeomanry are precisely the order of people with whom I feel I can have nothing to do. A degree or two lower, and a creditable appearance might interest me; I might hope to be useful to their families in some way or other. But a farmer can need none of my help, and is, therefore, in one sense, as much above my notice, as in every other he is below it."

A FARMERESS

OUR VILLAGE
Mary Russell Mitford

Mrs. Sally Mearing, when I first became acquainted with her, occupied, together with her father (a superannuated man of ninety), a large farm very near our former habitation. It had been anciently a great manor-farm or court-house, and was still a stately, substantial building, whose lofty halls and spacious chambers gave an air of grandeur to the common offices to which they were applied. Traces of gilding might yet be seen on the panels which covered the walls, and on the huge carved chimney-pieces which rose almost to the ceilings; and the marble tables and the inlaid oak staircase still spoke of the former grandeur of the court. Mrs. Sally corresponded well with the date of her mansion, although she troubled herself little with its dignity. She was thoroughly of the old school, and had a most comfortable contempt for the new : rose at four in winter and summer, breakfasted at six, dined at eleven in the forenoon, supper at five, and was regularly in bed before eight, except when the hay-time or the harvest imperiously required her to sit up till sunset,—a necessity to which she submitted with no very good grace. To a deviation from these hours, and to the modern iniquities of white aprons, cotton stockings, and muslin handkerchiefs (Mrs. Sally herself always wore check, black worsted, and a sort of yellow compound which she was wont to call *susy*), together with the invention of drill-plough and thrashing-machines, and other agricultural novelties, she failed not to attribute all the mishaps or misdoings of the whole parish. The last-mentioned discovery especially aroused her indignation. Oh to hear her descant on the merits of the flail, wielded by a stout right arm, such as she had known in her youth (for by her account there was as great a deterioration in bones and sinews as in the other implements of husbandry), was enough to make the very inventor break his machine. She would even take up her favourite instrument, and thrash the air herself by way of illustrating her argument, and, to say truth, few men in these degenerate days could have matched the stout, brawny, muscular limb which Mrs. Sally displayed at sixty-five.

In spite of this contumacious rejection of agricultural improvements, the world went well with her at

Court Farm. A good landlord, an easy rent, incessant labour, unremitting frugality, and excellent times, insured a regular though moderate profit; and she lived on, grumbling and prospering, flourishing and complaining, till two misfortunes befell her at once—her father died, and her lease expired. The loss of her father, although a bedridden man, turned of ninety, who could not in the course of nature have been expected to live long, was a terrible shock to a daughter, who was not so much younger as to be without fears for her own life, and who had besides been so used to nursing the good old man, and looking to his little comforts, that she missed him as a mother would miss an ailing child. The expiration of the lease was a grievance and a puzzle of a different nature. Her landlord would have willingly retained his excellent tenant, but not on the terms on which she then held the land, which had not varied for fifty years; so that poor Mrs. Sally had the misfortune to find rent rising and prices sinking both at the same moment—a terrible solecism in political economy. Even this, however, I believe she would have endured, rather than have quitted the house where she was born, and to which all her ways and notions were adapted, had not a priggish steward, as much addicted to improvement and reform as she was to precedent and established usages, insisted on binding her by lease to spread a certain number of loads of chalk on every field. This tremendous innovation, for never had that novelty in manure whitened the crofts and pightles of Court Farm, decided her at once. She threw the proposals into the fire, and left the place in a week.

Her choice of a habitation occasioned some wonder, and much amusement in our village world. To be sure, upon the verge of seventy, an old maid may be permitted to dispense with the more rigid punctilio of her class, but Mrs. Sally had always been so tenacious on the score of character, so very a prude, so determined an avoider of the ' men folk ' (as she was wont contemptuously to call them), that we all were conscious of something like astonishment, on finding that she and her little handmaid had taken up their abode in one end of a spacious farmhouse belonging to the bluff old bachelor, George Robinson, of the Lea. Now Farmer Robinson was quite as notorious for his aversion to petticoated things, as Mrs. Sally for her hatred to the unfeathered bipeds who wear doublet and hose, so that there was a little astonishment in that quarter too, and plenty of jests, which the honest farmer speedily silenced, by telling all who joked on the subject that he had given his lodger fair warning, that, let people say what they would, he was quite determined not to marry her : so that if she had any views that way, it would be better for her to go elsewhere. This declaration, which must be admitted to have been more remarkable for frankness than civility, made, however, no ill impression on Mrs. Sally. To the farmer's she went, and at his house she lives still, with her little maid, her tabby cat, a decrepit sheep-dog, and much of the lumber of Court Farm, which she could not find in her heart to part from. There she follows her old ways and her old hours, untempted by matrimony, and unassailed (as far as I hear) by love or by scandal, with no other grievance than an occasional dearth of employment for herself and her young lass (even pewter dishes do not always want scouring), and now and then a twinge of the rheumatsim.

Here she is, that good relique of the olden time—for, in spite of her whims and prejudices, a better and a kinder woman never lived—here she is, with the hood of her red cloak pulled over her close black bonnet, of that silk which once (it may be presumed) was fashionable, since it is still called mode, and her whole stout figure huddled up in a miscellaneous and most substantial covering of thick petticoats, gowns, aprons, shawls and cloaks—a weight which it requires the strength of a thrasher to walk under—here she is, with her square honest visage, and her loud frank voice;—and we hold a pleasant disjointed chat of rheumatisms and early chickens, bad weather, and hats with feathers in them;—the last exceedingly sore subject being introduced by poor Jane Davis (a cousin of Mrs. Sally), who, passing us in a beaver bonnet, on her road from school, stopped to drop her little curtsy, and was soundly scolded for her civility. Jane, who is a gentle, humble, smiling lass, about twelve years old, receives so many rebukes from her worthy relative, and bears them so meekly, that I should not wonder if they were to be followed by a legacy: I sincerely wish they may. Well, at last we said good-bye; when, on inquiring my destination, and hearing that I was bent to the ten-acre copse (part of the farm which she ruled so long), she stopped me to tell a dismal story of two sheep-stealers who, sixty years ago, were found hidden in that copse, and only taken after great difficulty and resistance, and the maiming of a peace-officer.—' Pray don't go there, Miss! For mercy's sake don't be so venturesome! Think if they should kill you!' were the last words of Mrs. Sally.

ONCE A BEAUTY

OUR VILLAGE
Mary Russell Mitford

This rustic dwelling belongs to what used to be called in this part of the country 'a little bargain': thirty or forty acres, perhaps, of arable land, which the owner and his sons cultivated themselves, whilst the wife and daughters assisted in the husbandry, and eked out the slender earnings by the produce of the dairy, the poultry yard, and the orchard;—an order of cultivators now passing rapidly away, but in which much of the best part of the English character, its industry, its frugality, its sound sense, and its kindness might be found. Farmer Allen himself is an excellent specimen, the cheerful venerable old man with his long white hair, and his bright grey eye, and his wife is a still finer. They have had a hard struggle to win through the world and keep their little property undivided; but good management and good principles, and the assistance afforded them by an admirable son, who left our village a poor 'prentice boy, and is now a partner in a great house in London, have enabled them to overcome all the difficulties of these trying times, and they are now enjoying the peaceful evenings of a well-spent life as free from care and anxiety as their best friends could desire.

Ah! there is Mr. Allen in the orchard, the beautiful orchard, with its glorious gardens of pink and white, its pearly pear-blossoms and coral apple-buds. What a flush of bloom it is! How brightly delicate it appears, thrown into strong relief by the dark house and the weather-stained barn, in this soft evening light! The very grass is strewed with the snowy petals of the pear and the cherry. And there sits Mrs. Allen, feeding her poultry, with her three little grand-daughters from London, pretty fairies from three years old to five (only two-and-twenty months elapsed between the birth of the eldest and the youngest) playing round her feet.

Mrs. Allen, my dear Mrs. Allen, has been that rare thing a beauty, and although she be now an old woman I had almost said that she is so still. Why should I not say so? Nobleness of feature and sweetness of expression are surely as delightful in age as in youth. Her face and figure are much like those which are stamped indelibly on the memory of every one who ever saw that grand specimen of woman—Mrs. Siddons. The outline of Mrs. Allen's face is exactly the same; but there is more softness, more gentleness, a more feminine composure in the eye and in the smile. Miss Allen never played Lady Macbeth. Her hair, almost as black as at twenty, is parted on her large fair forehead, and combed under her exquisitely neat and snowy cap; a muslin neckerchief, a grey stuff gown and a white apron complete the picture.

A DAIRY WOMAN

OUR VILLAGE
Mary Russell Mitford

His young daughter, Hannah, a girl of twelve years old, was the eldest of the family, and had, ever since her mother's death, which event had occurred two or three years before, been accustomed to take the direction of their domestic concerns, to manage her two brothers, to feed the pigs and the poultry, and to keep house during the almost constant absence of her father. She was a quick, clever lass, of a high spirit, a firm temper, some pride, and a horror of accepting parochial relief, which is every day becoming rarer amongst the peasantry; but which forms the surest safeguard to the sturdy independence of the English character. Our little damsel possessed this quality in perfection; and when her father talked of giving up their comfortable cottage, and removing to the workhouse, whilst she and her brothers must go to service, Hannah formed a bold resolution, and without disturbing the sick man by any participation of her hopes and fears, proceeded after settling their trifling affairs to act at once on her own plans and designs.

Careless of the future as the poor drover had seemed, he had yet kept clear of debt, and by subscribing constantly to a benefit club, had secured a pittance that might at least assist in supporting him during the long years of sickness and helplessness to which he was doomed to look forward. This his daughter knew. She knew also, that the employer in whose service his health had suffered so severely, was a rich and liberal cattle-dealer in the neighbourhood, who would willingly aid an old and faithful servant, and had, indeed, come forward with offers of money. To assistance from such a quarter Hannah saw no objection. Farmer Oakley and the parish were quite distinct things. Of him, accordingly, she asked, not money, but something much in his own way—' a cow ! any cow ! old or lame, or what not, so that it were a cow ! she would be bound to keep it well ; if she did not, he might take it back again. She even hoped to pay for it by and by, by instalments, but that she would not promise !' and, partly amused, partly interested by the child's earnestness, the wealthy yeoman gave her, not as a purchase, but as a present, a very fine young Alderney. She then went to the lord of the manor, and, with equal knowledge of character, begged his permission to keep her cow on the Shaw Common. ' Farmer Oakley had given her a fine Alderney, and she would be bound to pay the rent, and keep her father off the parish, if he would only let it graze on the waste ; and he, too, half from real good nature—half, not to be outdone in liberality by his tenant, not only granted the requested permission, but reduced the rent so much, that the produce of the vine seldom fails to satisfy their kind landlord.

Now Hannah showed great judgment in setting up as a dairy-woman. She could not have chosen an occupation more completely unoccupied, or more loudly called for. One of the most provoking of the petty difficulties which beset people with a small establishment in this neighbourhood, is the trouble, almost the impossibility, of procuring the pastoral luxuries of milk, eggs and butter, which rank, unfortunately, amongst the indispensable necessaries of house-keeping. To your thoroughbred Londoner, who, whilst grumbling over his own breakfast, is apt to fancy that thick cream, and fresh butter, and new-laid eggs, grow, so to say, in the country—from an actual part of its natural produce—it may be some comfort to learn, that in this great grazing district, however the calves and the farmers may be the better for cows, nobody else is; that farmers' wives have ceased to keep poultry; and that we unlucky villagers sit down often to our first meal in a state of destitution, which may well make him content with his thin milk and his Cambridge butter, when compared to our imputed pastoralities.

Hannah's Alderney restored us to one rural privilege. Never was so cleanly a little milkmaid. She changed away some of the cottage finery, which, in his prosperous days, poor Jack had pleased himself with bringing home, the china tea-service, the gilded mugs, and the painted waiters, for the useful utensils of the dairy, and speedily established a regular and gainful trade in milk, eggs, butter, honey and poultry—for poultry they had always kept.

Her domestic management prospered equally. Her father, who retained the perfect use of his hands, began a manufacture of mats and baskets, which he constructed with great nicety and adroitness; the eldest boy, a sharp and clever lad, cut for him his rushes and osiers; erected, under his sister's direction, a shed for the cow, and enlarged and cultivated the garden (always with the good leave of her kind patron he lord of the manor) until it became so ample, that the produce not only kept the pig, and half kept the family, but afforded another branch of merchandise to the indefatigable directress of the establishment. For the younger boy, less quick and active, Hannah contrived to obtain an admission to the charity-school, where he made good progress—retaining him at home, however, in the hay-making and leasing season, or whenever his services could be made available, to the great annoyance of the schoolmaster, whose favourite he is, and who piques himself so much on George's scholarship (your heavy sluggish boy at country work often turns out quick at his book), that it is the general opinion that this much-vaunted pupil will, in process of time, be promoted to the post of assistant, and may, possibly, in course of years, rise to the dignity of a parish pedagogue in his own person; so that his sister, although still making him useful at odd times, now considers George as pretty well off her hands, whilst his elder brother, Tom, could take an under-gardener's place directly, if he were not too important at home to be spared even for a day.

"SIXPENCE A JOKE"

ESSAYS OF ELIA
Lamb

In those days, every Morning Paper, as an essential retainer to its establishment, kept an author, who was bound to furnish daily a quantum of witty paragraphs. Sixpence a joke—and it was thought pretty high too—was Dan Stuart's settled remuneration in these cases. The chat of the day—scandal, but, above all, *dress*—furnished the material. The length of no paragraph was to exceed seven lines. Shorter they might be, but they must be poignant.

A fashion of *flesh*, or rather *pink*-coloured hose for

the ladies, luckily coming up at the juncture when we were on our probation for the place of Chief Jester to S.'s Paper, established our reputation in that line. We were pronounced a 'capital hand.' O the conceits which we varied upon *red* in all its prismatic differences! from the trite and obvious flower of Cytherea, to the flaming costume of the lady that has her sitting upon 'many waters.' Then there was the collateral topic of ankles. What an occasion to a truly chaste writer, like ourself, of touching that nice brink, and yet never tumbling over it, of a seemingly ever approximating something 'not quite proper'; while, like a skilful posture-master, balancing betwixt decorums and their opposites, he keeps the line, from which a hair's-breadth deviation is destruction; hovering in the confines of light and darkness, or where 'both seem either'; a hazy uncertain delicacy; Autolycus-like in the Play, still putting off his expectant auditory with 'Whoop, do me no harm, good man!' But above all, that conceit arrided us most at the time, and still tickles our midriff to remember, where allusively to the flight of Astræa—*ultima Cœlestum terras reliquit*—we pronounced—in reference to the stockings still—that MODESTY, TAKING HER FINAL LEAVE OF MORTALS, HER LAST BLUSH WAS VISIBLE IN HER ASCENT TO THE HEAVENS BY THE TRACT OF THE GLOWING INSTEP. This might be called the crowning conceit; and was esteemed tolerable writing in those days.

But the fashion of jokes, with all other things, passes away; as did the transient mode which had so favoured us. The ankles of our fair friends in a few weeks began to reassume their whiteness, and left us scarce a leg to stand upon. Other female whims followed, but none, methought, so pregnant, so invitatory of shrewd conceits, and more than single meanings.

Somebody has said, that to swallow six cross-buns daily consecutively for a fortnight, would surfeit the stoutest digestion. But to have to furnish as many jokes daily, and that not for a fortnight, but for a long twelvemonth, as we were constrained to do, was a little harder exaction. ' Man goeth forth to his work until the evening '—from a reasonable hour in the morning, we presume it was meant. Now, as our main occupation took us from eight till five every day in the city; and as our evening hours, at that time of life, had generally to do with anything rather than business, it follows, that the only time we could spare for this manufactory of jokes—our supplementary livelihood, that supplied us in every want beyond mere bread and cheese—was exactly that part of the day which (as we have heard of No Man's Land) may be fitly denominated No Man's Time; that is, no time in which a man ought to be up, and awake, in. To speak more plainly, it is that time of an hour, or an hour and a half's duration, in which a man, whose occasions call him up so preposterously, has to wait for his breakfast.

O those head-aches at dawn of day, when at five, or half-past five in summer, and not much later in the dark seasons, we were compelled to rise, having been perhaps not above four hours in bed—(for we were no go-to-beds with the lamb, though we anticipated the lark ofttimes in her rising—we like a parting cup at midnight, as all young men did before these effeminate times, and to have our friends about us—we were not constellated under Aquarius that watery sign, and therefore incapable of Bacchus, cold, washy, bloodless—we were none of your Basilian watersponges, nor had taken our degrees at Mount Ague—we were right toping Capulets, jolly companions, we and they) —but to have to get up, as we said before, curtailed of half our fair sleep, fasting, with only a dim vista of refreshing bohea in the distance—to be necessitated to rouse ourselves at the detestable rap of an old hag of a domestic, who seemed to take a diabolical pleasure in her announcement that it was 'time to rise'; and whose chappy knuckles we have often yearned to amputate, and string them up at our chamber door, to be a terror to all such unseasonable rest-breakers in future——

'Facil,' and sweet, as Virgil sings, had been the 'descending' of the over-night, balmy the first sinking of the heavy head upon the pillow; but to get up, as he goes on to say,—revocare gradus, superasque evadere ad auras—and to get up, moreover, to make jokes with malice pretended—there was the 'labour,' there the 'work.'

No Egyptian taskmaster ever devised a slavery like to that, our slavery. No fractious operants ever turned out for half the tyranny which this necessity exercised upon us. Half a dozen jests in a day (bating Sundays too), why, it seems nothing! We make twice the number every day in our lives as a matter of course, and claim no Sabbatical exemptions. But then they come into our head. But when the head has to go out to them—when the mountain must go to Mahomet—

Reader try it for once, only for a short twelvemonth.

It was not every week that a fashion of pink stockings came up; but mostly, instead of it, some rugged untractable subject; some topic impossible to be contorted into the risible; some feature, upon which no smile could play; some flint, from which no process of ingenuity could procure a scintillation. There they lay; there your appointed tale of brick-making was set before you, which you must finish, with or without straw, as it happened. The craving dragon—*the Public*—like him in Bel's Temple—must be fed, it expected its daily rations; and Daniel, and ourselves, to do us justice, did the best we could on this side bursting him.

While we were wringing out coy sprightliness for the *Post*, and writhing under the toil of what is called ' easy writing,' Bob Allen, our *quondram* schoolfellow, was tapping his impracticable brains in a like service for the *Oracle*. Not that Robert troubled himself much about wit. If his paragraphs had a sprightly air about them, it was sufficient. He carried this non-chalance so far at last, that a matter of intelligence, and that no very important one, was not seldom palmed off upon his employers for a good jest; for example sake—' *Walking yesterday morning casually down Snow Hill, who should we meet but Mr. Deputy Humphreys! we rejoice to add that the worthy Deputy appeared to enjoy a good state of health. We do not remember ever to have seen him look better.*' This gentleman so surprisingly met upon Snow Hill, from some peculiarities in gait or gesture, was a constant butt for mirth to the small paragraph-mongers of the day; and our friend thought that he might have his fling at him with the rest. We met A. in Holborn shortly after this extraordinary rencounter, which he told with tears of satisfaction in his eyes, and chuckling at the anticipated effects of its announcement next day in the paper.

We did not quite comprehend where the wit of it lay at the time; nor was it easy to be detected, when the thing came out advantaged by type and letterpress. He had better have met anything that morning than a Common Council Man. His services were shortly after dispensed with, on the plea that his paragraphs of late had been deficient in point. The one in question, it must be owned, had an air, in the opening especially, proper to awaken curiosity; and the sentiment, or moral, wears the aspect of humanity and good neighbourly feeling. But somehow the conclusion was not judged altogether to answer to the magnificent promise of the premises. We traced our friend's pen afterwards in the *True Briton*, the *Star*, the *Traveller*—from all which he was successively dismissed, the Proprietors having 'no further occasion for his services.' Nothing was easier than to detect him. When wit failed, or topics ran low, there constantly appeared the following—'*It is not generally known that the three Blue Balls at the Pawnbrokers' shops are the ancient arms of Lombardy. The Lombards were the first money-brokers in Europe.*' Bob has done more to set the public right on this important point of blazonry, than the whole College of Heralds.

AN ASSEMBLY

PRIDE AND PREJUDICE
Jane Austen

A report soon followed, that Mr. Bingley was to bring twelve ladies and seven gentlemen with him to the assembly. The girls grieved over such a number of ladies, but were comforted the day before the ball by hearing, that instead of twelve he had brought only six with him from London,—his five sisters and a cousin. And when the party entered the assembly room it consisted only of five all together —Mr. Bingley, his two sisters, the husband of the eldest, and another young man.

Mr. Bingley was good-looking and gentlemanlike: he had a pleasant countenance, and easy, unaffected manners. His sisters were fine women, with an air of decided fashion. His brother-in-law, Mr. Hurst, merely looked the gentleman; but his friend Mr. Darcy soon drew the attention of the room by his fine, tall person, handsome features, noble mien, and the report which was in general circulation within

The Diversions

five minutes after his entrance, of his having ten thousand a year. The gentleman pronounced him to be a fine figure of a man, the ladies declared he was much handsomer than Mr. Bingley, and he was looked at with great admiration for about half the evening, till his manners gave a disgust which turned the tide of his popularity; for he was discovered to be proud, to be above his company, and above being pleased; and not all his large estate in Derbyshire could then save him from having a most forbidding, disagreeable countenance, and being unworthy to be compared with his friend.

Mr. Bingley had soon made himself acquainted with all the principal people in the room; he was lively and unreserved, danced every dance, was angry that the ball closed so early, and talked of giving one himself at Netherfield. Such amiable qualities must speak for themselves. What a contrast between him and his friend! Mr. Darcy danced only once with Mrs. Hurst and once with Miss Bingley, declined being introduced to any other lady, and spent the rest of the evening in walking about the room, speaking occasionally to one of his own party. His character was decided. He was the proudest, most disagreeable man in the world, and everybody hoped that he would never come there again.....

The evening altogether passed off pleasantly to the whole family. Mrs. Bennet had seen her eldest daughter much admired by the Netherfield party. Mr. Bingley had danced with her twice, and she had been distinguished by his sisters. Jane was as much gratified by this as her mother could be, though in a quieter way. Elisabeth felt Jane's pleasure. Mary had heard herself mentioned to Miss Bingley as the most accomplished girl in the neighbourhood; and Catherine and Lydia had been fortunate enough to

CARICATURE "RESTORATION DRESSES," 1789
From a print of the period.

be never without partners, which was all that they had yet learnt to care for at a ball. They returned, therefore, in good spirits to Longbourn, the village where they lived, and of which they were the principal inhabitants. They found Mr. Bennet still up. With a book he was regardless of time; and on the present occasion he had a good deal of curiosity as to the event of an evening which had raised such splendid expectations. He had rather hoped that all his wife's views on the stranger would be disappointed; but he soon found that he had a very different story to hear.

"Oh! my dear Mr. Bennet," as she entered the room, "we have had a most delightful evening, a most excellent ball. I wish you had been there. Jane was so admired, nothing could be like it. Everybody said how well she looked; and Mr. Bingley thought her quite beautiful, and danced with her twice! Only think of *that*, my dear; he danced with her twice! and she was the only creature in the room that he asked a second time. First of all, he asked Miss Lucas. I was so vexed to see him stand up with her! but however, he did not admire her at all; nobody can, you know; and he seemed quite struck with Jane as she was going down the dance. So he inquired who she was, and got introduced, and asked her for the two next. Then the two third he danced with Miss King, and the two fourth with Maria Lucas, and the two fifth with Jane again, and the two sixth with Lizzy, and the *Boulanger*."

"If he had had any compassion for *me*," cried her husband impatiently, "he would not have danced half so much! For God's sake, say no more of his partners. Oh that he had sprained his ankle in the first dance!"

A FÊTE

BELINDA
Maria Edgworth

'What a cursed unlucky overturn that was of yours, Lady Delacour, with those famous young horses! Why, what with this sprain, and this nervous business, you've not been able to stir out since the birthday, and you've missed the breakfast, and all that, at Frogmore—why, all the world stayed broiling in town on purpose for it, and you that had a card too—how damned provoking!'

'I regret extremely that my illness prevented me from being at this charming *fete*; I regret it more on Miss Portman's account than on my own,' said her ladyship. Belinda assured her that she felt no mortification from the disappointment.

'Oh, damme! but I would have driven you in my curricle,' said Sir Philip: 'it was the finest sight and best conducted I ever saw, and only wanted Miss Portman to make it complete. We had gipsies, and Mrs. Mills the actress for queen of the gipsies; and she gave us a famous good song, Rochfort, you know—and then there *was* two children upon an *ass*—damme, I don't know how they came there, for they're things one sees every day—and belonged only to two of the soldiers' wives—for we had the whole band of the Staffordshire playing at dinner, and we had some famous glees—and Fawcett gave us his laughing song, and then we had the launching of the ship, and only it was a boat, it would have been well enough—but damme, the song of Polly Oliver was worth the whole—except the Flemish Hercules, Ducrow, you know, dressed in light blue and silver, and—Miss Portman, I wish you had seen this—three great coach-wheels on his chin, and a ladder and two chairs and two children on them—and after that, he sported a musket and bayonet with the point of the bayonet on his chin—faith! that was really famous! But I forgot the Pyrrhic dance, Miss Portman, which was damned fine too—danced in boots and spurs by those Hungarian fellows—they jump and turn about, and clap their knees with their hands, and put themselves in all sorts of ways—and then we had that song of Polly Oliver, as I told you before, and Mrs. Mills gave us—no, no—it was a drummer of the Staffordshire dressed as a gipsy girl, gave us *The Cottage on the Moor*, the most charming thing, and would suit your voice. Miss Portman—damme, you'd sing it like an angel—But where was I ?— Oh, then they had tea—and fireplaces built of brick, out in the air—and then the entrance to the ballroom was all a colonnade done with lamps and flowers, and that sort of thing—and there was some *bon-mot* (but that was in the morning) amongst the gipsies about an orange and the stadtholder—and then there was a Turkish dance, and a Polonese dance, all very fine, but nothing to come up to the Pyrrhic touch, which was a great deal the most knowing, in boots and spurs—damme, now, I can't describe the thing to you, 'tis a cursed pity you weren't there, damme.'

Lady Delacour assured Sir Philip that she had been more entertained by the description than she could have been by the reality.—' Clarence, was not it the best description you ever heard ? But pray favour us with a *touch* of the Pyrrhic dance, Sir Philip.'

Lady Delacour spoke with such polite earnestness, and the baronet had so little penetration and so much conceit, that he did not suspect her of irony : he eagerly began to exhibit the Pyrrhic dance, but in such a manner that it was impossible for human gravity to withstand the sight—Rochfort laughed first, Lady Delacour followed him, and Clarence Harvey and Belinda could no longer restrain themselves.

WAGERS

BELINDA
Maria Edgworth

In his way to St. James's Street, where the wine-merchant lived, Sir Philip Baddely picked up several young men of his acquaintance, who were all eager to witness a trial of *taste*, of epicurean taste, between the baronet and Clarence Harvey. Amongst his other accomplishments our hero piqued himself upon the exquisite accuracy of his organs of taste. He neither loved wine, nor was he fond of eating; but at fine dinners, with young men who were real epicures, Harvey gave himself the airs of a connoisseur, and asserted superiority even in judging of wine and sauces. Harvey gained immortal honour at an entertainment by gravely protesting that some turtle would have been excellent if it had not been done *a bubble too much*, he presumed, elate as he was with the applauses of the company, to assert, that no man in England had a more correct taste than himself.—Sir Philip Baddely could not passively submit to this arrogance; he loudly proclaimed, that though he would not dispute Mr. Harvey's judgment as far as eating was concerned, yet he would defy him as a connoisseur in wines, and he offered to submit the competition to any eminent wine-merchant in London, and to some common friend of acknowledged taste and experience.—Mr. Rochfort was chosen as the common friend of acknowledged taste and experience; and a fashionable wine-merchant was pitched upon to decide with him the merits of these candidates for bacchanalian fame. Sir Philip, who was just going to furnish his cellars, was a person of importance to the wine-merchant, who produced accordingly his choicest treasures. Sir Philip and Clarence tasted of all in their turns; Sir Philip with real, and

Clarence with affected gravity; and they delivered their opinions of the positive and comparative merits of each. The wine-merchant evidently, as Mr. Harvey thought, leaned towards Sir Philip. ' Upon my word, Sir Philip, you are right—that wine is the best I have —you certainly have a most discriminating taste,' said the complaisant wine-merchant.

' I'll tell you what,' cried Sir Philip, ' the thing is this : by Jove ! now, there's no possibility now—no possibility now, by Jove ! of imposing upon me.'

' Then,' said Clarence Harvey, ' would you engage to tell the differences between these two wines ten times running, blindfold ?'

' Ten times ! that's nothing,' replied Sir Philip : ' yes, fifty times I would, by Jove !'

But when it came to the trial, Sir Philip had nothing left but oaths in his own favour. Clarence Harvey was victorious; and his sense of the importance of this victory was much increased by the fumes of the wine, which began to operate upon his brain. His triumph was, as he said it ought to be, bacchanalian : he laughed and sang anacreontic spirit, and finished by declaring that he deserved to be crowned with vine leaves.

' Dine with me, Clarence,' said Rochfort, and we'll crown you with three times three ; and,' whispered he to Sir Philip, ' we'll have another trial after dinner.'

' But as it's not near dinner-time yet—what shall we do with ourselves till dinner-time ?' said Sir Philip, yawning pathetically.

Clarence not being used to drink in a morning, though all his companions were, was much affected by the wine, and Rochfort proposed that they should take a turn in the park to cool Harvey's head. To Hyde Park they repaired ; Sir Philip boasting, all the way they walked, of the superior strength of his head. Clarence protested that his own was stronger than any man's in England, and observed, that at this instant he walked better than any person in company, Sir Philip Baddely not excepted. Now Sir Philip Baddely was a noted pedestrian, and he immediately challenged our hero to walk with him for any money he pleased. 'Done,' said Clarence, 'for ten guineas—for any money you please': and instantly they set out to walk, as Rochfort cried ' one, two, three, and away; keep the path, and whichever reaches that elm tree first has it.'

They were exactly even for some yards, then Clarence got ahead of Sir Philip and he reached the elm tree first; but, as he waved his hat, exclaiming, ' Clarence has won the day,' Sir Philip came up with his companions, and coolly informed him that he had lost his wager—' Lost! lost! lost! Clarence—fairly lost.'

' Didn't I reach the tree first?' said Clarence.

'Yes,' answered his companions; 'but you didn't keep the path. You turned out of the way when you met that crowd of children yonder.'

'Now *I*,' said Sir Philip, 'dashed fairly through them—kept the path, and won my bet.'

' But,' said Harvey, 'would you have had me run over that little child, who was stooping down just in my way?'

'*I*! not I,' said Sir Philip; ' but I would have you go through with your civility: if a man will be polite, he must pay for his politeness sometimes.—You said you'd lay me *any money* I pleased, recollect—now I'm very moderate—and as you are a particular friend, Clarence, I'll only take your ten guineas.'

A loud laugh from his companions provoked Clarence; they were glad to have a laugh against him, because he excited universal envy by the real superiority of his talents, and by his perpetually taking the lead in those trifles which were beneath his

CROPP'D LOUNGERS IN BOND STREET, 1791
The origin of the shingle. From a print of the period.

ambition, and exactly suited to engage the attention of his associates.

'Be it so, and welcome; I'll pay ten guineas for having better manners than any of you,' cried Harvey, laughing; 'but remember, though I've lost this bet, I don't give up my pedestrian fame—Sir Philip, there are no women to throw golden apples in my way now, and no children for me to stumble over: I dare you to another trial—double or quit.'

'I'm off, by Jove!' said Sir Philip. 'I'm too hot, damme, to walk with you any more—but I'm your man if you've a mind for a swim—here's the Serpentine river, Clarence—hey? damn it!—hey?'

Sir Philip and all his companions knew that Clarence had never learned to swim.

'You may wink at one another, as wisely as you please,' said Clarence, 'but come on, my boys—I *am* your man for a swim—a hundred guineas upon it!

> Darest thou, Rochfort, now
> Leap in with me into this weedy flood,
> And swim to yonder point?'

and instantly Harvey, who had in his confused head some recollection of an essay of Dr. Franklin on swimming, by which he fancied that he could ensure at once his safety and his fame, threw off his coat and jumped into the river—luckily he was not in boots. Rochfort, and all the other young men stood laughing by the river-side.

'Who the devil are these two that seem to be making up to us?' said Sir Philip, looking at two gentlemen who were coming towards them; 'St. George, hey? you know everybody.'

'The foremost is Percival, of Oakly Park, I think, 'pon my honour,' replied Mr. St. George, and then he began to settle how many thousands a year Mr. Percival was worth. This point was not decided when the gentlemen came up to the spot where Sir Philip was standing.

The child for whose sake Clarence Harvey had lost his bet was Mr. Percival's, and he came to thank him for his civility.—The gentleman who accompanied Mr. Percival was an old friend of Clarence Harvey's; he had met him abroad, but had not seen him for some years.

'Pray, gentlemen,' said he to Sir Philip and his party, 'is Mr. Clarence Harvey amongst you? I think I saw him pass by me just now.'

'Damn it, yes—where is Clary, though?' exclaimed Sir Philip suddenly recollecting himself—Clarence Harvey at this instant was drowning; he had got out of his depth, and had struggled in vain to recover himself.

'Curse me, if it's not all over with Clary,' continued Sir Philip. 'Do any of you see his head anywhere? Damn you, Rochfort, yonder it is.'

'Damme, so it is,' said Rochfort; 'but he's so heavy in his clothes, he'd pull me down along with him to Davy's locker;—damme, if I'll go after him.'

'Damn it, though, can't some of ye swim? Can't some of ye jump in?' cried Sir Philip, turning to his companions: 'damn it, Clarence will go to the bottom.'

And so he inevitably would have done, had not Mr. Percival at this instant leaped into the river, and seized hold of the drowning Clarence. It was with great difficulty that he dragged him to the shore.—Sir Philip's party, as soon as the danger was over, officiously offered their assistance. Clarence Harvey was absolutely senseless. 'Damn it, what shall we do with him now?' said Sir Philip; 'Damn it, we must call some of the people from the boat-house—he's as heavy as lead: damn me, if I know what to do with him.'

THE UPPER ROOMS, BATH

NORTHANGER ABBEY
Jane Austen

Mrs. Allen was so long in dressing that they did not enter the ball-room till late. The season was full the room crowded, and the two ladies squeezed in as well as they could. As for Mr. Allen, he repaired directly to the card-room, and left them to enjoy a mob by themselves. With more care for the safety of her new gown than for the comfort of her protegée, Mrs. Allen made her way through the throng of men by the door, as swiftly as the necessary caution would allow; Catherine, however, kept close at her side, and linked her arm too firmly within her friend's to be torn asunder by any common effort of a struggling assembly. But, to her utter amazement, she found that to proceed along the room was by no means the way to disengage themselves from the crowd; it seemed rather to increase as they went on; whereas she had imagined that, when once fairly within the door, they should easily find seats, and be able to watch the dances with perfect convenience. But this was far from being the case; and though by unwearied diligence they gained even the top of the room, their situation was just the same: they saw nothing of the dancers, but the high feathers of some of the ladies. Still they moved on: something better was yet in view; and by a continued exertion of strength and ingenuity, they found themselves at last in the passage behind the highest bench. Here there was something less of a crowd than below; and hence Miss Morland had a comprehensive view of all the company beneath her, and of all the dangers of her late passage through them. It was a splendid sight; and she began, for the first time that evening, to feel herself at a ball: she longed to dance, but she had not an acquaintance in the room. Mrs. Allen did all that she could do in such a case, by saying very placidly, every now and then, " I wish you could dance, my dear ; I wish you could get a partner." For some time her young friend felt obliged to her for these wishes, but they were repeated so often, and proved so totally ineffectual, that Catherine grew tired at laſt, and would thank her no more.

They were not long able, however, to enjoy the repose of the eminence they had so laboriously gained. Everybody was shortly in motion for tea, and they muſt squeeze out like the reſt. Catherine began to feel something of disappointment : she was tired of being continually pressed againſt by people, the generality of whose faces possessed nothing to interest, and with all of whom she was so totally unacquainted that she could not relieve the irksomeness of imprisonment by the exchange of a syllable with any of her fellow-captives ; and when at laſt arrived in the tea-room, she felt yet more the awkwardness of having no party to join, no acquaintance to claim, no gentleman to assiſt them. They saw nothing of Mr. Allen ; and after looking about them in vain for a more eligible situation, were obliged to sit down at the end of a table, at which a large party were already placed, without having anything to do there, or anybody to speak to, except each other.

Mrs. Allen congratulated herself, as soon as they were seated, on having preserved her gown from injury. " It would have been very shocking to have it torn," said she, " would not it ? It is such a delicate muslin. For my part, I have not seen anything I like so well in the whole room, I assure you."

" How uncomfortable it is," whispered Catherine, " not to have a single acquaintance here !"

" Yes, my dear," replied Mrs. Allen, with perfeƈt serenity, " it is very uncomfortable, indeed."

" What shall we do ? The gentlemen and ladies at this table look as if they wondered why we came here ; we seem forcing ourselves into their party."

" Ay, so we do. That is very disagreeable. I wish we had a large acquaintance here."

" I wish we had *any* ; it would be somebody to go to."

" Very true, my dear ; and if we knew any body, we would join them directly. The Skinners were here last year ; I wish they were here now."

" Had not we better go away as it is ? Here are no tea-things for us, you see."

" No more there are, indeed. How very provoking ! But I think we had better sit still, for one gets so tumbled in such a crowd. How is my head, my dear ? Somebody gave me a push that has hurt it, I am afraid."

" No, indeed, it looks very nice. But, dear Mrs. Allen, are you sure there is nobody you know in all this multitude of people ? I think you *must* know somebody."

" I don't, upon my word ; I wish I did. I wish I had a large acquaintance here with all my heart, and then I should get you a partner. I should be so glad to have you dance. There goes a strange-looking woman ! What an odd gown she has got on ! How old-fashioned it is ! Look at the back."

After some time they received an offer of tea from one of their neighbours ; it was thankfully accepted, and this introduced a light conversation with the gentleman who offered it, which was the only time that anybody spoke to them during the evening, till they were discovered and joined by Mr. Allen when the dance was over.

" Well, Miss Morland," said he directly, " I hope you have had an agreeable ball."

" Very agreeable, indeed," she replied, vainly endeavouring to hide a great yawn.

"I wish she had been able to dance," said his wife; "I wish we could have got a partner for her. I have been saying how glad I should be if the Skinners were here this winter instead of last; or if the Parrys had come, as they talked of once, she might have danced with George Parry. I am sorry she has not had a partner."

"We shall do better another evening, I hope," was Mr. Allen's consolation.

The company began to disperse when the dancing was over: enough to leave space for the remainder to walk about in some comfort; and now was the time for a heroine, who had not yet played a very distinguished part in the events of the evening, to be noticed and admired. Every five minutes, by removing some of the crowd, gave greater openings for her charms. She was now seen by many young men who had not been near her before. Not one, however, started with rapturous wonder on beholding her, no whisper of eager inquiry ran round the room, nor was she once called a divinity by anybody. Yet Catherine was in very good looks, and, had the company only seen her three years before, they would *now* have thought her exceedingly handsome.

She *was* looked at, however, and with some admiration; for, in her own hearing, two gentlemen pronounced her to be a pretty girl. Such words had their due effect: she immediately thought the evening pleasanter than she had found it before; her humble vanity was contented; she felt more obliged to the two young men for this simple praise, than a true quality heroine would have been for fifteen sonnets in celebration of her charms, and went to her chair in good humour with everybody, and perfectly satisfied with her share of public attention.

CHAPTER VI

THE NINETEENTH CENTURY—II

AN OLD BEAU

PENDENNIS
Thackeray

ONE fine morning in the full London season, Major Arthur Pendennis came over from his lodgings, according to his custom, to breakfast at a certain Club in Pall Mall, of which he was a chief ornament... At a quarter past ten the Major invariably made his appearance in the best blacked boots in all London, with a checked morning cravat that never was rumpled until dinner-time, a buff waistcoat which bore the crown of his sovereign on the buttons, and linen so spotless that Mr. Brummel himself asked the name of his laundress, and would probably have employed her had not misfortunes compelled that great man to fly the country. Pendennis's coat, his white gloves, his whiskers, his very cane, were perfect of their kind as specimens of the costume of a military man *en retraite*. At a distance, or seeing his back merely, you would have taken him to be not more than thirty years old: it was only by a nearer inspection that you saw the factitious nature of his rich brown hair, and that there were a few crow's-feet round about the somewhat faded eyes of his handsome mottled face. His nose was of the Wellington pattern. His hands and wristbands were beautifully long and white. On the

In Society

latter he wore handsome gold buttons given to him by his Royal Highness the Duke of York, and on the others more than one elegant ring, the chief and largest of them being emblazoned with the famous arms of Pendennis.

He always took possession of the same table in the same corner of the room, from which nobody ever now thought of ousting him. One or two mad wags and wild fellows had, in former days, and in freak or bravado, endeavoured twice or thrice to deprive him of this place; but there was a quiet dignity in the Major's manner as he took his seat at the next table, and surveyed the interlopers, which rendered it impossible for any man to sit and breakfast under his eye; and that table—by the fire, and yet near the window—became his own. His letters were laid out there in expectation of his arrival, and many was the young fellow about town who looked with wonder at the number of those notes, and at the seals and franks which they bore. If there was any question about etiquette, society, who was married to whom, of what age such and such a duke was, Pendennis was the man to whom every one appealed. Marchionesses used to drive up to the Club, and leave notes for him, or fetch him out. He was perfectly affable. The young men liked to walk with him in the Park or down Pall Mall; for he touched his hat to everybody, and every other man he met was a lord.

The Major sate down at his accustomed table then, and while the waiters went to bring him his toast and his hot newspaper, he surveyed his letters through his gold double eye-glass—he carried it so gaily, you would hardly have known it was spectacles in disguise, and examined one pretty note after another, and laid them by in order. There were large solemn dinner cards, suggestive of three courses and heavy conversation; there were neat little confidential notes, conveying female entreaties; there was a note on thick official paper from the Marquis of Steyne, telling him to come to Richmond to a little party at the Star and Garter, and speak French, which language the Major possessed very perfectly; and another from the Bishop of Ealing and Mrs. Trail, requesting the honour of Major Pendennis's company at Ealing House, all of which letters Pendennis read gracefully, and with the more satisfaction, because Glowry, the Scotch surgeon breakfasting opposite to him, was looking on, and hating him for having so many invitations, which nobody ever sent to Glowry.

These perused, the Major took out his pocket-book to see on what days he was disengaged, and which of these many hospitable calls he could afford to accept or decline.

He threw over Cutler, the East India Director, in Baker Street, in order to dine with Lord Steyne and the little French party at the Star and Garter—the Bishop he accepted, because, though the dinner was slow, he liked to dine with bishops—and so went through his list and disposed of them according to his fancy or interest. Then he took his breakfast and looked over the paper, the gazette, and the births and deaths, and the fashionable intelligence, to see that his name was down among the guests at my Lord So-and-so's fête, and in the intervals of these occupations carried on cheerful conversation with his acquaintances about the room.

—AND HIS "TOILET"

PENDENNIS
Thackeray

The London season was now blooming in its full vigour, and the fashionable newspapers abounded with information regarding the grand banquets, routs, and balls which were enlivening the polite world. Our gracious Sovereign was holding levees and drawing-rooms at St. James's: the bow-windows of the clubs were crowded with the heads of respectable red-faced newspaper-reading gentlemen: along the Serpentine trailed thousands of carriages: squadrons of dandy horsemen trampled over Rotten Row: everybody was in town in a word; and of course Major Arthur Pendennis, who was somebody, was not absent.

With his head tied up in a smart bandanna handkerchief, and his meagre carcass enveloped in a brilliant Turkish dressing-gown, the worthy gentlemen sate on a certain morning by his fireside, letting his feet gently simmer in a bath, whilst he took his early cup of tea, and perused his *Morning Post*. He could not have faced the day without his two hours' toilet, without his early cup of tea, without his *Morning Post*. I suppose nobody in the world except Morgan, not even Morgan's master himself, knew how feeble and ancient the Major was growing, and what numberless little comforts he required.

If men sneer, as our habit is, at the artifices of an old beauty, at her paint, perfumes, ringlets; at those innumerable, and to us unknown, stratagems with which she is said to remedy the ravages of time and reconstruct the charms whereof years have bereft her; the ladies, it is to be presumed, are not on their side altogether ignorant that men are vain as well as they, and that the toilets of old bucks are to the full as elaborate as their own. How is it that old Blushington keeps that constant little rose-tint on his cheeks; and where does old Blondel get the preparation which makes his silver hair pass for golden? Have you ever seen Lord Hotspur get off his horse when he thinks nobody is looking? Taken out of his stirrups, his shiny boots can hardly totter up the steps of Hotspur House. He is a dashing young nobleman still as you see the back of him in Rotten Row: when you behold him on foot, what an old, old fellow! Did you ever form to yourself any idea of Dick Lacy (Dick has been Dick these sixty years) in a natural state, and without his stays? All these men are objects whom the observer of human life and manners may contemplate with as much profit as the most elderly Belgravian Venus, or inveterate Mayfair Jezebel. An old reprobate daddy-longlegs, who has never said his prayers (except perhaps in public) these fifty years: an old buck who still clings to as many of the habits of youth as his feeble grasp of health can hold by: who has given up the bottle, but sits with young fellows over it, and tells naughty stories upon toast-and-water—who has given up beauty, but still talks about it as wickedly as the youngest *roué* in company—such an old fellow, I say, if any parson in Pimlico or St. James's were to order the beadles to bring him into the middle aisle, and there set him in an arm-chair, and make a text of him, and preach about him to the congregation, could be turned to a wholesome use for once in his life, and might be surprised to find that some good thoughts came out of him. But we are wandering from our text, the honest Major, who sits all this while with his feet cooling in the bath: Morgan takes them out of that place of purification, and dries them daintily, and proceeds to set the old gentleman on his legs, with waistband and wig, starched cravat, and spotless boots and gloves.

"A NEW GENERATION"

PENDENNIS
Thackeray

As became a man of fashion, Major Pendennis spent the autumn passing from house to house of such country friends as were at home to receive him, and if the Duke happened to be abroad, or the Marquis in Scotland, condescending to sojourn with Sir John or the plain Squire. To say the truth, the old gentleman's reputation was somewhat on the wane: many of the men of his time had died out, and the occupants of their halls and the present wearers of their titles knew not Major Pendennis; and little cared for his traditions of 'the wild Prince and Poins,' and the heroes of fashion passed away. It must have struck the good man with melancholy as he walked by many a London door, to think how seldom it was now opened for him, and how often he used to knock at it—to what banquets and welcome he used to pass through it—a score of years back. He began to own that he was no longer of the present age, and dimly to apprehend that the young men laughed at him. Such melancholy musings must come across many a Pall Mall philosopher. The men, thinks he, are not such as they used to be in his time: the old grand manner and courtly grace of life are gone: what is Castlewood House and the present Castlewood compared to the magnificence of the old mansion and owner? The late lord came to London with four post-chaises and sixteen horses; all the North Road hurried out to look at his cavalcade: het people in London streets even stopped as his procession passed them. The present lord travels with five bagmen in a railway carriage, and sneaks away from the station, smoking a cigar in a brougham. The late lord in autumn filled Castlewood with company, who drank claret till midnight: the present man buries himself in a hut on a Scotch mountain, and passes November in two or three closets in an *entresol* at Paris, where his amusements are a dinner at a *café* and a box at a little theatre. What a contrast there is between *his* Lady Lorraine, the Regent's Lady Lorraine, and her little Ladyship of the present era! He figures to himself the first, beautiful, gorgeous, magnificent in diamonds and velvets, daring in rouge, the wits of the world (the old wits, the old polished gentlemen—not the *canaille* of to-day with their language of the cabstand, and their coats smelling of smoke) bowing at her feet; and then thinks of to-day's Lady Lorraine —a little woman in a black silk gown, like a governess, who talks astronomy, and labouring classes, and emigration, and the deuce knows what, and lurks to church at eight o'clock in the morning. Abbots-Lorraine, that used to be the noblest house in the county, is turned into a monastery—a regular La Trappe. They don't drink two glasses of wine after dinner, and every other man at table is a country curate, with a white neckcloth, whose talk is about Polly Higson's progress at school, or Widow Watkins' lumbago. " And the other young men, those lounging guardsmen and great lazy dandies—sprawling over sofas and billiard-tables, and stealing off to smoke pipes in each other's bedrooms, caring for nothing, reverencing nothing, not even an old gentleman who has known their fathers and their betters, not even a pretty woman—what a difference there is between these men, who poison the very turnips and stubble-fields with their tobacco, and the gentlemen of our time!" thinks the Major; " the breed is gone—there's no use for 'em; they're replaced by a parcel of damned cotton-spinners and utilitarians, and young sprigs of parsons with their hair combed down their backs. I'm getting old: they're getting past me: they laugh at us old boys," thought old Pendennis. And he was not far wrong; the times and manners which he admired were pretty nearly gone—the gay young men "larked" him irreverently, whilst the serious youth had a grave pity and wonder at him, which would have been even more painful to bear, had the old gentleman been aware of its extent. But he was rather simple; his examination of moral questions had never been very deep; it had never struck him, perhaps, until very lately, that he was otherwise than a most respectable and rather fortunate man. Is there no old age but his without reverence? Did youthful folly never jeer at other bald pates? For the past two or three years, he had begun to perceive that his day was well-nigh over, and that the men of the new time had begun to reign.

After a rather unsuccessful autumn season, then, during which he was faithfully followed by Mr. Morgan, his nephew Arthur being engaged, as we have seen, at Clavering, it happened that Major Pendennis came back for a while to London, at the dismal end of October, when the fogs and lawyers come to town. Who has not looked with interest at those loaded cabs, piled boxes, and crowded children, rattling through the streets on the dun October evenings; stopping at the dark houses, where they discharge nurse and infant, girls, matron and father, whose holidays are over? Yesterday it was France and sunshine, or Broadstairs and liberty; to-day comes work and a yellow fog; and, ye gods! what a heap of bills there lies in Master's study. And the clerk has brought the lawyer's papers from Chambers; and in half-an-hour the literary man knows that the printer's boy will be in the passage: and Mr. Smith with that little account (that particular little account) has called presentient of your arrival, and has left word that he will call to-morrow morning at ten. Who amongst us has not said good-bye to his holiday; returned to dun London, and his fate; surveyed his labours and liabilities laid out before him, and been aware of that inevitable little account to settle? Smith and his little account in the morning, symbolise duty, difficulty, struggle, which you will meet, let us hope, friend, with a manly and honest heart.—And you think of him, as the children are slumbering once more in their own beds, and the watchful housewife tenderly pretends to sleep.

A COMPANION

VANITY FAIR
Thackeray

An article as necessary to a lady in this position as her brougham or her bouquet, is her companion. I have always admired the way in which the tender creatures, who cannot exist without sympathy, hire an exceedingly plain friend of their own sex from whom they are almost inseparable. The sight of that inevitable woman in her faded gown seated behind her dear friend in the opera-box, or occupying the back seat of the barouche, is always a wholesome and moral one to me, as jolly a reminder as that of the death's-head which figured in the repasts of Egyptian *bon-vivants*, a strange sardonic memorial of Vanity Fair. What?—even battered, brazen, beautiful, conscienceless, heartless Mrs. Firebrace, whose father died of her shame: even lovely, daring Mrs. Mantrap, who will ride at any fence which any man in England will take, and who drives her grays in the Park, while her mother keeps a huxter's shop in Bath still—even those who are so bold, one might fancy they could face anything, dare not face the world without a female friend. They must have somebody to cling to, the affectionate creatures ! And you will hardly see them in any public place without a shabby companion in a dyed silk, sitting somewhere in the shade close behind them.

"Rawdon," said Becky, very late one night as a party of gentlemen were seated round the crackling drawing-room fire (for the men came to her house to finish the night; and she had ice and coffee for them, the best in London) "I must have a sheep-dog."

"A what?" said Rawdon, looking up from an *écarté* table.

"A sheep-dog," said young Lord Southdown. "My dear Mrs. Crawley, what a fancy! Why not have a Danish dog? I know of one as big as a camel-leopard, by Jove. It would almost pull your brougham. Or a Persian greyhound, eh? (I propose, if you please;) or a little pug that would go into one of Lord Steyne's snuff-boxes? There's a man at Bayswater got one with such a nose that you might—I mark the King and play—that you might hang your hat on it."

"I mark the trick," Rawdon gravely said. He attended to his game commonly, and didn't much meddle with the conversation except when it was about horses and betting.

"What *can* you want with a shepherd's-dog?" the lively little Southdown continued.

"I mean a *moral* shepherd's-dog," said Becky, laughing and looking up at Lord Steyne.

"What the devil's that?" said his lordship.

"A dog to keep the wolves off me," Rebecca continued. "A companion."

"Dear little innocent lamb, you want one," said the marquis; and his jaw thrust out, and he began to grin hideously, his little eyes leering towards Rebecca.

The great Lord of Steyne was standing by the fire sipping coffee. The fire crackled and blazed pleasantly. There was a score of candles sparkling round the mantelpiece, in all sorts of quaint sconces, of gilt

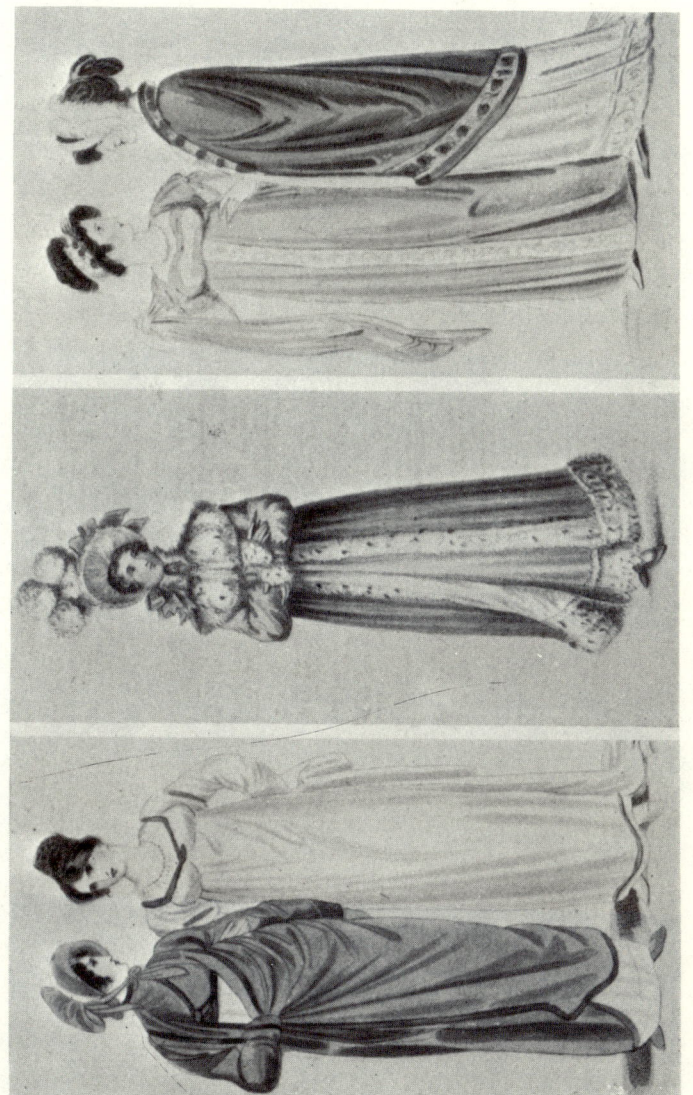

LADIES' DRESSES, 1816
From the *Lady's Magazine*.

and bronze and porcelain. They lighted up Rebecca's figure to admiration, as she sat on a sofa covered with a pattern of gaudy flowers. She was in a pink dress, that looked as fresh as a rose; her dazzling white arms and shoulders were half covered with a thin hazy scarf through which they sparkled; her hair hung in curls round her neck; one of her little feet peeped out from the fresh crisp folds of the silk; the prettiest little foot in the prettiest little sandal in the finest silk stocking in the world.

The candles lighted up Lord Steyne's shining bald head, which was fringed with red hair. He had thick, bushy eyebrows, with little twinkling, bloodshot eyes, surrounded by a thousand wrinkles. His jaw was underhung, and when he laughed, two white back-teeth protruded themselves and glistened savagely in the midst of the grin. He had been dining with royal personages, and wore his garter and ribbons. A short man was his lordship, broad-chested, and bow-legged, but proud of the firmness of his foot and ankle, and always caressing his garter-knee.

" And so the shepherd is not enough," said he, " to defend his lambkin ?"

" The shepherd is too fond of playing at cards and going to his clubs," answered Becky laughing.

" Gad, what a debauched Corydon !" said my lord— " what a mouth for a pipe !"

" I take your three to two," here said Rawdon, at the card-table.

" Hark at Melibœus," snarled the noble marquis: " he's pastorally occupied too : he's shearing a South-down. What an innocent mutton, hey ? Damme, what a snowy fleece !"

Rebecca's eyes shot out gleams of scornful humour. " My lord," she said, " you are a Knight of the order." He had the collar round his neck, indeed—a gift of the restored Princes of Spain.

BELOW STAIRS

PICKWICK PAPERS
Dickens

By this time they had reached a small greengrocer's shop, which Mr. John Smauker entered, followed by Sam: who, the moment he got behind him, relapsed into a series of the very broadest and most unmitigated grins, and manifested other demonstrations of being in a highly enviable state of inward merriment.

Crossing the greengrocer's shop, and putting their hats on the stairs in the little passage behind it, they walked into a small parlour; and here the full splendour of the scene burst upon Mr. Weller's view.

A couple of tables were put together in the middle of the parlour, covered with three or four cloths of different ages and dates of washing, arranged to look as much like one as the circumstances of the case would allow. Upon these were laid knives and forks for six or eight people. Some of the knife handles were green, others red, and a few yellow; and as all the forks were black, the combination of colours was exceedingly striking. Plates for a corresponding number of guests were warming behind the fender; and the guests themselves were warming before it: the chief and most important of whom appeared to be a stoutish gentleman in a bright crimson coat with long tails, vividly red breeches, and a cocked hat, who was standing with his back to the fire, and had apparently just entered, for besides retaining his cocked hat on his head, he carried in his hand a high stick, such as gentlemen of his profession usually elevate in a sloping position over the roofs of carriages.

"Smauker, my lad, your fin," said the gentleman with the cocked hat.

Mr. Smauker dovetailed the top joint of his right hand little finger into that of the gentleman with the cocked hat, and said he was charmed to see him looking so well.

"Well, they tell me I am looking pretty blooming," said the man with the cocked hat, "and it's a wonder, too. I've been following our old woman about, two hours a-day, for the last fortnight; and if a constant contemplation of the manner in which she hooks-and-eyes that infernal lavender coloured old gown of hers behind, isn't enough to throw anybody into a low state of despondency for life, stop my quarter's salary."

At this, the assembled selections laughed very heartily; and one gentleman in a yellow waistcoat, with a coach trimming border, whispered a neighbour in green-foil smalls, that Tuckle was in spirits to-night.

"By the bye," said Mr. Tuckle, "Smauker, my boy, you—" The remainder of the sentence was forwarded into Mr. John Smauker's ear, by whisper.

"Oh, dear me, I quite forgot," said Mr. John Smauker. "Gentlemen, my friend Mr. Weller."

"Sorry to keep the fire off you, Weller," said Mr. Tuckle with a familiar nod. "Hope you're not cold, Weller."

"Not by no means, Blazes," replied Sam. "It 'ud be a wery chilly subject as felt cold wen you stood opposit. You'd save coals if they put you behind the fender in the waitin' room at a public office, you would."

As this retort appeared to convey rather a personal illusion to Mr. Tuckle's crimson livery, that gentleman looked majestic for a few seconds, but gradually edging away from the fire, broke into a forced smile, and said it wasn't bad.

"Very much obliged for your good opinion, sir," replied Sam. "We shall get on by degrees, I des-say. We'll try a better one, bye-and-bye."

At this point the conversation was interrupted by

the arrival of a gentleman in orange-coloured plush, accompanied by another selection in purple cloth, with a great extent of stocking. The new-comers having been welcomed by the old ones, Mr. Tuckle put the question that supper be ordered in, which was carried unanimously.

The greengrocer and his wife then arranged upon the table a boiled leg of mutton, hot, with caper sauce, turnips, and potatoes. Mr. Tuckle took the chair, and was supported at the other end of the board by the gentleman in orange plush. The greengrocer put on a pair of wash-leather gloves to hand the plates with, and stationed himself behind Mr. Tuckle's chair.

"Harris," said Mr. Tuckle, in a commanding tone.

"Sir," said the greengrocer.

"Have you got your gloves on?"

"Yes, sir."

"Then take the kiver off."

"Yes, sir."

The greengrocer did as he was told, with a show of great humility, and obsequiously handed Mr. Tuckle the carving knife; in doing which, he accidentally gaped.

"What do you mean by that, sir?" said Mr. Tuckle, with great asperity.

"I beg your pardon, sir," replied the crest-fallen greengrocer, "I didn't mean to do it, sir; I was up very late last night, sir."

"I tell you what my opinion of you is, Harris," said Mr. Tuckle with a most impressive air, "you're a wulgar beast."

"I hope, gentlemen," said Harris, "that you won't be severe with me, gentlemen. I'm very much obliged to you indeed, gentlemen, for your patronage, and also for your recommendations, gentlemen, whenever additional assistance in waiting is required. I hope, gentlemen, I give satisfaction."

"No, you don't, sir," said Mr. Tuckle. "Very far from it, sir."

"We consider you an inattentive reskel," said the gentleman in the orange plush.

"And a low thief," added the gentleman in the green-foil smalls.

"And an unreclaimable blaygaird," added the gentleman in purple.

The poor greengrocer bowed very humbly while these little epithets were bestowed upon him, in the true spirit of the very smallest tyranny; and when everybody had said something to show his superiority, Mr. Tuckle proceeded to carve the leg of mutton, and to help the company.

This important business of the evening had hardly commenced, when the door was thrown briskly open, and another gentleman in a light-blue suit, and leaden buttons, made his appearance.

"Against the rules," said Mr. Tuckle. "Too late, too late."

"No, no; positively I couldn't help it," said the gentleman in blue. "I appeal to the company. An affair of gallantry now, an appointment at the theayter."

"Oh, that indeed," said the gentleman in the orange plush.

"Yes; raly now, honour bright," said the man in blue. "I made a promese to fetch our youngest daughter at half-past ten, and she is such an uncauminly fine gal, that I raly hadn't the 'art to disappoint her. No offence to the present company, sir, but a petticut, sir, is irrevokeable."

"I begin to suspect there's something in that quarter," said Tuckle, as the new-comer took his seat next Sam. "I've remarked, once or twice, that she leans very heavy on your shoulder when she gets in and out of the carriage."

"Oh, raly, raly, Tuckle, you shouldn't," said the

man in blue. " It's not fair. I may have said to one or two friends that she was a very divine creechure, and had refused one or two offers without any hobvus cause, but—no, no, no, indeed, Tuckle—before strangers, too—it's not right—you shouldn't. Delicacy, my dear friend, delicacy!" And the man in blue, pulling up his neckerchief, and adjusting his coat cuffs, nodded and frowned as if there were more behind, which he could say if he liked, but was bound in honour to suppress.

The man in blue being a light-haired, stiff-necked, free and easy sort of footman, with a swaggering air and pert face, had attracted Mr. Weller's especial attention at first, but when he began to come out in this way, Sam felt more than ever disposed to cultivate his acquaintance; so he launched himself into the conversation at once, with characteristic independence.

"Your health, sir," said Sam. "I like your conwersation much. I think it's wery pretty."

At this the man in blue smiled, as if it were a compliment he was well used to; but looked approvingly on Sam at the same time, and said he hoped he should be better acquainted with him, for without any flattery at all he seemed to have the makings of a very nice fellow about him, and to be just the man after his own heart.

"You're wery good, sir," said Sam. "What a lucky feller you are!"

"How do you mean?" inquired the gentleman in blue.

"That 'ere young lady," replied Sam. "She knows wot's wot, she does. Ah! I see." Mr. Weller closed one eye, and shook his head from side to side, in a manner which was highly gratifying to the personal vanity of the gentleman in blue.

"I'm afraid you're a cunning fellow, Mr. Weller," said that individual.

"No, no," said Sam. "I leave all that 'ere to you. It's a great deal more in your way than mine, as the gen'l'm'n on the right side o' the garden vall said to the man on the wrong 'un, ven the mad bull wos a comin' up the lane."

"Well, well, Mr. Weller," said the gentleman in blue, "I think she has remarked my air and manner, Mr. Weller."

"I should think she couldn't wery well be off o' that," said Sam.

"Have you any little thing of that kind in hand, sir?" inquired the favoured gentleman in blue, drawing a toothpick from his waistcoat pocket.

"Not exactly," said Sam. "There's no daughters at my place, else o' course I should ha' made up to vun of 'em. As it is, I don't think I can do anythin' under a female markis. I might take up with a young 'ooman o' large property as hadn't a title, if she made wery fierce love to me. Not else."

"Of course not, Mr. Weller," said the gentleman in blue, "one can't be troubled, you know; and *we* know, Mr. Weller—we, who are men of the world—that a good uniform must work its way with the women, sooner or later. In fact, that's the only thing, between you and me, that makes the service worth entering into."

"Just so," said Sam. "That's it, o'course."

When this confidential dialogue had gone thus far, glasses were placed round, and every gentleman ordered what he liked best, before the public-house shut up. The gentleman in blue, and the man in orange, who were the chief exquisites of the party, ordered "cold srub and water," but with the others, gin and water, sweet, appeared to be the favourite beverage. Sam called the greengrocer a "desp'rate willin," and ordered a large bowl of punch; two circumstances which seemed to raise him very much in the opinion of the selections.

"Gentlemen," said the man in blue, with an air of the most consummate dandyism, "I'll give you the ladies; come."

"Hear, hear!" said Sam. "The young mississes."

Here there was a loud cry of "Order," and Mr John Smauker, as the gentleman who had introduced Mr. Weller into that company, begged to inform him that the word he had just made use of, was unparliamentary.

"Which word was that 'ere, sir?" inquired Sam.

"Missesses, sir," replied Mr. John Smauker, with an alarming frown.

"We don't recognise such distinctions here."

"Oh, wery good," Sam said; "then I'll amend the observation, and call them the dear creeturs, if Blazes vill allow me."

Some doubt appeared to exist in the mind of the gentleman in the greenfoil smalls, whether the chairman could be legally appealed to, as "Blazes," but as the company seemed more disposed to stand upon their own rights than his, the question was not raised. The man with the cocked hat breathed short, and looked long at Sam, but apparently thought it as well to say nothing, in case he should get the worst of it.

After a short silence, a gentleman in an embroidered coat reaching down to his heels, and a waistcoat of the same which kept one half of his legs warm, stirred his gin and water with great energy, and putting himself upon his feet, all at once, by a violent effort, said he was desirous of offering a few remarks to the company: whereupon the person in the cocked hat, had no doubt that the company would be very happy to hear any remarks that the man in the long coat might wish to offer.

"I feel a great delicacy, gentlemen, in coming forard," said the man in the long coat, "having the misforchune to be a coachman, and being only admitted as a honorary member of these agreeable swarrys, but I do feel myself bound, gentlemen—drove into a corner, if I may use the expression—to make known an afflicting circumstance which has come to my knowledge; which has happened I may say within the soap of my every day contemplation. Gentlemen, our friend Mr. Whiffers (everybody looked at the individual in orange), our friend Mr. Whiffers has resigned."

Universal astonishment fell upon the hearers. Each gentleman looked in his neighbour's face, and then transferred his glance to the upstanding coachman.

"You may well be sapparised, gentlemen," said the coachman. "I will not wenchure to state the reasons of this irrepairabel loss to the service, but I will beg Mr. Whiffers to state them himself, for the improvement and imitation of his admiring friends."

The suggestion being loudly approved of, Mr. Whiffers explained. He said he certainly could have wished to have continued to hold the appointment he had just resigned. The uniform was extremely rich and expensive, the females of the family was most agreeable, and the duties of the situation was not, he was bound to say, too heavy; the principal service that was required of him, being, that he should look out the hall window as much as possible, in company with another gentleman, who had also resigned. He could have wished to have spared that company the painful and disgusting detail on which he was about to enter, but as the explanation had been demanded of him, he had no alternative but to state, boldly and distinctly, that he had been required to eat cold meat.

It is impossible to conceive the disgust which this

avowal awakened in the bosoms of the hearers. Loud cries of " Shame !" mingled with groans and hisses, prevailed for a quarter of an hour.

DINNERS IN HALL
PENDENNIS
Thackeray

The Professions A long morning's reading, a walk in the park, a pull on the river, a stretch up the hill to Hampstead, and a modest tavern dinner ; a bachelor night passed here or there, in joviality, not vice (for Arthur Pendennis admired women so heartily that he could never bear the society of any of them that were not, in his fancy at least, good and pure) ; a quiet evening at home, alone with a friend and a pipe or two, and a humble potation of British spirits, whereof Mrs. Flanagan, the laundress, invariably tested the quality,—these were our young gentleman's pursuits, and it must be owned that his life was not unpleasant. In term-time, Mr. Pen showed a most praiseworthy regularity in performing one part of the law-student's course of duty, and eating his dinners in Hall. Indeed, that Hall of the Upper Temple is a sight not uninteresting, and with the exception of some trifling improvements and anachronisms which have been introduced into the practice there, a man may sit down and fancy that he joins in a meal of the seventeenth century. The bar have their messes, the students their tables apart ; the benchers sit at the high table on the raised platform, surrounded by pictures of judges of the law and portraits of royal personages who have honoured its festivities with their presence and patronage. Pen looked about, on his first introduction, not a little amused with the scene which he witnessed. Among his comrades of the student class there were gentlemen of all ages, from sixty to seventeen; stout greyheaded attorneys who were proceeding to take the superior dignity,—dandies and men about town who wished for some reason to be barristers of seven years' standing,—swarthy, black-eyed natives of the Colonies, who came to be called here before they practised in their own islands,—and many gentlemen of the Irish nation, who make a sojourn in Middle Temple Lane before they return to the green country of their birth. There were little squads of reading students who talked law all dinner-time; there were rowing men, whose discourse was of sculling matches, the Red House, Vauxhall, and the Opera; there were others great in politics, and orators of the students' debating clubs; with all of which sets, except the first, whose talk was an almost unknown and a quite uninteresting language to him, Mr. Pen made a gradual acquaintance, and had many points of sympathy.

The ancient and liberal Inn of the Upper Temple provides in its Hall, and for a most moderate price, an excellent wholesome dinner of soup, meat, tarts, and port wine or sherry, for the barristers and students who attend that place of refection. The parties are arranged in messes of four, each of which quartets has its piece of beef or leg of mutton, its sufficient apple-pie, and its bottle of wine. But the honest *habitués* of the Hall, amongst the lower rank of students, who have a taste for good living, have many harmless arts by which they improve their banquet, and innocent " dodges " (if we may be permitted to use an excellent phrase that has become vernacular since the appearance of the last dictionaries) by which they strive to attain for themselves more delicate food than the common everyday roast meat of the students' tables.

"Wait a bit," said Mr. Lowton, one of these Temple gourmands. " Wait a bit," said Mr. Lowton, tugging at Pen's gown—" the tables are very full, and there's only three benchers to eat ten side dishes—if we wait, perhaps we shall get something from their table." And Pen looked with some amusement, as did Mr. Lowton with eyes of fond desire, towards the benchers' high table, where three old gentlemen were standing up before a dozen silver dish-covers, while the clerk was quavering out a grace.

Lowton was great in the conduct of the dinner. His aim was to manage so as to be the first, or captain of the mess, and to secure for himself the thirteenth glass of the bottle of port wine. Thus he would have the command of the joint on which he operated his favourite cuts, and made rapid dexterous appropriations of gravy, which amused Pen infinitely. Poor Jack Lowton! thy pleasures in life were very harmless; an eager epicure, thy desires did not go beyond eighteenpence.

Pen was somewhat older than many of his fellow-students, and there was that about his style and appearance which, as we have said, was rather haughty and impertinent, that stamped him as a man of *ton*—very unlike those pale students who were talking law to one another, and those ferocious dandies, in rowing shirts and astonishing pins and waistcoats, who represented the idle part of the little community. The humble and good-natured Lowton had felt attracted by Pen's superior looks and presence—and had made acquaintance with him at the mess by opening the conversation.

"This is boiled beef day, I believe, sir," said Lowton to Pen.

"Upon my word, sir, I'm not aware," said Pen, hardly able to contain his laughter, but added, "I'm a stranger; this is my first term"; on which Lowton began to point out to him the notabilities in the Hall.

"That's Bossey the bencher, the bald one sitting under the picture and 'aving soup; I wonder whether it's turtle? They often 'ave turtle. Next is Balls, the King's Counsel, and Swettenham—Hodge and Swettenham, you know. That's old Grump, the senior of the bar; they say he's dined here forty years. They often send 'em down their fish from the benchers to the senior table. Do you see those four fellows seated opposite us? They are regular swells—tip-top fellows. I can tell you—Mr. Trail, the Bishop of Ealing's son, Honourable Fred Ringwood, Lord Cinqbars' brother, you know. *He'll* have a good place, I bet any money: and Bob Suckling, who's always with him—a high fellow too. Ha! ha!" Here Lowton burst into a laugh.

"What is it?" said Pen, still amused.

"I say, I like to mess with those chaps," Lowton said, winking his eye knowingly, and pouring out his glass of wine.

"And why?" asked Pen.

"Why! they don't come down here to dine, you know, they only make believe to dine. *They* dine here, Law bless you! They go to some of the swell clubs, or else to some grand dinner party. You see their names in the *Morning Post* at all the fine parties in London. Why, I bet anything that Ringwood has his cab, or Trail his brougham (he's a devil of a fellow, and makes the bishop's money spin, I can tell you) at the corner of Essex Street at this minute. They dine! They won't dine these two hours, I dare say."

"But why should you like to mess with them, if they don't eat any dinner?" Pen asked, still puzzled. "There's plenty, isn't there?"

"How green you are!" said Lowton. "Excuse me, but you *are* green. They don't drink any wine, don't you see, and a fellow gets the bottle to himself if he likes it when he messes with those three chaps. That's why Corkoran got in with 'em."

"Ah, Mr. Lowton, I see you are a sly fellow," Pen

said, delighted with his acquaintance : on which the other modestly replied, that he had lived in London the better part of his life, and of course had his eyes about him ; and went on with his catalogue to Pen.

"There's a lot of Irish here," he said; "that Corkoran's one, and I can't say I like him. You see that handsome chap with the blue neckcloth, and pink shirt, and yellow waistcoat, that's another; that's Molloy Maloney, of Ballymaloney, and nephew to Major-General Sir Hector O'Dowd, he, he," Lowton said, trying to imitate the Hibernian accent. "He's always bragging about his uncle ; and came into Hall in silver-striped trousers the day he had been presented. That other near him, with the long black hair, is a tremendous rebel. By Jove, sir, to hear him at the Forum it makes your blood freeze ; and the next is an Irishman, too, Jack Finucane, reporter of a newspaper. They all stick together, those Irish. It's your turn to fill your glass. What ? you won't have any port ? Don't like port with your dinner ? Here's your health." And this worthy man found himself not the less attached to Pendennis because the latter disliked port wine at dinner.

"BEHIND THE SCENES"

NICHOLAS NICKLEBY
Dickens

As Mr. Crummles had a strange four-legged animal in the inn stables, which he called a pony, and a vehicle of unknown design, on which he bestowed the appellation of a four-wheeled phaeton, Nicholas proceeded on his journey next morning with greater ease than he had expected : the manager and himself occupying the front seat, and the Master Crummleses and Smike being packed together behind, in company with a wicker basket defended from wet by a stout oilskin, in which were the broad-swords, pistols, pigtails, nautical costumes, and other professional necessaries of the aforesaid young gentlemen.

The pony took his time upon the road, and—possibly in consequence of his theatrical education—evinced, every now and then, a strong inclination to lie down. However, Mr. Vincent Crummles kept him up pretty well, by jerking the rein, and plying the whip; and when these means failed, and the animal came to a stand, the elder Master Crummles got out and kicked him. By dint of these encouragements, he was persuaded to move from time to time, and they jogged on (as Mr. Crummles truly observed) very comfortably for all parties.

" He's a good pony at bottom," said Mr. Crummles, turning to Nicholas.

He might have been at bottom, but he certainly was not at top, seeing that his coat was of two roughest and most ill-favoured kinds. So Nicholas merely observed that he shouldn't wonder if he was.

" Many and many is the circuit this pony has gone," said Mr. Crummles, flicking him skilfully on the eyelid for old acquaintance' sake. " He is quite one of us. His mother was on the stage."

" Was she ?" rejoined Nicholas.

" She ate apple-pie at a circus for upwards of fourteen years," said the manager; " fired pistols, and went to bed in a nightcap; and, in short, took the low comedy entirely. His father was a dancer."

" Was he at all distinguished ?"

" Not very," said the manager. " He was rather a low sort of pony. The fact is, he had originally been jobbed out by the day, and he never quite got over his old habits. He was clever in melodrama too, but too broad—too broad. When the mother died, he took the port-wine business."

"The port-wine business!" cried Nicholas.

"Drinking port-wine with the clown," said the manager; "but he was greedy, and one night bit off the bowl of the glass, and choked himself, so his vulgarity was the death of him at laſt."

The descendant of this ill-starred animal requiring increasing attention from Mr. Crummles as he progressed in his day's work, that gentleman had very little time for conversation. Nicholas was thus left at leisure to entertain himself with his own thoughts, until they arrived at the drawbridge at Portsmouth, where Mr. Crummles pulled up.

"We'll get down here," said the manager, "and the boys will take him round to the ſtable, and call at my lodgings with the luggage. You had better let yours be taken there, for the present."

Thanking Mr. Vincent Crummles for his obliging offer, Nicholas jumped out, and, giving Smike his arm, accompanied the manager up High Street on their way to the theatre; feeling nervous and uncomfortable enough at the prospect of an immediate introduction to a scene so new to him.

They passed a great many bills, pasted againſt the walls and displayed in windows, wherein the names of Mr. Vincent Crummles, Mrs. Vincent Crummles, Master Crummles, Master P. Crummles, and Miss Crummles, were printed in very large letters, and everything else in very small ones; and, turning at length into an entry, in which was a ſtrong smell of orange-peel and lamp-oil, with an under-current of saw-duſt, groped their way through a dark passage, and, descending a step or two, threaded a little maze of canvas screens and paint-pots, and emerged upon the stage of the Portsmouth Theatre.

"Here we are," said Mr. Crummles.

It was not very light, but Nicholas found himself close to the firſt entrance on the prompt side, among bare walls, dusty scenes, mildewed clouds, heavily daubed draperies, and dirty floors. He looked about him; ceiling, pit, boxes, gallery, orchestra, fittings and decorations of every kind,—all looked coarse, cold, gloomy and wretched.

"Is this a theatre?" whispered Smike, in amazement; "I thought it was a blaze of light and finery."

"Why, so it is," replied Nicholas, hardly less surprised; "but not by day, Smike—not by day."

The manager's voice recalled him from a more careful inspection of the building to the opposite side of the proscenium, where, at a small mahogany table with rickety legs and of an oblong shape, sat a stout, portly female, apparently between forty and fifty, in a tarnished silk cloak, with her bonnet dangling by the strings in her hand, and her hair (of which she had a great quantity) braided in a large festoon over each temple.

"Mr. Johnson," said the manager (for Nicholas had given the name which Newman Noggs had bestowed upon him in his conversation with Mrs. Kenwigs), "let me introduce Mrs. Vincent Crummles."

"I am glad to see you, sir," said Mrs. Vincent Crummles, in a sepulchral voice. " I am very glad to see you, and still more happy to hail you as a promising member of our corps."

The lady shook Nicholas by the hand as she addressed him in these terms; he saw it was a large one, but had not expected quite such an iron grip as that with which she honoured him.

"And this," said the lady, crossing to Smike, as tragic actresses cross when they obey a stage direction, "and this is the other. You, too, are welcome, sir."

"He'll do, I think, my dear?" said the manager, taking a pinch of snuff.

"He is admirable," replied the lady. "An acquisition, indeed."

As Mrs. Vincent Crummles recrossed back to the table, there bounded on to the stage from some mysterious inlet, a little girl in a dirty white frock with tucks up to the knees, short trousers, sandaled shoes, white spencer, pink gauze bonnet, green veil and curl-papers; who turned a pirouette, cut twice in the air, turned another pirouette, then, looking off at the opposite wing, shrieked, bounded forward to within six inches of the footlights, and fell into a beautiful attitude of terror, as a shabby gentleman in an old pair of buff slippers came in at one powerful slide, and chattering his teeth, fiercely brandished a walking-stick.

" They are going through the Indian Savage and the Maiden," said Mrs. Crummles.

" Oh!" said the manager, " the little ballet interlude. Very good, go on. A little this way if you please, Mr. Johnson. That'll do. Now!"

The manager clapped his hands as a signal to proceed, and the Savage, becoming ferocious, made a slide towards the maiden; but the maiden avoided him in six twirls, and came down, at the end of the last one, upon the very points of her toes. This seemed to make some impression upon the Savage; for, after a little more ferocity and chasing of the maiden into corners, he began to relent, and stroked his face several times with his right thumb and four fingers, thereby intimating that he was struck with admiration of the maiden's beauty. Acting upon the impulse of this passion, he (the Savage) began to hit himself severe thumps in the chest, and to exhibit other indications of being desperately in love, which being rather a prosy proceeding, was very likely the cause of the maiden's falling asleep; whether it was or no, asleep she did fall, sound as a church, on a sloping bank, and the Savage perceiving it, leant his left ear on his right hand, and nodded sideways, to intimate

THE NINETEENTH CENTURY

to all whom it might concern that she *was* asleep, and no shamming. Being left to himself, the Savage had a dance, all alone. Just as he left off, the maiden woke up, rubbed her eyes, got off the bank, and had a dance all alone too—such a dance that the savage looked on in ecstasy all the while, and when it was done, plucked from a neighbouring tree some botanical curiosity, resembling a small pickled cabbage, and offered it to the maiden, who at first wouldn't have it, but on the Savage shedding tears relented. Then the Savage jumped for joy ; then the maiden jumped for rapture at the sweet smell of the pickled cabbage. Then the Savage and the maiden danced violently together, and, finally, the Savage dropped down on one knee, and the maiden stood on one leg upon his other knee ; thus concluding the ballet, and leaving the spectators in a state of pleasing uncertainty, whether she would ultimately marry the Savage, or return to her friends.

" Very well indeed," said Mr. Crummles ; " bravo !"

" Bravo !" cried Nicholas, resolved to make the best of everything. " Beautiful !"

" This, sir," said Mr. Vincent Crummles, bringing the maiden forward, " this is the infant phenomenon—Miss Ninetta Crummles."

" Your daughter ?" inquired Nicholas.

" My daughter—my daughter," replied Mr. Vincent Crummles ; " the idol of every place we go into, sir. We have had complimentary letters about this girl, sir, from the nobility and gentry of almost every town in England."

" I am not surprised at that," said Nicholas ; " she must be quite a natural genius."

" Quite a— !" Mr. Crummles stopped : language was not powerful enough to describe the infant phenomenon. " I'll tell you what, sir," he said ; " the talent of this child is not to be imagined. She must be seen, sir—seen—to be ever so faintly appreciated. There; go to your mother, my dear."

"May I ask how old she is" enquired Nicholas.

"You may, sir," replied Mr. Crummles, looking steadily in his questioner's face, as some men do when they have doubts about being implicitly believed in what they are going to say. "She is ten years of age, sir."

"Not more?"

"Not a day?"

"Dear me!" said Nicholas, "it's extraordinary."

It was; for the infant phenomenon, though of short stature, had a comparatively aged countenance, and had moreover been precisely the same age—not perhaps to the full extent of the memory of the oldest inhabitant, but certainly for five good years. But she had been kept up late every night, and put upon an unlimited allowance of gin-an-water from infancy, to prevent her growing tall, and perhaps this system of training had produced in the infant phenomenon these additional phenomena.

While this short dialogue was going on, the gentleman who had enacted the Savage came up, with his walking shoes on his feet, and his slippers in his hand, to within a few paces, as if desirous to join in the conversation. Deeming this a good opportunity, he put in his word.

"Talent there, sir!" said the Savage, nodding towards Miss Crummles.

Nicholas assented.

"Ah!" said the actor, setting his teeth together, and drawing in his breath with a hissing sound, "She oughtn't to be in the provinces, she oughtn't."

"What do you mean?" asked the manager.

"I mean to say," replied the other warmly, "that she is too good for country boards, and that she ought to be in one of the large houses in London, or nowhere;

and I tell you more, without mincing the matter, that if it wasn't for envy and jealousy in some quarter that you know of, she would be. Perhaps you'll introduce me here, Mr. Crummles."

"Mr. Folair," said the manager, presenting him to Nicholas.

"Happy to know you, sir." Mr. Folair touched the brim of his hat with his forefinger, and then shook hands." "A recruit, sir, I understand?"

"An unworthy one," replied Nicholas.

"Did you ever see such a set-out as that?" whispered the actor, drawing him away, as Crummles left them to speak to his wife.

"As what?"

Mr. Folair made a funny face from his pantomime collection, and pointed over his shoulder.

"You don't mean the infant phenomenon?"

"Infant humbug, sir," replied Mr. Folair. "There isn't a female child of common sharpness in a charity school, that couldn't do better than that. She may thank her stars she was born a manager's daughter."

"You seem to take it to heart," observed Nicholas, with a smile.

"Yes, by Jove, and well I may," said Mr. Folair, drawing his arm through his, and walking him up and down the stage. "Isn't it enough to make a man crusty to see that little sprawler put up in the best business every night, and actually keeping money out of the house, by being forced down the people's throats, while other people are passed over? Isn't it extraordinary to see a man's confounded family conceit blinding him, even to his own interest? Why I *know* of fifteen and sixpence that came to Southampton one night last month, to see me dance the Highland Fling; and what's the consequence? I've never been put up in it since—never once— while the 'infant phenomenon' has been grinning through artificial flowers at five people and a baby in the pit, and two boys in the gallery, every night."

"If I may judge from what I have seen of you," said Nicholas, "you must be a valuable member of the company."

"Oh!" replied Mr. Folair, beating his slippers together, to knock the dust out; "I *can* come it pretty well—nobody better, perhaps, in my own line—but having such business as one gets here, is like putting lead on one's feet instead of chalk, and dancing in fetters without the credit of it. Holloa, old fellow, how are you?"

The gentleman addressed in these latter words was a dark-complexioned man, inclining indeed to sallow, with long thick black hair, and very evident indications (though he was close shaved) of a stiff beard, and whiskers of the same deep shade. His age did not appear to exceed thirty, though many at first sight would have considered him much older, as his face was long, and very pale, from the constant application of stage paint. He wore a checked shirt, an old green coat with new gilt buttons, a neckerchief of broad red and green stripes, and full blue trousers; he carried, too, a common ash walking-stick, apparently more for show than use, as he flourished it about, with the hooked end downwards, except when he raised it for a few seconds, and throwing himself into a fencing attitude, made a pass or two at the side-scenes, or at any other object, animate or inanimate, that chanced to afford him a pretty good mark at the moment.

"Well, Tommy," said this gentleman, making a thrust at his friend, who parried it dexterously with his slipper, "what's the news?"

"A new appearance, that's all," replied Mr. Folair, looking at Nicholas.

"Do the honours, Tommy, do the honours," said

the other gentleman, tapping him reproachfully on the crown of the hat with his stick.

" This is Mr. Lenville, who does our first tragedy, Mr. Johnson," said the pantomimist.

" Except when old bricks and mortar takes it into his head to do it himself, you should add, Tommy," remarked Mr. Lenville. " You know who bricks and mortar is, I suppose, sir ?"

" I do not, indeed," replied Nicholas.

" We call Crummles that, because his style of acting is rather in the heavy and ponderous way," said Mr. Lenville. " I mustn't be cracking jokes though, for I've got a part of twelve lengths here, which I must be up in to-morrow night, and I haven't had time to look at it yet ; I'm a confounded quick study, that's one comfort."

Consoling himself with this reflection, Mr. Lenville drew from his coat-pocket a greasy and crumpled manuscript, and, having made another pass at his friend, proceeded to walk to and fro, conning it himself and indulging occasionally in such appropriate action as his imagination and the text suggested.

A pretty general muster of the company had by this time taken place ; for besides Mr. Lenville and his friend Tommy, there were present, a slim young gentleman with weak eyes, who played the low-spirited lovers and sang tenor songs, and who had come arm-in-arm with the comic countryman—a man with a turned-up nose, large mouth, broad face, and staring eyes. Making himself very amiable to the infant phenomenon, was an inebriated elderly gentleman in the last depths of shabbiness, who plryed the calm and virtuous old men ; and paying especial court to Mrs. Crummles was another elderly gentleman, a shade more respectable, who played the irascible old men—those funny fellows who have nephews in the army, and perpetually run about with thick sticks to compel them to marry heiresses. Besides these, there was a roving-looking person in a rough great-coat, who strode up and down in front of the lamps, flourishing a dress-cane, and rattling away, in an undertone, with great vivacity for the amusement of an ideal audience. He was not quite so young as he had been, and his figure was rather running to seed; but there was an air of exaggerated gentility about him, which bespoke the hero of swaggering comedy. There was, also, a little group of three or four young men, with lantern jaws and thick eyebrows, who were conversing in one corner; but they seemed to be of secondary importance, and laughed and talked together without attracting any attention.

The ladies were gathered in a little knot by themselves round the rickety table before mentioned. There was Miss Snevellicci—who could do anything from a medley dance to Lady Macbeth, and also always played some part in blue silk knee-smalls at her benefit—glancing, from the depths of her coal-scuttle straw bonnet, at Nicholas, and affecting to be absorbed in the recital of a diverting story to her friend Miss Ledbrook, who had brought her work, and was making up a ruff in the most natural manner possible. There was Miss Belvawney—who seldom aspired to speaking parts, and usually went on as a page in white silk hose, to stand with one leg bent, and contemplate the audience, or to go in and out after Mr. Crummles in stately tragedy—twisting up the ringlets of the beautiful Miss Bravassa, who had once had her likeness taken "in character" by an engraver's apprentice, whereof impressions were hung up for sale in the pastry-cook's window, and the green-grocer's, and at the circulating library, and the box-office, whenever the announce bills came out for her annual night. There was Mrs. Lenville, in a very limp bonnet and veil, decidedly in that way in which she would wish to be if she truly loved Mr. Lenville; there was Miss Gazingi, with an imitation ermine boa tied in a loose knot round her neck, flogging Mr. Crummles, junior, with both ends, in fun. Lastly, there was Mrs. Grudden in a brown cloth pelisse and a beaver bonnet, who assisted Mrs. Crummles in her domestic affairs, and took money at the doors, and dressed the ladies, and swept the house, and held the prompt book when everybody else was on for the last scene, and acted any kind of part on any emergency without ever learning it, and was put down in the bills under any name or names whatever, that occurred to Mr. Crummles as looking well in print.

AT VAUXHALL

VANITY FAIR
Thackeray

The party was landed at the Royal Gardens in due time. As the majestic Jos stepped out of the creaking vehicle the crowd gave a cheer for the fat gentleman, who blushed and looked very big and mighty, as he walked away with Rebecca under his arm. George, of course, took charge of Amelia. She looked as happy as a rose-tree in sunshine. *The Diversions*

"I say, Dobbin," says George, "just look to the shawls and things, there's a good fellow." And so while he paired off with Miss Sedley, and Jos squeezed through the gate into the Gardens with Rebecca at his side, honest Dobbin contented himself by giving an arm to the shawls, and by paying at the door for the whole party.

He walked very modestly behind them. He was not willing to spoil sport. About Rebecca and Jos he did not care a fig. But he thought Amelia worthy

w

even of the brilliant George Osborne, and as he saw that good-looking couple threading the walks to the girl's delight and wonder, he watched her artless happiness with a sort of fatherly pleasure. Perhaps he felt that he would have liked to have something on his own arm besides a shawl (the people laughed at seeing the gawky young officer carrying this female burthen); but William Dobbin was very little addicted to selfish calculation at all; and so long as his friend was enjoying himself, how should he be discontented? And the truth is, that of all the delights of the Gardens; of the hundred thousand *extra* lamps, which were always lighted; the fiddlers in cocked hats, who played ravishing melodies under the gilded cockle-shell in the midst of the Gardens; the singers, both of comic and sentimental ballads, who charmed the ears there; the country dances, formed by bouncing cockneys and cockneyesses, and executed amidst jumping, thumping and laughter; the signal which announced that Madame Saqui was about to mount skyward on a slack-rope ascending to the stars; the hermit that always sat in the illuminated hermitage; the dark walks, so favourable to the interviews of young lovers; the pots of stout handed about by the people in the shabby old liveries; and the twinkling boxes, in which the happy feasters made-believe to eat slices of almost invisible ham; of all these things, and of the gentle Simpson, that kind, smiling idiot, who, I dare say, presided even then over the place—Captain William Dobbin did not take the slightest notice.

He carried about Amelia's white cashmere shawl, and having attended under the gilt cockle-shell, while Mrs. Salmon performed the Battle of Borodino (a savage cantata against the Corsican upstart, who had lately met with his Russian reverses)—Mr. Dobbin tried to hum it as he walked away, and found he was

"MR. JOSEPH IN A STATE OF EXCITEMENT" AT VAUXHALL
From a drawing by Thackeray in "Vanity Fair."

humming—the tune which Amelia Sedley sang on the stairs, as she came down to dinner.

He burst out laughing at himself; for the truth is, he could sing no better than an owl. . . . .

It is to be understood, as a matter of course, that our young people, being in parties of two and two, made the most solemn promises to keep together during the evening, and separated in ten minutes afterwards. Parties at Vauxhall always did separate but 'twas only to meet again at supper-time, when they could talk of their mutual adventures in the interval.

What were the adventures of Mr. Osborne and Miss Amelia? That is a secret. But be sure of this—they were perfectly happy, and correct in their behaviour; and as they had been in the habit of being together any time these fifteen years, their *tête-à-tête* offered no particular novelty.

But when Miss Rebecca Sharp and her companion lost themselves in a solitary walk, in which there were not above five score more of couples similarly straying, they both felt that the situation was extremely tender and critical, and now or never was the moment, Miss Sharp thought, to provoke that declaration which was trembling on the timid lips of Mr. Sedley. They had previously been to the panorama of Moscow, where a rude fellow, treading on Miss Sharp's foot, caused her to fall back with a little shriek into the arms of Mr. Sedley, and this little incident increased the tenderness and confidence of that gentleman to such a degree, that he told her several of his favourite Indian stories over again for, at least, the sixth time.

" How I should like to see India !" said Rebecca.

" *Should* you ?" said Joseph, with a most killing tenderness ; and was no doubt about to follow up this artful interrogatory by a question still more tender (for he puffed and panted a great deal, and Rebecca's hand, which was placed near his heart, could count the feverish pulsations of that organ), when, oh, provoking, the bell rang for the fireworks, and, a great scuffling and running taking place, these interesting lovers were obliged to follow in the stream of people.

Captain Dobbin had some thoughts of joining the party at supper: as, in truth, he found the Vauxhall amusements not particularly lively—but he paraded twice before the box where the now united couples were met, and nobody took any notice of him. Covers were laid for four. The mated pairs were prattling away quite happily, and Dobbin knew he was as clean forgotten as if he had never existed in this world.

"I should only be *de trop*," said the Captain, looking at them rather wistfully. "I'd best go and talk to the hermit"—and so he strolled off out of the hum of men, and noise, and clatter of the banquet, into the dark walk, at the end of which lived that well-known pasteboard solitary. It wasn't very good fun for Dobbin—and, indeed, to be alone at Vauxhall, I have found from my own experience, to be one of the most dismal sports ever entered into by a bachelor.

The two couples were perfectly happy then in their box: where the most delightful and intimate conversation took place. Jos was in his glory, ordering about the waiters with great majesty. He made the salad; and uncorked the champagne; and carved the chickens; and ate and drank the greater part of the refreshments on the tables. Finally, he insisted upon having a bowl of rack punch; everybody had rack punch at Vauxhall. "Waiter, rack punch."

That bowl of rack punch was the cause of all this history. And why not a bowl of rack punch as well as any other cause? Was not a bowl of prussic acid the cause of Fair Rosamond's retiring from the world?

Was not a bowl of wine the cause of the demise of Alexander the Great, or, at least, does not Dr. Lempriere say so?—So did this bowl of rack punch influence the fates of all the principal characters in this " Novel without a Hero," which we are now relating. It influenced their life, although most of them did not taste a drop of it.

The young ladies did not drink it; Osborne did not like it; and the consequence was that Jos, that fat *gourmand*, drank up the whole contents of the bowl; and the consequence of his drinking up the whole contents of the bowl was, a liveliness which at first was astonishing, and then became almost painful; for he talked and laughed so loud as to bring scores of listeners round the box, much to the confusion of the innocent party within it; and, volunteering to sing a song (which he did in that maudlin high key peculiar to gentlemen in an inebriated state), he almost drew away the audience who were gathered round the musicians in the gilt scollop-shell, and received from his hearers a great deal of applause.

A FANCY DRESS BREAKFAST

PICKWICK PAPERS
Dickens

The morning came: it was a pleasant sight to behold Mr. Tupman in full Brigand's costume, with a very tight jacket, sitting like a pincushion over his back and shoulders: the upper portion of his legs encased in the velvet shorts, and the lower part thereof swathed in the complicated bandages to which all Brigands are peculiarly attached. It was pleasing to see his open and ingenuous countenance, well mustachioed and corked, looking out from an open shirt collar; and to contemplate the sugar-loaf hat, decorated with ribbons of all colours, which he was compelled to carry on his knee, inasmuch as no known conveyance with a top to it would admit of any man's carrying it between his head and the roof. Equally humorous and agreeable was the appearance of Mr. Snodgrass in blue satin trunks and cloak, white silk tights and shoes, and Grecian helmet: which everybody knows (and if they do not, Mr. Solomon Lucas did) to have been the regular, authentic, every-day costume of a Troubadour, from the earliest ages down to the time of their final disappearance from the face of the earth. All this was pleasant, but this was nothing compared with the shouting of the populace when the carriage drew up, behind Mr. Pott's chariot, which chariot itself drew up at Mr. Pott's door, which door itself opened, and displayed the great Pott accoutred as a Russian officer of justice, with a tremendous knout in his hand—tastefully typical of the stern and mighty power of the Eatanswill Gazette, and the fearful lashings it bestowed on public offenders.

" Bravo !" shouted Mr. Tupman and Mr. Snodgrass from the passaage, when they beheld the walking allegory.

" Bravo !" Mr. Pickwick was heard to exclaim, from the passage.

" Hoo-roar Pott !" shouted the populace. Amid these salutations, Mr. Pott, smiling with that kind of bland dignity which sufficiently testified that he felt his power, and knew how to exert it, got into the chariot.

Then there emerged from the house, Mrs. Pott, who would have looked very like Apollo, if she hadn't had a gown on: conducted by Mr. Winkle, who in his light-red coat, could not possibly have been mistaken for anything but a sportsman, if he had not borne an equal resemblance to a general postman.

"AND ABOVE ALL, THERE WAS MRS. LEO HUNTER IN THE CHARACTER OF MINERVA RECEIVING THE COMPANY" . . .
From an illustration by Phiz in the "*Pickwick Papers.*"

Last of all came Mr. Pickwick, whom the boys applauded as loud as anybody, probably under the impression that his tights and gaiters were some remnants of the dark ages; and then the two vehicles proceeded towards Mrs. Leo Hunter's: Mr. Weller (who was to assist in waiting) being stationed on the box of that in which his master was seated.

Every one of the men, women, boys, girls, and babies, who were assembled to see the visitors in their fancy dresses, screamed with delight and ecstasy, when Mr. Pickwick, with the Brigand on one arm, and the Troubadour on the other, walked solemnly up the entrance. Never were such shouts heard, as those which greeted Mr. Tupman's efforts to fix the sugar-loaf hat on his head, by way of entering the garden in style.

The preparations were on the most delightful scale; fully realising the prophetic Pott's anticipations about the gorgeousness of Eastern Fairyland, and at once affording a sufficient contradiction to the malignant statements of the reptile Independent. The grounds were more than an acre and a quarter in extent, and they were filled with people! Never was such a blaze of beauty, and fashion, and literature. There was the young lady who "did" the poetry in the Eatanswill Gazette, in the garb of a sultana, leaning upon the arm of the young gentleman who "did" the review department, and who was appropriately habited in a field marshal's uniform—the boots excepted. There were hosts of these geniuses, and any reasonable person would have thought it honour enough to meet them. But more than these, there were half a dozen lions from London—authors, real authors, who had written whole books, and printed them afterwards—and here you might see 'em, walking about, like ordinary men, smiling, and talking—aye, and talking pretty considerable nonsense too, no doubt with the benign intention of rendering themselves intelligible to the common people about them. Moreover, there was a band of music in pasteboard caps; four some-thing-ean singers in the costume of their country, and a dozen hired waiters in the costume of their country—and very dirty costume too. And above all, there was Mrs. Leo Hunter in the character of Minerva, receiving the company, and overflowing with pride and gratification at the notion of having called such distinguished individuals together.

CHAPTER VII

THE NINETEENTH CENTURY—III

TOWN AND COUNTRY

DOCTOR THORNE
Trollope

There is a county in the west of England not so *Our* full of life, indeed, nor so widely spoken of as some of *Grand-* its manufacturing leviathian brethren in the north, *parents* but which is, nevertheless, very dear to those who know it well. Its green pastures, its waving wheat, its deep and shady and—let us add—dirty lanes, its paths and stiles, its tawny-coloured, well-built rural churches, its avenues of beeches, and frequent Tudor mansions, its constant county hunt, its social graces, and the general air of clanship which pervades it, has made it to its own inhabitants a favoured land of Goshen. It is purely agricultural; agricultural in its produce, agricultural in its poor, and agricultural in its pleasures. There are towns in it, of course; depôts from which are brought seeds and groceries, ribbons and fire-shovels; in which markets are held and county balls are carried on; which return members to Parliament, generally—in spite of reform bills, past, present, and coming—in accordance with the dictates of some neighbouring land magnate: from whence emanate the country postmen, and where is located the supply of post-horses necessary for county visitings But these towns add nothing to the importance of the county; they consist, with the exception of the assize-town, of dull, all but death-like single streets. Each possesses two pumps, three hotels, ten shops, fifteen beer-houses, a beadle and a market-place.

Indeed, the town population of the county reckons for nothing when the importance of the county is discussed, with the exception, as before said, of the assize-town, which is also a cathedral city. Herein is a clerical aristocracy, which is certainly not without its due weight. A resident bishop, a resident dean, an archdeacon, three or four resident prebendaries, and all their numerous chaplains, vicars, and ecclesiastical satellites, do make up a society sufficiently powerful to be counted as something by the county squirearchy. In other respects the greatness of Barsetshire depends wholly on the landed powers.

Barsetshire, however, is not now so essentially one whole as it was before the Reform Bill divided it. There is in these days an East Barsetshire, and there is a West Barsetshire; and people conversant with Barsetshire doings declare that they can already decipher some difference of feeling, some division of interests. The eastern moiety of the county is more purely conservative than the western; there is, or was, a taint of Peelism in the latter; and then, too, the residence of two such great Whig magnates as the Duke of Omnium and the Earl de Courcy in that locality in some degree overshadows and renders less influential the gentlemen who live near them.

HER FIRST BALL

THE THREE CLERKS
Trollope

Katie's heart beat high as she got out of the carriage—Mrs. Val's private carriage had been kept on for the occasion—and saw before and above her on the stairs a crowd of muslin, crushing its way on towards the room prepared for dancing. Katie had never been to a ball before. We hope that the word ball may not bring down on us the adverse criticism of the ' Morning Post.' It was probably not a ball in the strictly fashionable sense of the word, but it was so to Katie to all intents and purposes. Her dancing had hitherto been done either at children's parties or as a sort of supplemental amusement to the evening tea-gatherings at Hampton or Hampton Court. She had never yet seen the muse worshipped with the premeditated ceremony of banished carpets, chalked floors, and hired musicians. Her heart consequently beat high as she made her way up stairs, linked arm-in-arm with Ugolina Neverbend.

' Shall you dance much ?' said Ugolina.

' Oh, I hope so,' said Katie.

' I shall not. It is an amusement of which I am peculiarly fond, and for which my active habits suit me.' This was probably said with some allusion to her sister, who was apt to be short of breath. ' But in the dances of the present day conversation is impossible, and I look upon any pursuit as barbaric which stops the " feast of reason and the flow of soul."

Katie did not quite understand this, but she thought in her heart that she would not at all mind giving up talking for the whole evening if she could only get dancing enough. But on this matter her heart misgave her. To be sure she was engaged to Charley for the first quadrille and second waltz ; but there her engagements stopped, whereas Clementina, as she was aware, had a whole book full of them. What if she could get no more dancing when Charley's goodnature should have been expended ? She had an idea that no one would care to dance with her when older partners were to be had. Ah, Katie, you do not yet know the extent of your riches, or half the wealth of your own attractions!

And then they all heard another little speech from Mrs. Val. 'She was really quite ashamed—she really was—to see so many people; she could not wish any of her guests away, that would be impossible—though perhaps one or two might be spared,' she said in a confidential whisper to Gertrude. Who the one or two might be it would be difficult to decide, as she had made the same whisper to every one; 'but she really was ashamed; there was almost a crowd, and she had quite intended that the house should be nearly empty. The fact was everybody asked had come, and as she could not, of course, have counted on that, why she had got, you see, twice as many people as she had expected.' And then she went on, and made the same speech to the next arrival.

Katie, who wanted to begin the play at the beginning, kept her eye anxiously on Charley, who was still standing with Lactimel Neverbend on his arm. 'Oh, now,' said she to herself, 'if he should forget me and begin dancing with Miss Neverbend!' But then she remembered how he had jumped into the water, and determined that, even with such provocation as that, she must not be angry with him.

But there was no danger of Charley's forgetting. 'Come,' said he, 'we must not lose any more time, if we mean to dance the first set. Alaric will be our *vis avis*—he is going to dance with Miss Neverbend,' and so they stood up. Katie tightened her gloves, gave her dress a little shake, looked at her shoes, and then the work of the evening began.

'I shouldn't have liked to have sat down for the first dance,' she said confidentially to Charley, 'because it's my first ball.'

'Sit down! I don't suppose you'll be let to sit

down the whole evening. You'll be crying out for mercy about three or four o'clock in the morning.'

'It's you to go on now,' said Katie, whose eyes were intent on the figure, and who would not have gone wrong herself, or allowed her partner to do so, on any consideration. And so the dance went on right merrily.

'I've got to dance the first polka with Miss Golightly,' said Charley.

'And the next with me,' said Katie.

'You may be sure I shan't forget that.'

'You lucky man to get Miss Golightly for a partner. I am told she is the most beautiful dancer in the world.'

'O no—Mademoiselle——is much better,' said Charley, naming the principal stage performer of the day. 'If one is to go the whole hog, one had better do it thoroughly.'

Katie did not quite understand then what he meant, and merely replied that she would look at the performance. In this, however, she was destined to be disappointed, for Charley had hardly left her before Miss Golightly brought up to her the identical M. Delabarbe de l'Empereur who had so terribly put her out in the gardens. This was done so suddenly, that Katie's presence of mind was quite insufficient to provide her with any means of escape. The Frenchman bowed very low and said nothing. Katie made a little curtsey, and was equally silent. Then she felt her own arm gathered up and put within his, and she stood up to take her share in the awful performance. She felt herself to be in such a nervous fright, that she would willingly have been home again at Hampton if she could; but as this was utterly impossible, she had only to bethink herself of her steps, and get through the work as best she might.

Away went Charley and Clementina leading the

throng; away went M. Jaquêtenàpe and Linda; away went another Frenchman clasping in his arms the happy Ugolina. Away went Lactimel with a young Weights and Measures—and then came Katie's turn. She pressed her lips together, shut her eyes, and felt the tall Frenchman's arms behind her back, and made a start. 'Twas like plunging into cold water on the first bathing day of the season—*ce n'est que le premier pas qui coûte*. When once off Katie did not find it so bad. The Frenchman danced well, and Katie herself was a wicked little adept. At home, at Surbiton, dancing with another girl, she had with great triumph tired out the fingers both of her mother and sister, and forced them to own that it was impossible to put her down. M. de l'Empereur, therefore, had his work before him, and he did it like a man— as long as he could.

Katie, who had not yet assumed the airs or will of a grown-up young lady, thought that she was bound to go on as long as her grand partner chose to go with her. He, on the other hand, accustomed in his gallantry to obey all ladies' wishes, considered himself bound to leave it to her to stop when she pleased. And so they went on with apparently interminable gyrations. Charley and the heiress had twice been in motion, and had twice stopped, and still they were going on; Ugolina had refreshed herself with many delicious observations, and Lactimel had thrice paused to advocate dancing for the million, and still they went on; the circle was gradually left to themselves, and still they went on;—people stood round, some admiring and others pitying; and still they went on. Katie, thinking of her steps and her business, did not perceive that she and her partner were alone; and ever and anon, others of course joined in—and so they went on—and on—and on.

M. Delabarbe de l'Empereur was a strong and active

man, but he began to perceive that the lady was too much for him. He was already melting away with his exertions, while his partner was as cool as a cucumber. She, with her active young legs, her lightly filled veins, and small agile frame, could have gone on almost for ever; but M. de l'Empereur was more encumbered. Gallantry was at last beat by nature, his overtasked muscles would do no more for him, and he was fain to stop, dropping his partner into a chair, and throwing himself in a state of utter exhaustion against the wall.

Katie was hardly out of breath as she received the congratulations of her friends; but at the moment she could not understand why they were quizzing her. In after times, however, she was often reproached with having danced a Frenchman to death in the evening, in revenge for his having bored her in the morning. It was observed that M. Delabarbe de l'Empereur danced no more that evening. Indeed he very soon left the house.

Katie had not been able to see Miss Golightly's performance, but it had been well worth seeing. She was certainly no ordinary performer, and if she did not quite come up to the remarkable movements which one sees on the stage under the name of dancing, the fault was neither in her will nor her ability, but only in her education. Charley also was peculiarly well suited to give her ' ample verge and room enough ' to show off all her perfections. Her most peculiar merit consisted, perhaps, in her power of stopping herself suddenly, while going on at the rate of a hunt one way, and without any pause or apparent difficulty going just as fast the other way. This was done by a jerk which must, one would be inclined to think, have dislocated all her bones and entirely upset her internal arrangements. But no; it was done without injury, or any disagreeable result either to her brain or elsewhere. We all know how a steamer is manœuvred when she has to change her course, how we stop her and ease her and back her; but Miss Golightly stopped and eased and backed all at once, and that without collision with any other craft. It was truly very wonderful, and Katie ought to have looked at her.

Katie soon found occasion to cast off her fear that her evening's happiness would be destroyed by a dearth of partners. Her troubles began to be of an exactly opposite description. She had almost envied Miss Golightly her little book full of engagements, and now she found herself dreadfully bewildered by a book of her own. Some one had given her a card and a pencil, and every moment she could get to herself was taken up in endeavouring to guard herself from perfidy on her own part. All down the card, at intervals which were not very far apart, there were great C's which stood for Charley, and her firmest feeling was that no earthly consideration should be allowed to interfere with those landmarks. And then there were all manner of hieroglyphics —sometimes, unfortunately, illegible to Katie herself— French names and English names mixed together in a manner most vexatious; and to make matters worse, she found that she had put down both Victoire Jaquêtanàpe and Mr. Johnson of the Weights, by a great I, and she could not remember with whom she was bound to dance the lancers, and to whom she had promised the last polka before supper. One thing, however, was quite fixed: when supper should arrive she was to go down stairs with Charley.

'What dreadful news, Linda!' said Charley; 'did you hear it?' Linda was standing up with Mr. Neverbend for a sober quadrille, and Katie also was close by with her partner. 'Dreadful news indeed!'

'What is it?' said Linda.

'A man can die but once to be sure; but to be killed in such a manner as that, is certainly very sad.'

'Killed! who has been killed?' said Neverbend.

'Well, perhaps I shouldn't say killed. He only died in the cab as he went home.'

'Died in a cab! how dreadful!' said Neverbend. 'Who? who was it, Mr. Tudor?'

'Didn't you hear? How very odd! Why M. de l' Empereur, to be sure. I wonder what the coroner will bring it in.'

'How can you talk such nonsense, Charley?' said Linda.

'Very well, Master Charley,' said Katie. 'All that comes of being a writer of romances. I suppose that's to be the next contribution to the "Daily Delight."'

Neverbend went off on his quadrille not at all pleased with the joke. Indeed, he was never pleased with a joke, and in this instance he ventured to suggest to his partner that the idea of a gentleman expiring in a cab was much too horrid to be laughed at.

'Oh, we never mind Charley Tudor,' said Linda; 'he always goes on in that way. We all like him so much.'

Mr. Neverbend, who, though not very young, still had a susceptible heart within his bosom, had been much taken by Linda's charms. He already began to entertain an idea that as a Mrs. Neverbend would be a desirable adjunct to his establishment at some future period, he could not do better than offer himself and his worldly goods to the acceptance of Miss Woodward; he therefore said nothing further in disparagement of the family friend; but he resolved that no such alliance should ever induce him to make Mr. Charles Tudor welcome at his house. But what could he have expected? The Internal Navigation had ever been a low place, and he was surprised that the Hon. Mrs. Val should have admitted one of the navvies inside her drawing-room.

And so the ball went on. Mrs. Johnson came duly for the lancers, and M. Jaquêtanàpe for the polka. Johnson was great at the lancers, knowing every turn and vagary in that most intricate and exclusive of dances; and it need hardly be said that the polka with M. Jaquètanàpe was successful. The last honour, however, was not without evil results, for it excited the envy of Ugolina, who, proud of her own performance, had longed, but hitherto in vain, to be whirled round the room by that wondrously expert foreigner.

IN THE FASHION

DOCTOR THORNE
Trollope

Sir Louis was dressed in what he considered the most fashionable style of the day. He had on a new dress-coat lined with satin, new dress-trousers, a silk waistcoat covered with chains, a white cravat, polished pumps, and silk stockings, and he carried a scented handkerchief in his hand; he had rings on his fingers, and carbuncle studs in his shirt, and he smelt as sweet as patchouli could make him . . . . When Frank came in, the doctor hardly did know him. His hair was darker than it had been, and so was his complexion; but his chief disguise was in a long silken beard. which hung down over his cravat. The doctor had hitherto not been much in favour of long beards, but he could not deny that Frank looked very well with the appendage.

" Oh, doctor, I am so delighted to find you here,"

LADIES' DRESSES, EARLY VICTORIAN PERIOD
From a fashion paper of the time

said he, coming up to him; "so very, very glad;" and, taking the doctor's arm, he led him away into a window, where they were alone. "And how is Mary?" said he, almost in a whisper. "Oh, I wish she were here! But doctor, it shall all come in time. But tell me, doctor, there is no news about her, is there?"

"News—what news?"

"Oh, well; no news is good news; you will give her my love, won't you?"

The doctor said that he would. What else could he say? It appeared quite clear to him that some of Mary's fears were groundless.

Frank was again very much altered. It has been said, that though he was a boy at twenty-one, he was a man at twenty-two. But now, at twenty-three, he appeared to be almost a man of the world. His manners were easy, his voice under his control, and words were at his command: he was no longer either shy or noisy; but, perhaps, was open to the charge of seeming, at least, to be too conscious of his own merits. He was, indeed, very handsome; tall, manly, and powerfully built, his form was such as women's eyes have ever loved to look upon. "Ah, if he would but marry money!" said Lady Arabella to herself, taken up by a mother's natural admiration for her son. His sisters clung round him before dinner, all talking to him at once. How proud a family of girls always are of one big, tall, burly brother!

"You don't mean to tell me, Frank, that you are going to eat soup with that beard?" said the squire, when they were seated round the table. He had not ceased to rally his son as to this patriarchal adornment; but, nevertheless, any one could have seen, with half an eye, that he was as proud of it as were the others.

"Don't I, sir? All I require is a relay of napkins for every course:" and he went to work, covering it with every spoonful, as men with beards always do.

"Well, if you like it!" said the squire, shrugging his shoulders.

"But I do like it," said Frank.

"Oh, papa! you wouldn't have him cut it off," said one of the twins. "It is so handsome."

"I should like to work it into a chair-back instead of floss-silk," said the other twin.

"Thank'ee, Sophy; I'll remember you for that."

"Doesn't it look nice, and grand, and patriarchal?" said Beatrice, turning to her neighbour.

"Patriarchal, certainly," said Mr. Oriel. "I should grow one myself if I had not the fear of the archbishop before my eyes."

What was next said to him was in a whisper, audible only to himself.

"Doctor, did you know Wildman, of the 9th? He was left as surgeon at Scutari for two years. Why, my beard to his is only a little down."

"A little way down, you mean," said Mr. Gazebee.

"Yes," said Frank, resolutely set against laughing at Mr. Gazebee's pun. "Why, his beard descends to his ankles, and he is obliged to tie it in a bag at night, because his feet get entangled in it when he is asleep!"

"SOMETHING FAST"

THE THREE CLERKS
Trollope

Charley had not been so resolute with the usurer, so determined to get 5*l.* from him on this special day, without a special object in view. His credit was at stake in a more than ordinary manner; he had about a week since borrowed money from the woman who kept the public-house in Norfolk Street, and having borrowed it for a week only, felt that this was a debt of honour which it was incumbent on him to pay. Therefore, when he had walked the length of one street on his road towards his lodgings, he retraced his steps and made his way back to his old haunts.

The house which he frequented was hardly more like a modern London gin-palace than was that other house in the city which Mr. M'Ruen honoured with his custom. It was one of those small tranquil shrines of Bacchus in which the god is worshipped perhaps with as constant a devotion, though with less noisy demonstrations of zeal than in his larger and more public temples. None absolutely of the lower orders were encouraged to come thither for oblivion. It had about it nothing inviting to the general eye. No gas illuminations proclaimed its midnight grandeur. No huge folding doors, one set here and another there, gave ingress and egress to a wretched crowd of poverty-stricken midnight revellers. No reiterated assertions in gaudy letters, each a foot long, as to the peculiar merits of the old tom or Hodge's cream of the valley, seduced the thirsty traveller. The panelling over the window bore the simple announcement, in modest letters, of the name of the landlady, Mrs. Davis; and the same name appeared with equal modesty on the one gas lamp opposite the door.

Mrs. Davis was a widow, and her customers were chiefly people who knew her and frequented her house regularly. Lawyers' clerks, who were either unmarried, or whose married homes were perhaps not so comfortable as the widow's front parlour; tradesmen, not of the best sort, glad to get away from the noise of their children; young men who had begun the cares of life in ambiguous positions, just on the confines of respectability, and who finding themselves too weak in flesh to cling on to the round of the ladder above them, were sinking from year to year to lower steps, and depths even below the level of Mrs. Davis's public-house. To these might be added some few of a somewhat higher rank in life, though perhaps of a lower rank of respectability; young men who, like Charley Tudor and his comrades, liked their ease and self-indulgence, and were too indifferent as to the class of companions against whom they might rub their shoulders while seeking it.

The 'Cat and Whistle,' for such was the name of Mrs. Davis's establishment, had been a house of call for the young men of the Internal Navigation long before Charley's time. What first gave rise to the connection it is not now easy to say; but Charley had found it, and had fostered it into a close alliance, which greatly exceeded any amount of intimacy which existed previously to his day.

It must not be presumed that he, in an ordinary way, took his place among the lawyers' clerks, and general run of customers in the front parlour; occasionally he condescended to preside there over the quiet revels, to sing a song for the guests, which was sure to be applauded to the echo, and to engage in a little skirmish of politics with a retired lamp-maker and a silversmith's foreman from the Strand, who always called him 'Sir,' and received what he said with the greatest respect; but, as a rule, he quaffed his Falernian in a little secluded parlour behind the bar, in which sat the widow Davis, auditing her accounts in the morning, and giving out orders in the evening to Norah Geraghty, her barmaid, and to an attendant sylph, who ministered to the front parlour, taking in goes of gin and screws of tobacco, and bringing out the price thereof with praiseworthy punctuality.

Latterly, indeed, Charley had utterly deserted the front parlour; for there had come there a pestilent fellow, highly connected with the press, as the lamp-maker declared, but employed as an assistant short-hand writer somewhere about the Houses of Parliament, according to the silversmith, who greatly interfered with our navvy's authority. He would not at all allow that what Charley said was law, entertained fearfully democratic principles of his own, and was not at all the gentleman. So Charley drew himself up, declined to converse any further on politics with a man who seemed to know more about them than himself, and confined himself exclusively to the inner room.

On arriving at this elysium, on the night in question, he found Mrs. Davis usefully engaged in darning a stocking, while Scatterall sat opposite with a cigar in his mouth, his hat over his nose, and a glass of gin and water before him.

'I began to think you weren't coming,' said Scatterall, and 'I was getting so deuced dull that I was positively thinking of going home.'

'That's very civil of you, Mr. Scatterall,' said the widow.

'Well, you've been sitting there for the last half hour without saying a word to me; and it is dull. Looking at a woman mending stockings is dull, ain't it, Charley?'

'That depends,' said Charley, 'partly on whom the woman may be, and partly on whom the man may be.'

'Where's Norah, Mrs. Davis?'

'She's not very well to-night; she has got a headache; there ain't many of them here to-night, so she's lying down.'

'A little seedy, I suppose,' said Scatterall.

Charley felt rather angry with his friend for applying such an epithet to his lady-love; however he did not resent it, but sitting down, lighted his pipe and sipped his gin and water.

And so they sat for the next quarter of an hour, saying very little to each other. What was the nature of the attraction which induced two such men as Charley Tudor and Dick Scatterall to give Mrs. Davis the benefit of their society, while she was mending her stockings, it might be difficult to explain. They could have smoked in their own rooms as well, and have drunk gin and water there, if they had had any real predilection for that mixture. Mrs. Davis was neither young nor beautiful, nor more than ordinarily witty. Charley, it is true, had an allurement to entice him thither, but this could not be said of Scatterall, to whom the lovely Norah was never more than decently civil. Had they been desired, in their own paternal halls, to sit and see their mother's housekeeper darn the family stockings, they would, probably, both of them have rebelled, even though the supply of tobacco and gin and water should be gratuitous and unlimited.

It must be presumed that the only charm of the pursuit was in its acknowledged impropriety. They both understood that there was something fast in frequenting Mrs. Davis's inner parlour, something slow in remaining at home; and so they both sat there, and Mrs. Davis went on with her darning needle, nothing abashed.

ON BOARD

FRANK MILDMAY
Marryat

The Professions I had now more leisure to contemplate my new residence and new associates, who, having returned from the duty of the dockyard, were all assembled in the berth, seated round the table on the lockers, which paid 'the double debt' of seats and receptacles; but in order to obtain a sitting, it was requisite either to climb over the backs of the company, or submit to 'high pressure' from the last comer. Such close contact, even with our best friends, is never desirable; but in warm weather, in a close, confined air, with a manifest scarcity of clean linen, it became particularly inconvenient. The population here very far exceeded the limits usually allotted to human beings in any situation of life, except in a slave ship. The midshipmen, of whom there were eight full-grown, and four youngsters, were without either jackets or waistcoats; some of them had their shirt-sleeves rolled up, either to prevent the reception or to conceal the absorption of dirt in the region of the wristbands. The repast on the table consisted of a can or large black-jack of small beer, and a japan bread-basket full of sea-biscuit. To compensate for this simple fare, and at the same time to cool the close atmosphere of the berth, the table was covered with a large green cloth with a yellow border, and many yellow spots withal, where the colour had been discharged by slops of vinegar, hot tea, etc., etc.; a sack of potatoes stood in one corner, and the shelves all round, and close over our heads, were stuffed with plates, glasses, quadrants, knives and forks, loaves of sugar, dirty stockings and shirts, and still fouler table-cloths, small tooth-combs, and ditto large, clothes brushes and shoe brushes, cocked hats, dirks, German flutes, mahogany writing-desks, a plate of salt butter, and some two or three pair of naval half-boots. A single candle served to make darkness visible, and the stench had nearly overpowered me.

The reception I met with tended in no way to relieve these horrible impressions. A black man, with no other dress than a dirty check shirt and trousers, not smelling of amber, stood within the door ready to obey all and any one of the commands with which he was loaded. The smell of the towel he held in his hand to wipe the plates and glasses with, completed my discomfiture; and I fell sick upon the seat nearest to me. Recovering from this without the aid of any 'ministering angel,' I contracted the pupils of my eyes, and ventured to look around me. The first who met my gaze was my recent foe; he bore the marks of contention by having his eye bound up with brown paper and a dirty silk pocket-handkerchief; the other was quickly turned on me; and with a savage and brutal countenance he swore and denounced the severest vengeance on me for what I had done. In this he was joined by another ill-looking fellow with large whiskers.

I shall not repeat the elegant philippics with which I was greeted. Suffice it to say that I found all the big ones against me, and the little ones neuter; the caterer, supposing that I had received suitable admonition for my future guidance, and that I was completely bound over to keep the peace, turned all the youngsters out of the berth: 'As for you, Mr. Fistycuff,' said he, addressing himself to me, 'you may walk off with the rest of the gang, so make yourself scarce, like the Highlander's breeches.'

The boys all obeyed the command in silence, and I was not sorry to follow them. As I went out he added, ' So, Mr. Rumbusticus, you can obey orders, I see, and it is well for you; for I had a biscuit ready to shy at your head.' This affront, after all I had suffered, I was forced to pocket; but I could not understand what the admiral could mean, when he said that people went to sea ' to learn manners.'

I soon made acquaintance with the younger set

of my messmates, and we retreated to the forecastle as the only part of the ship suitable to the nature of the conversation we intended to hold. After one hour's deliberation, and notwithstanding it was the first night I had ever been on board a ship, I was unanimously elected leader of this little band. I became the William Tell of the party, as having been the first to resist the tyranny of the oldsters, and especially of the tyrant Murphy. I was let into all the secrets of the mess in which the youngsters were placed by the captain to be instructed and kept in order. Alas! what instruction did we get but blasphemy? What order where we kept in, except that of paying our mess, and being forbidden to partake of those articles which our money had purchased? My blood boiled when they related all they had suffered, and I vowed I would sooner die than submit to such treatment.

The hour of bed-time arrived. I was instructed how to get into my hammock, and laughed at for tumbling out on the opposite side. I was forced to submit to this pride of conscious superiority of these urchins who could only boast of a few months more practical experience than myself, and who therefore called me a greenhorn. But all this was done in good nature; and after a few hearty laughs from my companions, I gained the centre of my suspended bed, and was very soon in a sound sleep. This was only allowed to last till about four o'clock in the morning, when down came the head of my hammock, and I fell to the deck, with my feet still hanging in the air, like poor Sally, when she caught the crab. Stunned and stupefied by the fall, bewildered by the violent concussion and the novelty of all around me, I continued in a state of somnambulism, and it was some minutes before I could recollect myself.

The marine sentinel at the gun-room door seeing

what had happened, and also espying the person to whom I was indebted for this favour, very kindly came to my assistance. He knotted my lanyard, and restored my hammock to its place, but he could not persuade me to confide myself again to such treacherous bed-posts, for I thought the rope had broken; and so strongly did the fear of another tumble possess my mind, that I took a blanket, and lay down on a chest at some little distance, keeping a sleepless eye directed to the scene of my late disaster.

This was fortunate; for not many minutes had elapsed when Murphy, who had been relieved from the middle watch, came below, and seeing my hammock again hanging up, and supposing me in it, took out his knife and cut it down. ' So then,' said I to myself, ' it was you, was it, who invaded my slumbers, and nearly dashed my brains out, and have now made the second attempt.' I vowed to Heaven that I would have revenge; and I acquitted myself of that vow. Like the North American savage, crouching lest he should see me, I waited patiently till he had got into his hammock, and was in a sound sleep. I then gently pushed a shot-case under the head of his hammock, and placed the corner of it so as to receive his head; for had it split his skull I should not have cared, so exasperated was I, and so bent on revenge. Subtle and silent, I then cut his lanyard; he fell, and his head coming in contact with the edge of the shot-case, he gave a deep groan, and there he lay. I instantly retreated to my chest and blanket, where I pretended to snore, while the sentinel, who, fortunately for me, had seen Murphy cut me down the first time, came with his lanthorn, and seeing him apparently dead, removed the shot-case out of the way, and then ran to the sergeant of marines, desiring him to bring the surgeon's assistant.

While the sergeant was gone, he whispered softly to me, ' Lie still ; I saw the whole of it, and if you are found out it may go hard with you.'

Murphy, it appeared, had few friends in the ship ; all rejoiced at his accident. I lay very quietly in my blanket while the surgeon's assistant dressed the wound ; and, after a considerable time, succeeded in restoring the patient to his senses ; he was, however, confined a fortnight to his bed. I was either not suspected, or if I was, it was known that I was not the aggressor. The secret was well kept. I gave the marine a guinea, and took him into my service as *valet de place*.

A PHYSICIAN

DOCTOR THORNE
Trollope

And thus Dr. Thorne became settled for life in the little village of Greshambury. As was then the wont of many country practitioners, and as should be the wont with them all if they consulted their own dignity a little less and the comforts of their customers somewhat more, he added the business of a dispensing apothecary to that of physician. In doing so, he was of course much reviled. Many people around him declared that he could not truly be a doctor, or at any rate, a doctor to be so called ; and his brethren in the art living around him, though they knew that his diplomas, degrees, and certificates were all *en régle*, rather countenanced the report. There was much about this new-comer which did not endear him to his own profession. In the first place he was a new-comer, and, as such, was of course to be regarded by other doctors as being *de trop*. Greshambury was only fifteen miles from Barchester, where there was a regular depôt of medical skill, and but eight from Silverbridge, where a properly-established physician had been in residence for the last forty years. Dr. Thorne's predecessor at Greshambury had been a humble-minded, general practitioner, gifted with a due respect for the physicians of the county; and he, though he had been allowed to physic the servants, and sometimes the children at Greshambury, had never had the presumption to put himself on a par with his betters.

Then, also, Dr. Thorne, though a graduated physician, though entitled beyond all dispute to call himself a doctor, according to all the laws of all the colleges, made it known to the East Barsetshire world, very soon after he had seated himself at Greshambury, that his rate of pay was to be seven-and-sixpence a visit within a circuit of five miles, with a proportionately increased charge at proportionately increased distances. Now there was something low, mean, unprofessional, and democratic in this; so, at least, said the children of Æsculapius gathered together in conclave at Barchester. In the first place, it showed that this Thorne was always thinking of his money, like an apothecary, as he was; whereas, it would have behoved him, as a physician, had he had the feelings of a physician under his hat, to have regarded his own pursuits in a purely philosophical spirit, and to have taken any gain which might have accrued as an accidental adjunct to his station in life. A physician should take his fee without letting his left hand know what his right hand was doing; it should be taken without a thought, without a look, without a move of the facial muscles; the true physician should hardly be aware that the last friendly grasp of the hand had been made more precious by the touch of gold. Whereas, that fellow Thorne would lug out half-a-crown from his breeches pocket and give it in change for a ten shilling piece. And then it was clear that this man had no appreciation of the dignity of a learned profession. He might constantly be seen compounding medicines in the shop, at the left hand of his front door; not making experiments philosophically in materia medica for the benefit of coming ages— which, if he did, he should have done in the exclusion of his study, far from profane eyes—but positively putting together common powders for rural bowels, or spreading vulgar ointments for agricultural ailments.

A COURT MARTIAL

FRANK MILDMAY
Marryat

While I was on board of this ship two poor men were executed for mutiny. The scene was far more solemn to me than anything I had ever beheld. Indeed, it was the first thing of the kind I had been present at. When we hear of executions on shore, we are always prepared to read of some foul, atrocious crime, some unprovoked and unmitigated offence against the laws of civilised society, which a just and a merciful government cannot allow to pass unpunished. With us at sea there are many shades of difference; but that which the law of our service considers a serious offence is often no more than an ebullition of local and temporary feeling, which in some cases might be curbed, and in others totally suppressed, by timely firmness and conciliation.

The ships had been a long time at sea, the enemy did not appear—and there was no chance either of bringing him to action, or of returning into port. Indeed, nothing can be more dull and monotonous than a blockading cruise 'in the team,' as we call it, that is, the ships of the line stationed to watch an enemy. The frigates have, in this respect, every advantage; they are always employed on shore, often in action, and the more men they have killed, the happier are the survivors. Some melancholy ferment on board of the flagship I was in, caused an open mutiny. Of course it was very soon quelled, and the ringleaders having been tried by a court-martial, two of them were condemned to be hanged at the yardarm of their own ship, and were ordered for execution on the following day but one.

Our courts-martial are always arrayed in the most pompous manner, and certainly are calculated to strike the mind with awe—even of a captain himself. A gun is fired at eight o'clock in the morning from the ship where it is to be held, and a union flag is displayed at the mizzen-peak. If the weather be fine, the ship is arranged with the greatest nicety; her decks are as white as snow—her hammocks are stowed with care—her ropes are taut—her yards square—her guns run out—and a guard of marines, under the orders of a lieutenant, prepared to receive every member of the court with the honours due to his rank. Before nine o'clock they are all assembled; the officers in their undress uniform, unless an admiral is to be tried. The great cabin is prepared, with a long table covered with a green cloth. Pens, ink, paper, prayer-books, and the articles of war, are laid round to every member.

'Open the court,' says the president.

The court is opened, and officers and men indiscriminately stand round. The prisoners are now brought in under the charge of the prevost-marshal, a master-at-arms, with his sword drawn and placed at the foot of the table, on the left hand of the judge-advocate. The court is sworn to do its duty impartially, and if there is any doubt, to let it go in favour of the prisoner. Having done this, the members sit down, covered, if they please.

The judge-advocate is then sworn, and the order for the court-martial read. The prisoner is put on his trial: if he says anything to commit himself, the court stops him, and kindly observes, 'We do not want your evidence against yourself; we want only to know what others can prove against you.' The unfortunate man is offered any assistance he may require; and when the defence is over, the court is cleared, the doors are shut, and the minutes which have been taken down by the judge-advocate, are carefully read over, the credibility of the witnesses weighed, and the president puts the question to the youngest member first, 'Proved, or not proved?'

All having given their answer, if seven are in favour of proved, and six against, proved is recorded. The next question—if for mutiny or desertion, or other capital crime—'Flogging or death?' The votes are given in the same way: if the majority be for death, the judge-advocate writes the sentence, and it is signed by all the members, according to seniority, beginning with the president, and ending with the judge-advocate.

The court is now opened again, the prisoner brought in, and an awful and deep silence prevails. The members of the court all put their hats on, and are seated; every one else, except the provost-marshal, is uncovered. As soon as the judge-advocate has read the sentence, the prisoner is delivered to the custody of the provost-marshal, by a warrant from the president, and he has charge of him till the time for the execution of the sentence.

. . . The fatal morning came. It was eight o'clock. The gun fired—the signal for punishment flew at our mast-head. The poor men gave a deep groan, exclaiming, 'Lord have mercy upon us! —our earthly career and troubles are nearly over!' The master-at-arms came in, unlocked the padlock at the end of the bars, and, slipping off the shackles, desired the marine sentinels to conduct the prisoners to the quarter-deck.

Here was a scene of solemnity which I hardly dare attempt to describe. The day was clear and beautiful, the top-gallant yards were crossed on board of all the ships; the colours were flying; the crews were all dressed in white trousers and blue jackets, and hung in clusters, like bees, on the side of the rigging facing our ship; a guard of marines, under arms, was placed along each gangway, but on board of our ship they were on the quarter-deck. Two boats from each ship lay off upon their oars alongside of us, with a lieutenant's and a corporal's guard in each, with fixed bayonets. The hands were all turned up by the boatswain and his mates with a shrill whistle and calling down each hatchway, 'All hands, attend punishment!'

You now heard the quick trampling of feet up the ladders, but not a word was spoken. The prisoners stood on the middle of the quarter-deck, while the captain read the sentence of the court-martial and the order from the commander-in-chief for the execution. The appropriate prayers and psalms having been read by the chaplain with much feeling and devotion, the poor men were asked if they were ready; they both replied in the affirmative, but each requested to have a glass of wine, which was instantly brought. They drank it off, bowing most respectfully to the captain and officers.

The admiral did not appear, it not being etiquette; but the prisoners desired to be kindly and gratefully remembered to him: they then begged to shake hands with the captain and all the officers, which having done, they asked permission to address the ship's company. The captain ordered them all to come aft on the top and quarter-deck. The most profound silence reigned, and there was not an eye but had a tear in it.

William Strange, the man who had sent for me, then said, in a clear and audible tone of voice, ' Brother sailors, attend to the last words of a dying man. We are brought here at the instigation of some of you who are now standing in safety among the crowd ; you have made fools of us, and we are become the victims to the just vengeance of the laws. Had you succeeded in the infamous design you contemplated, what would have been the consequences ? Ruin, eternal ruin, to yourselves and to your families ; a disgrace to your country, and the scorn of those foreigners to whom you proposed delivering up the ship. Thank God! you did not succeed. Let our fate be a warning to you ; and endeavour to show by your future acts your deep contrition for the past. Now, sir,' turning to the captain, ' we are ready.'

This beautiful speech from the mouth of a common sailor, must as much astonish the reader as it then did the captain and officers of the ship. But Strange, as I have shown, was no common man ; he had had the advantage of education, and, like many of the ringleaders at the mutiny of the Nore, was led into the error of refusing to *obey*, from the conscious feeling that he was born to *command*.

The arms of the prisoners were then pinioned, and the chaplain led the way, reading the funeral service ; the master-at-arms with two marine sentinels, conducted them along the starboard gangway to the forecastle ; here a stage was erected on either side, over the cathead, with steps to ascend to it ; a tail block was attached to the boom iron, as the outer extremity of each fore-yard arm, and through this a rope was rove, one end of which came down to the stage. The other was led along the yard into the catharpings, and thence down upon the main-deck. A gun was primed and ready to fire, on the fore-part of the ship, directly beneath the scaffold.

I attended poor Strange to the very last moment, he begged me to see that the halter, which was a piece of line like a clothes line, was properly made fast round his neck, for he had known men suffer dreadfully from the want of this precaution. A white cap was placed on the head of each man, and when both mounted the platform, the cap was drawn over their eyes. They shook hands with me, with their messmates and with the chaplain, assuring him that they died happy, and confident in the hopes of redemption. They then stood still while the yard-ropes were fixed to the halter by a toggle in the running noose of the latter; the other ends of the yard-ropes were held by some twenty or thirty men on each side of the main-deck, where two lieutenants of the ship attended.

All being ready, the captain waved a white handkerchief, the gun fired, and in an instant the poor fellows were seen swinging at either yard-arm. They had on blue jackets and white trousers, and were remarkably fine-looking young men. They did not appear to suffer any pain, and at the expiration of an hour, the bodies were lowered down, placed in coffins, and sent on shore for interment.

AN EXAMINATION

FRANK MILDMAY
Marryat

On my own name being called, I felt a flutter about the heart which I did not feel in action, or in the hurricane, or when, in a case more desperate than either, I jumped overboard at Spithead to swim to my dear Eugenia. 'Powers of Impudence, as well as Algebra,' said I, 'lend me your aid, or I am undone.' In a moment the cabin door flew open, the sentinel closed it after me, and I found myself in the presence of this most awful triumovate. I felt very like Daniel in the lions' den. I was desired to take a chair, and a short discussion ensued between the judges, which I neither heard nor wished to hear; but while it lasted, I had time to survey any antagonists from head to foot. I encouraged myself to think that I was equal to one of them; and if I could only neutralise him, I thought I should very easily floor the other two.

One of these officers had a face like a painted pumpkin; and his hand, as it lay on the table, looked more like the fin of a turtle; the nails were bitten so close off, that the very remains of them seemed to have retreated into the flesh, for fear of farther depredation, which the other hand was at the moment suffering. Thinks I to myself, 'If ever I saw "lodgings to let, unfurnished," it is in that cocoanut, or pumpkin, or gourd of yours.'

The next captain to him was a little, thin, dark, dried-up, shrivelled fellow, with keen eyes, and a sharp nose. The midshipmen called him 'Old Chili Vinegar,' or 'Old Hot and Sour.' He was what we term a martinet. He would keep a man two months on his black list, giving him a breech of a gun to polish and keep bright, never allowing him time to mend his clothes, or keep himself clean, while he was cleaning that which, for all the purposes of war, had better have been black. He seldom flogged a man; but he tormented him into sullen discontent, by what he called 'Keeping the devil out of his mind.' This little nightmare, who looked like a dried eel-skin, I so found was the leader of the band.

The third captain was a tall, well-looking, pompous

man (he was the junior officer of the three), with a commanding and most unbending countenance: 'He would not ope his mouth in way of smile, though Nestor swore the jest was laughable.'

I had just time to finish my survey, and form a rough estimate of the qualities of my examiners, when I was put upon my trial by the president, who thus addressed me,

'You are perfect in the theory of navigation, I presume, sir, or you would not come here?'

I replied that I hope I should be found so, if they would please to try me.

'Ready enough with his answer,' said the tall captain; 'I daresay this fellow is jaw-master-general in the cockpit. Whom did you serve your time with, sir?'

I stated the different captains I had served with, particularly Lord Edward.

'Oh, ay, that's enough; you *must* be a smart fellow, if you have served with Lord Edward.'

I understood the envious and sarcastic manner in which this was uttered, and prepared accordingly for an arduous campaign, quite sure that this man, who was no seaman, would have been too happy in turning back one of Lord Edward's midshipmen. Several problems were given to me, which I readily solved, and returned to them. They examined my logs and certificates with much seeming scrutiny, and then ventured a question in the higher branches of mathematics. This I also solved; but I found talent was not exactly what they wanted. The little skinny captain seemed rather disappointed that he could not find fault with me. A difficult problem in spherical trigonometry lay before them, carefully drawn out, and the result distinctly marked at the bottom; but this I was not, of course, permitted to see. I soon answered the question; they compared my work with that which had

THE CHILDREN, EARLY VICTORIAN PERIOD
From a fashion paper of the time,

been prepared for them; and as they did not exactly agree, I was told that I was wrong. I was not disconcerted, and very deliberately looking over my work I told them that I could not discover any error, and was able to prove it by inspection, by Canon, by Gunter, or by figure.

'You think yourself a very clever fellow, I daresay,' said the little fat captain.

'A second Euclid,' said the tall captain. 'Pray, sir, do you know the meaning of "*Pons Asinorum*?"'

'Bridge of Asses, sir,' said I, staring him full in the face, with a smile under the skin.

Now it was very clear to me that the little fat captain had never heard of the Asses' Bridge before, and therefore supposed I was quizzing the tall captain, who, from having been what we used to term a 'harbour-duty man' all his life, had heard of the "*Pons Asinorum*," but did not know which of the problems of Euclid it was, nor how it was applicable to navigation. The fat captain, therefore, burst into a hoarse laugh, saying, 'I think he hits you hard; you had better let him alone: he will puzzle you presently.'

Nettled at this observation of his brother officer, the tall captain was put upon his mettle, and insisted that the question last proposed was not satisfactorily answered, and swore by G— that he never would sign my certificate until I did it.

I persisted; the two works were compared: I was threatened to be turned back; when, lo, to the dismay of the party, the error was found in their own work. The fat captain, who was a well-meaning man, laughed heartily; the other two looked very silly and very angry.

'Enough of this, sir,' said the martinet: 'now stand up; and let us see what you can do with a ship.' A ship was supposed to be on the stocks; she was launched; I was appointed to her, and as first lieutenant, ordered to prepare her for sea. I took her into dock, and saw her coppered; took her along the sheer-hulk, masted her; laid her to the ballast wharf, took in and stowed her iron ballast and her tanks; moved off to a hulk or receiving ship, rigged her completely, bent her sails, took in guns, stores, and provisions; reported her ready for sea, and made the signal for a pilot; took her out of harbour, and was desired to conduct her into other harbours, pointing out the shoals and dangers of Plymouth, Plymouth, Falmouth, the Downs, Yarmouth Roads, and even to Shetland.

But the little martinet and the tall captain had not forgiven me for being right in the problem, and my examination continued. They put my ship into every possible situation which the numerous casualties of a sea life present in such endless variety. I set and took in every sail, from a skysail to a trysail. I had my masts shot away, and I rigged jury-masts: I made sail on them, and was getting fairly into port, when the little martinet very cruelly threw my ship on her beam-ends on a dead lee-shore, a dark night, and blowing a hurricane, and told me to get her out of the scrape if I could. I replied that, if there was anchorage, I should anchor, and take my chance; but if there was no anchorage, neither he nor any one else could save the ship, without a change of wind, or the special interference of Providence. This did not satisfy old Chili Vinegar. I saw that I was persecuted, and that the end would be fatal to my hopes: I therefore became indifferent; was fatigued with the endless questions put to me; and, very fortunately for me, made a mistake, at least in the opinion of the tall captain. The question at that time was one which was much controverted in the service; namely, whether, on being taken flat aback, you should put your helm a turn or two alee, or keep it amidship? I preferred th latter mode; but the tall captain insisted on the former, and gave his reasons. Finding myself on debatable ground, I gave way, and thanked him for his advice, which I said I should certainly follow whenever the case occurred to me; not that I felt convinced then, and have since found that he was wrong; still my apparent tractability pleased his self-love, and he became my advocate. 'He grinned horribly a ghastly smile,' and, turning to the other captains, asked if they were satisfied.

This question, like the blow of the auctioneer's hammer, ends all discussion; for captains, on these occasions, never gainsay each other; I was told that my passing certificate would be signed. I made my best bow and my exit, reflecting, as I returned to the 'sheep-pen,' that I had nearly lost my promotion by wounding their vanity, and had regained my ground by flattering it. Thus the world goes on; and from my earliest days, my mind was strengthened and confirmed in every vice by the pernicious example of my superiors.

RENEWALS 691-4574

DATE DUE

DEC 0 2

Demco, Inc. 38-293